The Cambridge Introduction to
French Poetry

The Cambridge Introduction to French Poetry is the most comprehensive survey of French poetry available. The poets discussed – all quoted in the original, followed by an English translation – belong to every period from the eleventh century to the present, and include Francophone authors from areas other than France. The goals of this Introduction are to provide tools for the analysis of French poems, while assessing ever-changing distinctions and hierarchies between verse and prose, forms and genres, and levels of style; and to give a sense of French poetry's endless quest for self-definition, by examining its ambivalent relations with political realities, philosophical ideas, and the achievements of other arts. Accessible, wide-ranging and designed specifically for use in courses, this *Introduction* contains a useful glossary of poetic terms, and will prove invaluable to students and teachers alike.

The Cambridge Introduction to
French Poetry

MARY LEWIS SHAW

CAMBRIDGE
UNIVERSITY PRESS

PUBLISHED BY THE PRESS SYNDICATE OF THE UNIVERSITY OF CAMBRIDGE
The Pitt Building, Trumpington Street, Cambridge CB2 1RP, United Kingdom

CAMBRIDGE UNIVERSITY PRESS
The Edinburgh Building, Cambridge, CB2 2RU, UK
40 West 20th Street, New York, NY 10011–4211, USA
477 Williamstown Road, Port Melbourne, VIC 3207, Australia
Ruiz de Alarcón 13, 28014 Madrid, Spain
Dock House, The Waterfront, Cape Town 8001, South Africa

http://www.cambridge.org

© Mary Lewis Shaw 2003

First published 2003

Printed in the United Kingdom at the University Press, Cambridge

Typefaces Bembo 11/12.5 pt., Plantin and Univers   *System* LaTeX 2$_\varepsilon$ [TB]

A catalogue record for this book is available from the British Library

ISBN 0 521 80876 6 hardback
ISBN 0 521 00485 3 paperback

For my parents, Elizabeth and Ellsworth Shaw

Contents

Illustrations

Acknowledgements

I would first like to thank Linda Bree of Cambridge University Press for encouraging me to undertake this book and for her editorial guidance during its writing. I am also very grateful to Rachel DeWachter and David Watson of Cambridge for their reading and comments on the manuscript and for supporting me through the final phases of the book's preparation. Anonymous readers at Cambridge also provided me with many generous and useful comments. As always, I remain much indebted to Michael Riffaterre, my own principal teacher, for my critical formation and approach to teaching poetic analysis. Steven Winspur and Peter Schofer of the University of Wisconsin at Madison kindly gave me advice on how to design books oriented toward the teaching of French poetry, when I first conceived that I might write one. All of my colleagues at Rutgers University have been extremely helpful and supportive of this project. In particular, I am indebted to Dennis Cate, for introducing me to many rare fin-de-siècle texts held in the collections of the Jane Voorhees Zimmerli Art Museum; to Richard Serrano, for his reading and comments on sections dealing with contemporary "Francophone" poetry, and for introducing me to J.-J. Rabéarivelo's rewritings of Mallarmé; to James Swenson, for assisting me with many a translation; and to Richard Lockwood, for helping me to coordinate the writing of this book with the teaching of courses in which its usefulness could be tested. My students' feedback in these courses has been gracious and constructive. Many friends have sustained me through this project, especially Susann Carroll, Anna Duhl, Jerry Flieger, Debbie Keates, and Madhuri Mukherjee. Nothing, finally, has been more essential than the support and love of all my family, and the presence of my children, Ben, Elizabeth, and Pierre. Most of all I would like to thank my husband and colleague, François Cornilliat. An invaluable source of knowledge on all periods of French poetry, and a reader as insightful as meticulous, he has offered countless suggestions and aided in many a task at every stage of this book's development. For this and infinitely more, I cannot express enough my gratitude to him.

Permission to reproduce the following copyright materials in French and in English translations is hereby gratefully acknowledged (unless otherwise indicated, permission to publish English translations specially prepared for *The Cambridge Introduction to French Poetry* has been granted by the publishers of the French text):

To Éditions Gallimard
for the following whole poems:
  'Congé au vent' by René Char (in *Fureur et mystère*)
  'La terre est bleue…' by Paul Éluard (in *L'Amour la poésie*)
  'Aujourd'hui…' by Raymond Queneau (in "Littérature potentielle")
  'Méditation de la comparaison' by Jacques Roubaud (in *Quelque chose noir*)
and for extracts from
  'J'ai tant rêvé de toi' by Robert Desnos (in *Corps et biens*)
  'Zone' by Guillaume Apollinaire (in *Alcools*)
  'Première ode' by Paul Claudel (in *Cinq grandes odes*)
  'Le Mimosa' and 'Le Soleil placé en abîme' by Francis Ponge (in *La Rage de l'expression* and *Pièces*)
  'Dernière levée' and 'L'Union libre' by André Breton (in *Le Revolver à cheveux blancs*)
  'Glu et gli' (in *Qui je fus*) and 'Lecture de huit lithographies de Zao Wou-Ki' by Henri Michaux
  Anabase by Saint-John Perse
  Feuillets d'Hypnos by René Char
  'Le Rameur' and 'Le Cimetière marin' by Paul Valéry (in *Charmes*)
  'Ave' by Catherine Pozzi (in *Poèmes*)
  Art poétique by Eugène Guillevic
  'Au petit jour' by Philippe Jaccottet (in *L'Ignorant*)
  'L'Iconoclaste' by Michel Deguy (in *Gisants. Poèmes III 1980–1995*)
  'Présentation' by Édouard Glissant (in *Les Grands Chaos*)

To Éditions Mercure de France
for the full poem
  'Vrai corps' by Yves Bonnefoy (in *Du mouvement et de l'immobilité de Douve*)
and for extracts from
  'Perdre le midi quotidien' and 'Conseils au bon voyageur' by Victor Segalen (in *Stèles*)
  'Fairy' by Pierre Jean Jouve (in *Diadème*)
  'Vrai nom' by Yves Bonnefoy (in *Du mouvement et de l'immobilité de Douve*)

To Éditions Denoël for an extract from
  Prose du Transsibérien et de la petite Jeanne de France by Blaise Cendrars

To Éditions Flammarion for an extract from
  'Chanson Dada' by Tristan Tzara (in *De nos oiseaux*)

To Éditions de Minuit for an extract from
  'Liberté' by Paul Éluard (in *Poésie et vérité*)

To Presses Universitaires de France for the full poem
  'Nuit blanche' by Léon-G. Damas (in *Pigments*, reprinted in L. S. Senghor's *Anthologie de la nouvelle poésie nègre et malgache de langue française*)

To Éditions Présence Africaine for extracts from
  Cahier d'un retour au pays natal by Aimé Césaire

To Éditions Seghers for the full poem
  'Noyée au fond d'un rêve ennuyeux' by Joyce Mansour (in *Rapaces*)

To Éditions P.O.L. for an extract from
  'Des pommes et de la marée' by Michelle Grangaud (in *Poèmes fondus*)

To The University of Michigan Press for extracts from
  Richard A. Seaver's and Helen R. Lane's English translation of André Breton's *Manifesto of Surrealism* (1924)

To The Feminist Press for an extract from
  Mary Ann Caws' 'Men po men with glasses,' an English translation of 'Hommes po hommes à lunettes' by Thérèse Plantier

To Sun & Moon Press for permission to publish the present English translations (specially prepared here for *The Cambridge Introduction to French Poetry*) of extracts from André Breton's *Le Revolver à cheveux blancs*

To The University of Nebraska Press for permission to publish the present English translation (specially prepared here for *The Cambridge Introduction to French Poetry*) of Raymond Queneau's 'Aujourd'hui,' from "Littérature potentielle"

To Dalkey Archive Press for permission to publish the present English translation (specially prepared here for *The Cambridge Introduction to*

French Poetry) of Jacques Roubaud's 'Méditation de la comparaison,' from *Quelque chose noir*

To The University of Minnesota Press and the Regents of the University of Minnesota for permission to publish the present English translation (specially prepared here for *The Cambridge Introduction to French Poetry*) of an extract from Édouard Glissant's 'Présentation,' from *Les Grands Chaos* (to be published in the English language in a volume-entitled *Collected Poems of Édouard Glissant*, trans. Jefferson Humphries, forthcoming)

Prologue: French poetry?

From France or other countries, modern or from older times, poems written in French often tell us themselves what poetry is, how it operates on language, and what status and function it should hold in cultural life. And in France, perhaps more than elsewhere, poetry has been marked by programmatic attempts to define its nature and expand its role in the world. The fate of such efforts and the corollary development of French poetry through its relations with other languages, other discourses, and other arts: these are the themes to be woven in this book.

Neither chronological nor exhaustive in its approach to poets and movements, this is not a "history" of French poetry. My aim has been, rather, to provide the reader with a synthetic appreciation of the main forms, techniques, and traditions informing great poems written in French. And yet, because poems are always composed within a particular historical, cultural, and linguistic context, they will consistently be placed here in a framework of evolving conventions and perceptions as to what poetry itself is: presentations are organized around chapters designed to highlight (rather than to artificially resolve) the struggles that have shaped French poetry from its inception.

Beginning with an examination of the world of French poems from within, the first three chapters introduce and explore the unstable distinctions defining verse and prose (chapter 1), forms and genres (chapter 2), and words and figures (chapter 3). Building on this formal foundation, the last two chapters, on poetry and politics (chapter 4) and poetry and philosophy (chapter 5), as well as an Epilogue on poetry and other arts, move toward a more panoramic view, considering crucial ways in which poetry has situated and imposed itself within the wider world of French culture.

For now, let us sample, by way of introduction, famous theoretical statements from a few poets: judgments and reflections in which we can trace, along with the contest of generations, the expression of a collective will and the binding of poetry to changing linguistic, social, and political realities.

Joachim du Bellay's 1549 *Deffence et illustration de la langue françoyse* (*Defense and Illustration of the French Language*) takes on the general cause of the

1

French language and culture before calling to arms a group of young poets –
whom Pierre de Ronsard (1524–1585), the most prominent of these, later
named after the "Pléiade" constellation – and explaining to them just how
their labors might lift the French realm to the stars. Rendered illustrious
through poetry and rhetoric patterned on the great works of Antiquity, the
French language could one day, Du Bellay (1522–1560) argues, equal the
languages of Ancient Greece and Rome, producing supreme literary heroes,
the likes of Homer, Demosthenes, Virgil, and Cicero, as France rises up and
procures "the reins of monarchy" (in the sense of universal dominion).[1]
Because of its "magnificence de motz" (verbal magnificence) and "divinité
d'invention" (divinely inspired invention), poetry was supposed to spearhead
this endeavor.[2]

To "defend" the French language against accusations of poverty and "bar-
barie," the *Deffence* begins by accepting the charges, accusing French poets
of either a lazy or a pretentious refusal to cultivate their vulgate.[3] Using
the image of the garden and other natural metaphors, Du Bellay advocates
enriching the French vocabulary with words imported from Greek, Latin,
or Italian, and urges the French to imitate, as Rome had done with Greek
letters, all forms and varieties of Ancient literature, undertaking a sort of
grafting that would make all this Antique wealth their own. In short, French
poets needed to join in and take over the Renaissance movement that had
begun in Italy two centuries before.

That a thriving humanist culture based on knowledge recovered from
Antiquity could be reborn in France had already been proven by the
widespread translations of Greek, Latin, and Italian texts. However, the
glorification of the French language would require more, Du Bellay argued, than straight translation. It would require art: the "painter's" hand
and the poet's inventive "genius" – which is to say, the direct expression of
the French soul in works at once deliberately imitative of Antique models
and true to nature itself.[4] Thus, the Pléiade's notion of imitation, which
encourages a relation between texts – the rewriting of classical forms and
genres in original French works – also implies from the beginning imitation in the sense of mimesis*[5] (the imitation of reality in art). Du Bellay's
images for the imitative project he is prescribing are very natural and mobile, evoking a physical assimilative process: for example, new poems might
take their "skin and color" from previous French authors, but their "flesh,
bones, nerves, and blood" should be taken from Ancient writers, just as
their Roman predecessors had "devoured" Greek texts, converting them
into their own "blood and nourishment."[6] And while Du Bellay admits
that "nature," in the sense of talent and inspiration, is equally if not more
important for poets than "culture" in the sense of erudition and hard work,
he takes French poets' innate abilities for granted, just as he presents France's

military, political, and religious superiority over Italy and other countries to be in the normal order of things.[7]

What shocks the modern reader, however, is the utter rudeness with which Du Bellay treats his poetic forefathers throughout the *Deffence*. Toward the end he goes so far as to pray to Apollo that his language, a long-sterile mother, might at last give birth to a (true) poet.[8] This image is as false and self-deceiving as it is strategic, designed primarily to promote the Pléiade poets themselves. The most deceptive aspect consists in Du Bellay's blanket denial of the wealth of his own poetic tradition. On the one hand, by the time of the *Deffence*, the French language had been accumulating riches for five centuries, magnificent works in all genres from the epic *Chanson de Roland* (*Song of Roland, c.*1090) to the satirical lyricism of François Villon (1431–1463?), and had been propagating them throughout Europe (although it is true that since the fourteenth century Italian Renaissance authors such as Petrarch had taken to calling French literature "barbaric"). On the other hand, and more indicative still of the Pléiade's own unbridled bid for glory, Du Bellay also dismisses the innovations of his most immediate forebears, paying little respect to such noted Renaissance poets as the recently dead Clément Marot (1496–1544) and Maurice Scève (*c.*1501–1560), who together had already completed many of the poetic reforms he was shouting about. Finally, in calculating his own generation's prospects for success, Du Bellay acknowledges but refuses to factor in a major setback: the recent death of King Francis I (1547), the monarch who most enthusiastically supported and embodied Renaissance culture and arts in France.

Nevertheless, the Pléiade poets' break with late medieval and early sixteenth-century models did, in fact, galvanize and reshape French poetry. Their rejection of old French forms and their systematic experimentation with new ones, borrowed from Antiquity or from Italy, led to the increasing autonomy of poetry as an art in France (from such domains as music, rhetoric, and history, to which it had been variously subservient), and to the development of Classical French verse.

The Classical period itself begins with the stern rejection by François de Malherbe (1555–1628) of the "barbarismes," foreign borrowings, and pedantic excesses typical of the Pléiade poets and their heirs of the ornate "Baroque" school (late sixteenth to early seventeenth century). The austere court poet Malherbe strove above all to purify and standardize the French language and required that poetry reflect the values of reason and order, uniformity and clarity. Thus, it hardly seems coincidental that the crowning and most rigorous imposition of the regular alexandrine, a neglected old French meter which the Pléiade poets had revived and developed as a mainstay to uplift their native culture, occurs in the seventeenth century with the rise of the absolute monarchy and the creation of the Académie Française, an institution charged with dictating and preserving the norms of the French language. Forcefully articulated by Nicolas Boileau (1636–1711) in his *Art poétique*, the rules and conventions of French Classical poetry reigned supreme along with the Old Regime throughout most of the seventeenth and eighteenth centuries. Then they, too, were overthrown, succumbing in part to the foreign influence of Romanticism, a European movement that swept into France from England and Germany around 1800, promoting art as an absolute along with the exaltation of nature, the passions, personal genius, and individualism.

Whence, Stéphane Mallarmé's 1886 essay *Crise de vers* (*Crisis of Verse*) describes the Symbolist poets' "freeing" of French verse – an aesthetic liberation prepared earlier in the century by Victor Hugo (1802–1885) and other Romantic poets – as a moment of significance determined by and comparable to the (1789) French Revolution.[9] In the broadest sense, the French Symbolist movement includes all of the major French poets of the latter half of the nineteenth century following Charles Baudelaire (1821–1867): preeminently, Paul Verlaine (1844–1896), Arthur Rimbaud (1854–1891) and Mallarmé himself (1842–1898). But it is Jules Laforgue (1860–1887) and others in a narrower "school" of young Symbolist poets that Mallarmé credits for finalizing the break with traditional French meters. And, in a manner somewhat reminiscent of Du Bellay's strategy, he describes this break on the whole more as a natural process of decadence and renewal than as an organized political rebellion. However, Mallarmé, inversely to Du Bellay, tends to present his poetic forefathers as unsurpassable in their "illustration" of French verse, so that his essay defending the poetics of his own followers is presented not as a call to arms, but rather as a reflection on inevitable events that have already transpired, beginning with the natural death of Hugo.[10] Representing this national hero as the ultimate incarnation of French verse, Mallarmé attributes to his passing nearly the same gravity and consequence as Du Bellay fears might ensue from the loss of Francis I.

At the same time, the gain that Mallarmé sees coming out of his nation's poetic "crisis" is unmistakably great. He portrays the young practitioners of free verse as having insured once and for all French poets' access to individual modalities of expression – *musical* modalities free at once from authoritative linguistic conventions and metrical constraints, as well as from ordinary language's obligations to imitate or represent reality directly, in the manner of journalistic "reportage": freedoms all central to Mallarmé's own poetics of "suggestion."[11] Finally, and perhaps most importantly, he credits his own time for revealing the equivalence of all kinds of poetic writing, and especially of verse and prose.[12]

André Breton's 1924 *Manifeste du surréalisme* (*Manifesto of Surrealism*) is no doubt the twentieth century's most crucial theoretical statement subverting, refocusing, and centralizing French poetry. A quintessentially Parisian movement with global influence (heir to such European avant-gardes as Russian and Italian Futurism, and international nihilistic Dada), Surrealism, with its mystical elevation of poetic experimentation, its pseudo-scientific doctrine, and its revolutionary ambitions, nourishes and colors the vast majority of the last century's poems written in French. With a violence reminiscent of the *Deffence*, Breton (1896–1966) presents Surrealism as a clean break from the poetic tradition: only Isidore Ducasse (1846–1870), alias Lautréamont, the then barely known author of *Les Chants de Maldoror* (*The Lays of Maldoror*), was deemed a probable "surréaliste absolu," an appellation otherwise reserved for the members of the anointed group – such as Louis Aragon (1897–1982), Paul Éluard (1895–1952), and Robert Desnos (1900–1945). These are said to have "performed acts of ABSOLUTE SURREALISM," to have sworn themselves to a cause that encompasses not only poetry and other arts, but life itself.[13] In the same breath, on the sole basis of their works, Breton exercises (not without humor) the right to evaluate the partial, intermittent Surrealism of past and present authors (including Dante, and Shakespeare "in his finer moments"): thus, "Hugo is Surrealist when he isn't stupid," but "Rimbaud is Surrealist in the way he lived, and elsewhere";[14] Guillaume Apollinaire (1880–1918), who invented the term, only approached Surrealism in the "letter," whereas its "spirit" had been earlier embodied by the "SUPERNATURALISM" of Gérard de Nerval (1808–1855).[15]

As might be expected, the influence of this fiercely polemical movement registers itself negatively as much as positively, as Surrealism itself becomes a heritage. The very force of its pull and the binding character of its community trigger opposing, decentralizing trends in French poetry, breeding from the 1930s onward a wide variety of poetic orientations, an array of strongly individualistic poets who refuse group categorization, as well as scattered offshoots or rebellions of a more collective nature. In particular, the (not always consistent) social and political positions associated with Surrealism are often dramatically altered in the hands of women poets and Francophone poets from Africa, the Caribbean, or Québec, who in recent decades have called into question the very meaning of "French" language and culture. At the same time, insofar as Surrealism has not been replaced by a movement of comparable sway, contemporary French poetry – often judged obscure and feeling socially marginalized with respect to other genres – seems to be going through another protracted "crise de vers," continually experimenting with new ways to recover and expand its audience.

A number of structural, stylistic, and interpretive issues will recur throughout these pages as leitmotifs. We shall repeatedly see, for example, the important interplay of sameness and difference in such rudimentary elements as rhythm and rhyme,* in the patterning of fixed forms, in word choices and rhetorical figures. The nature of such basic poetic devices as metaphor,* allegory,* and symbol* is taken up repeatedly, in diverse historical contexts. The reader will also find frequent discussion of the varied and powerful means by which poetry can refer to the world, be this, for example, in mimetic effects such as onomatopoeia* (the verbal imitation of natural sounds), or in the pointed commentary of satire;* engage itself with other texts through various kinds of textual imitation or intertextuality* (any mode by which one text refers to another); or conversely appear, through self-reference or autoreferentiality,* to point our attention mainly to formal or philosophical aspects of the poem's own existence, thereby insisting on its autonomy. These broad issues, relevant to literature in general and to other arts, are especially crucial in poetry, perhaps because it strikes us – whatever its predominant formal, stylistic, or ideological features might be – first and foremost as a marked, or heightened, form of artistic language.

The discussion of these matters will entail a number of technical terms, which are generally defined in context (as they appear), as well as in the glossary. Every poem quoted is given in its original language, including Old, Middle, and Renaissance French (though from the seventeenth century forward, when differences become minimal, I conform to the tradition of using standardized spelling), and is accompanied (unless otherwise indicated) by a translation of my own, which aims to remain as literal as possible and harbors no poetic pretensions.[16]

Chapter 1

Verse and prose

While an absolute distinction between verse and prose is difficult to make, understanding the differences between these two kinds of discourse is fundamental to appreciating poetry. Verse can be defined as sequences of language in which we perceive a marked beat and a structured relationship between more or less regular accented measures, or recurrent rhythmic groups. Prose presents itself in sequences where there are no such evident rhythmic patterns. This is not to say that prose completely lacks rhythm, or that the rhythms of verse are always decisive. Indeed, our perception of French verse rhythms often depends on extra-rhythmic factors that underscore accent, such as syntax (word order) and rhyme. To make matters more complex, certain French prose styles, such as those imitating the Classical Latin period, tend to establish their own semi-regular rhythmic patterns, while free verse aims precisely to defy our rhythmic expectations. But despite these complications, as etymology suggests (the first meaning of the Latin noun *versus* was "the act of turning," whereas *prosa* came from *prosus*, "going straight"), it is the very practice of turning, or cutting, a line of language so as to signal its end and internal rhythmic proportions that first distinguishes verse from prose. Since prose does not separate sequences of language in this way, we experience its rhythms differently within a temporal flow.

Though verse makes up much of French poetry, it is important to avoid equating verse and poetry for a number of reasons. The most obvious is that a significant portion of modern French and Francophone poems have in fact been written in prose, the prose poem insinuating itself into lyric poetry in the middle of the nineteenth century, decades before the invention of free verse. But intersections and exchanges between verse and prose do not occur solely in modernity, nor in poetry alone. They haunt the history of all the major genres of French literature from the Middle Ages. Verse and prose are, for example, mixed in the medieval and Renaissance *prosimètres*,* texts such as *Le Chappelet des dames* (*The Garland of the Ladies*) by Jean Molinet (1435–1507), composed along the lines of Boethius' sixth-century *Consolation of Philosophy*, where the narrative progresses through alternating segments of Latin verse and prose. And while we normally think of fiction in terms of prose, the first "novels" of French literature, the Arthurian romances of

Chrétien de Troyes (*c.*1135–1185), were composed in octosyllables* of *rimes plates** (rhymed couplets), one of the earliest and longest-lasting varieties of French verse. Here, for example, are the opening lines from *Yvain*:

> Artus, li boens rois de Bretaingne
> La cui proesce nos enseigne
> Que nos soiens preu et cortois,
> Tint cort si riche come rois
> A cele feste qui tant coste,
> Qu' an doit clamer la Pantecoste.[1]

> *Arthur, the good king of Brittany,*
> *Who by his prowess teaches us*
> *To be brave and courteous,*
> *Held a court as rich as royal*
> *At the time of that feast so costly*
> *That we must call it Pentecost.*

Finally, the supreme realization of the *alexandrin*,* the classic twelve-syllable French equivalent of the English iambic pentameter, is generally considered to be found not in any seventeenth-century poem, but rather in the tragedies of Jean Racine (1639–1699).

Since it is with respect to the alexandrine that the rules of French verse have been the most rigorously defined, and since this verse form dominated French poetry for over 300 years, both in terms of prestige and frequency of use, much of this presentation of French prosody* will revolve around it. But the discussion of regular verse will also treat a number of other prominent meters,* as well as generally highlight the interdependency of rhythm, rhyme, and syntax in French verse.

The French language, like every other, has an inherent rhythm (or beat), which comes from the relative emphasis it places on certain sounds, that is, its accent. This "natural" rhythm plays an important role in the development of poetic meters. The way accent falls in a given language can involve the quantity of time, or duration, given to a sound (as with long and short syllables), or be simply a matter of intensity, or stress. It can be variably built into the pronunciation of words, as in English – for example, in the word *un*der the first syllable is accented, whereas the second syllable is accented in be*neath*. Or accent can be determined, as it is in French, primarily by the order in which a sound comes within a given sequence of sounds, whether this sequence be a word or a word-group. Over the course of its development from Latin, the French language's accent weakened little by little and became associated with endings: rather than being heavily marked, and varying, as in English, with particular words and parts of speech, it is relatively light and evenly distributed, the stress always falling on the last accentuable syllable, which is to say the last tonic (or pronounced) vowel of any word or syntactic word-group. As the *e atone* (the silent e, also called the "*e muet*") became gradually muted during the Middle Ages, and is not pronounced in modern French, the many French words ending with this particular vowel have their accents on the next to last vowel. Thus, one says: "hib*ou*," "plaf*ond*," "libert*é*," but "t*a*ble," "vis*i*ble," and "éc*ou*te."[2] Similarly, in word-groups, which are determined by grammar and syntax, it is always the last accentuable syllable of the last word that carries the strongest accent, weakening all the terminal vowel accents of all the previous words. Accordingly, in the phrase "un bon v*in*," the words "un" and "bon" would have their stress attenuated; in turn, the word "vin" would lose some of its stress in the longer word-group "un bon vin franç*ais*." So syntax plays a much more important role in the rhythm of French than it does in English.

The relative weakness of French accent and its association with endings may explain in part why French poetry, contrary to English, has no tradition of blank (or unrhymed) regular verse. On the one hand, owing to the subtlety and terminal position of its linguistic accent, French verse has both a built-in need and a natural inclination for the kind of end-line demarcation that rhyme provides. Well-marked recurring sound patterns supplement, as it were, for elusive linguistic rhythms, the repetition of the rhyme creating the effect of a phonetic accent strengthening the final, and therefore most critical, metrical one. On the other hand, French words, like Spanish ones, owing to the frequency of certain word endings (in the form of suffixes, for example, and grammatical inflections), lend themselves more easily than English words do to the requirements of rhyme.

Differences inherent in the patterns of rhythm, grammar, and acoustics in French and English also account in part for differences between the two languages' predominant poetic meters. French meters are isosyllabic:* that is, comprised of equal numbers of syllables, as opposed to rhythmic measures or "feet." As students of English poetry know, the foot is a pre-set rhythmic measure containing at least one accented syllable and one or more unac-cented syllables depending upon its variety: the iambic, trochaic, anapestic, dactylic, etc . . . English meters are generally counted by these measures loosely based on Latin and Greek models (which originally structured verse according to certain fixed patterns of long and short syllables). Though the aspect of duration central to accent in Classical meters is not generally rele-vant to English-language poetry, English words, contrary to French ones, do carry variable built-in accents of intensity and must therefore be arranged in verse in such a way as to fit a given meter, the pre-set sequence of ac-cented and unaccented syllables chosen for the poem. The words '*under*' and '*beneath*' are, for example, synonymous and have an equal number of sylla-bles. But they are not metrically interchangeable, since their accentuation is inherently different. In and of itself the word *un*der would make up a "trochee" (a foot comprized of one accented syllable and one unaccented syllable), while the word "be*neath*" would make up an iamb (a foot comprized of one unaccented syllable followed by one accented one). It has often been argued that spoken English naturally follows the iambic pattern. And iambic pentameter, the most traditional meter of English poetry, is defined as verse generally composed of five iambic feet. Paul Fussell offers the following stanza* from Edward Fitzgerald's 1859 rendering of Omar Khayyám's *Rubáiyát* (translated from the Persian) as a simple example of this particular meter, and more generally of English poetry's accentual-syllabic verse:

> Ĭ sómetĭmes thínk thăt névĕr blóws sŏ réd
> Thĕ Róse ăs whére sóme búrĭed Cáesăr bléd;
>   Thăt éverў Hўăcĭnth thĕ Gárdĕn wéars
> Drópt ĭn hĕr láp frŏm sóme ónce lóvelў héad.[3]

We note from the scansion of the verse that only the first line of the stanza is composed strictly of iambs; the regular pattern of one unstressed syllable followed by a stressed one is already broken in the second line, since the word *some* bears an accent. In the third line, the word *every* is also counted as having only two syllables, while it might arguably be counted as having three. These variations in accentuation and syllable count do not constitute a problem with respect to the poem's meter. Since accent is strong in English and the iambic pattern is generally maintained, the occasional use of other, substituted feet is a positive thing to be expected, and the precise number of syllables articulated in each line is inconsequential. The meter will be easily heard so long as the iamb dominates.

The conditions within which rhythmic regularity, or meter, can be created in French are very different. The fact that French words tend to lose their individual accents within the context of a word-group and that the terminal accent is syntactically determined, means that all syllables are inherently equal in French verse (with the crucial exception of those formed by the *e atone*): they may or may not be accented depending upon where they fall. Owing to the effect of syllable linking, or *enchaînement*, created by the grammatical rules of *élision* (the eliding of a word's final *e* in front of a word beginning with a vowel) and *liaison* (the linking of final consonants with beginning vowels), boundaries between words tend, moreover, to be inaudible in French. Accordingly, as Clive Scott has argued, we should think of a French verse-line not as "a string of words, but of syllables" and recognize that much of the beauty of French prosody stems from "its shifting accentuation and its phrasal nature."[4] French verse's requirement for rhyme, for a rigorous metrical system, and in particular for the return of equal numbers of syllables, appears then, by contrast, to correspond to an inverse need for balance – for clarity, stability, and order. Homophony, number, and symmetry strengthen and regulate the language's volatile, almost too subtle accent.

This is evident when we consider the massive appeal and sway of the even, binary-shaped, Classical alexandrine – a meter as central to the history of French poetry as is generally, for the history of French culture, the absolute monarchy of Louis XIV. Originally employed in Lambert le Tort's twelfth-century *Roman d'Alexandre* (*The Romance of Alexander*, a narrative of the exploits of Alexander the Great), developed and adapted to the aims of French poetry in the Renaissance, and fully institutionalized in the seventeenth century, the regular alexandrine can be most simply defined as follows: a twelve-syllable line divided by a caesura* (or metrical pivot) into two hemistichs* (half-lines), carrying fixed metrical accents on syllables 6 and 12, and, normally, two other mobile accents. In the following heterometric* (or mixed-meter) stanza by François de Malherbe (1555–1628), composed of four alexandrines followed by two hexasyllables,* note how the rhyme emphasizes the metrical accent at the end of each line, and how well the syntax, or phrasing, is fitted to the metrical pattern:

> N'espérons plus/ mon âme,// aux promes/ses du monde, (4+2+3+3)
> Sa lumière/ est un verre,// et sa faveur/ une onde, (3+3+4+2)
> Que toujours/ quelque vent// empê/che de calmer, (3+3+2+4)
> Quittons/ ses vanités,// lassons-nous/de les suivre: (2+4+3+3)
>> C'est Dieu/qui nous fait vivre, (2+4)
>> C'est Dieu/qu'il faut aimer.[5] (2+4)

> *Let us no longer hope, my soul, for the promises of the world,*
> *Its light is a glass, and its favor a wave,*
> *That some wind always keeps from calming,*
> *Let us leave these vanities, let us tire of their seeking:*
>> *It is God who gives us life,*
>> *It is God whom we must love.*

This stanza, which follows a rhyme scheme of aabccb – *rimes plates* followed by *rimes embrassées** – is the opening of 'Imitation du psaume *Lauda anima mea dominum*' ('Imitation of the Psalm *Praise the Lord O My Soul*'), by the early seventeenth-century court poet who established many of the rules of the Classical alexandrine. Generally simple and clear, Malherbe's lines provide a good introduction to the scanning of French verse, while allowing us to verify that the counting of syllables is not always an easy exercise, due to the sheer frequency and varied pronunciation of the *e atone*. The first cardinal rule of French prosody in fact concerns this vowel, which modern poets continue to recognize as one of the most fundamental resources of French verse.[6] The Classical rule can be articulated as follows: line-terminal *e atones* are never pronounced or marked as syllables, while line-internal ones must be pronounced and counted when they are followed by a consonant, but elided when they are followed by a vowel. Thus, in line 1, the *e atones* in "âme" and "monde" are not counted, but the *e atone* of "promesses" is, as it is followed by a consonant; in line 2, none of the *e atones* are counted, as they are either followed by vowels (in "lumière" and "verre") or terminal as in "monde"; in line 3, all of the *e atones* are counted, as they are internal and followed by consonants.

Line-terminal *e atones*, which become, like other *e atones*, progressively weaker in French pronunciation from the Middle Ages to the sixteenth century (they were generally heard to a certain extent in the early 1500s, and still are today in the Southern accent), play a crucial role in structuring French verse; they mark the "gender" of rhymes as "feminine," even when they no longer count as a metrical element. From the Renaissance forward, masculine and feminine rhymes are required to alternate; this means that a principle of variation is incorporated within the structure of homophony, so that each time there is a change of rhyme, there is a change of gender also. Before this time we find an unregulated interweaving of masculine and feminine rhymes, though alternation was sporadically recommended. Its becoming mandatory (by the mid-sixteenth century) marks an important stage in the general progression toward the clarification of French verse structure. And this rule is not developed in isolation. It accompanies several other rhyme-related regulations, designed to enhance the structural symmetry best featured in the binary alexandrine. Some of these include prohibiting the mixture of masculine and feminine terms within a rhyme pair (*veille/réveil*); prohibiting rhymes between the same words or derivatives of the same word; and generally encouraging, by contrast, semantic and other types of opposition to balance out the effect of repetition created by the rhyme. Many critics have insisted on the opposing phonetic qualities of masculine and feminine rhymes, characterizing the former as hard and abrupt, and the latter as soft and melting. The sexual overtones implicit in the norms of regular French verse were most meaningful, however, during the periods when the rule concerning rhyme gender was first established and then broken, that is, in the sixteenth and nineteenth centuries.

Though the *e atone* creates the greatest complications with regard to syllable count, rules concerning other vowels must also be considered. The prosodic separation into two syllables of two contiguous vowels normally pronounced as one syllable (with a semi-vowel) is called *diérèse** (diaeresis). This occurs frequently in Classical poetry, and is permissible whenever the contiguous vowels in question are etymologically distinct, that is, come from a Latin word implying the articulation of the original vowels in separate syllables. The contrary practice, whereby two contiguous vowels originating from one Latin vowel (through dipthonguing, for example) are pronounced as one syllable (instead of two), is called *synérèse** (synaeresis). There are examples of each of these practices in many of the poems that follow. Both occur in this famous decasyllable* from *La Chanson de Roland*, the eleventh-century foundational epic of the French nation:

Pour ço sunt Francs// si FIERS/ cume LE-ÜNS[7] (4+2+4)

This is why the Francs are as ferocious as lions

Here, "fiers," deriving from a dipthonguing of the Latin [e] in the term *fer-um*, collapses its contiguous vowels into one syllable (containing a vowel and a semi-vowel), creating a synaeresis; while "leuns" (Latin *lE-O-nem*, lion) separates them in a diaeresis.

But to return to our stanza from Malherbe: these lines also illustrate the extent to which syntax and symmetry converge with the metrics of French verse. In our scansion's numerical and visual representation of where the accents fall, we see, for example, that there is a rhythmic regularity that exceeds the recurrence of the obligatory metrical accents falling at the caesura and at the end of the line. Each of the alexandrines carries also two shifting secondary accents, as alexandrines normally do, so that the lines in fact consist, not only of two halves, or hemistichs, but also of four accented measures of varying numbers of syllables (here represented by the sequence of numbers in parentheses). Because of the predominance of this four-measure pattern, the regular alexandrine is generally qualified as a tetrameter.

Once we understand this basic metrical framework, we can begin to better appreciate the details of these lines' structure. Within our scansion, each single bar (representing the division of accented syllables into measures) is called a *coupe,** while the double bar representing the central pre-set metrical articulation marks the caesura. Note that while the caesura consistently falls, as it must, after the obligatory metrical accent on syllable 6, what determines the position of the *coupe* (following each other accentuated syllable) is fundamentally syntax, the structural composition of the word-group. Thus, while each line clearly divides itself syntactically into two equal halves, within these hemistichs syntactical variations determine accentual ones. In the first line, the insertion of the address "mon âme" necessarily causes a rhythmic grouping of four syllables, followed by two, while the second hemistich, like one of the hemistichs in each of the other lines, has a typical binary pattern of 3+3. What is more, if we look down the numbers of the four alexandrines taken together, we see that they form a symmetrical chiastic (or crossed) pattern.

Finally, the syntactic and semantic parallelism of the fourth alexandrine's two hemistichs, and of the two hexasyllables* closing the stanza, help us to appreciate that the alexandrine is a *vers composé*,* a composite of two halves divided by a caesura, each enjoying a certain limited independence, rather than an indifferently cut or accented "dodecasyllable," or twelve-syllable line. Conversely, the stanza's constitution also reveals that two hexasyllables, despite the extent of their parallelism, symmetry, and equality of number, cannot (in many cases) be realigned to forge an alexandrine. This is not because of particular rules regarding the hexasyllable's metrical accents; like all meters of less than eight syllables, the hexasyllable does not in fact have any caesura or other predetermined metrical articulation; treated as a *vers simple*,* or thought of in one piece, it can be accented in any number of ways. Rather, the two six-syllable lines could not make an alexandrine because the theoretical line's combined syllable count would in fact add up to an impossible thirteen, since the *e atone* of "vivre" (becoming internal before a consonant) would have to be pronounced. In addition, Malherbe himself helped to consolidate a finicky rule regarding the caesura, stating that within a twelve-syllable line, a non-elided *e atone* could not appear either at syllable 6 or 7, that is, either at the syllable where the metrical accent would fall, or at the first syllable of the second hemistich.

All kinds of liberties with respect to syllable count were taken before Malherbe, in the Renaissance and medieval periods, and would again be seized with the dawning of modern poetry. Some of these concerned the free or etymologically unjustified treatment of contiguous vowels in synaeresis or diaeresis; but the vast majority of pre- and post-Classical prosodic liberties concern, in one way or another, the treatment of the *e atone*. In medieval and early sixteenth-century versification, the hemistichs of alexandrines enjoyed, for example, considerably more autonomy than in the Classical age, and a theoretical alexandrine out of Malherbe's two hexasyllables would have been possible. This thanks to the convention of the *césure épique*,* a device widely used in medieval epic poetry, allowing the line-internal *e atone* of the caesura to be treated just like the line-teminal one. Here are examples of the *césure épique* in decasyllables, the first two drawn again from *La Chanson de Roland:*

Li emperer(e)s// Carles de Fran/ce dulc(e) (4+4+2)
The emperor Charles of sweet France

De vasselag(e)//[8] fut asez/ chevaler (4+3+3)
By his valiance was very chivalrous

And a third from the *Voyage de Gênes* (*Voyage of Genoa*) of Jean Marot (*c.*1463–1526?):

> Ainsi que frer(e)// doit es/tre pour la seur[9] (4+3+3)
>
> *Just as the brother should be for the sister*

The metrical pattern of the decasyllable – the most commonly used type of French verse after the alexandrine and octosyllable – is not as rigorously determined as that of the alexandrine, but like all verses over eight syllables, it is a *vers composé*, requiring some sort of caesura. Typically, the decasyllable's caesura comes after the fourth syllable, as in the examples above. Note that an *e atone* immediately follows the fourth accented syllable in each line, falling at the end of a word just before the caesura. In the *césure épique* these non-elided *e atones* can be simply dropped. When an *e atone* falls before the caesura, but is, by contrast, pronounced to ensure an even syllable count, as often occurs in medieval and Renaissance poems set to music, we have what is called a *césure lyrique*.* Here are two examples of it in lines from François Villon (1431–1463?), the first drawn from the 'Ballade pour prier Nostre Dame' ('Ballade to Pray Our Lady'):

> Emperiere// des infernaulx/ paluz[10] (4+4+2)
>
> *Empress of infernal swamps*

the second from 'Les Contredits Franc Gontier' ('Franc Gontier's Counterings'):

> Sy se vantent// couchier /soubz le rosier![11] (4+2+4)
>
> *And they boast that they lie under the rosebush!*

Like the *césure épique*, the *césure lyrique* (rare by the mid-sixteenth century) is not permitted in Classical prosody, but the *coupe lyrique*,* which incorporates in effect a non-elided *e muet* into the measure that precedes the *coupe*, is allowed. We find a clear necessity for such a *coupe lyrique* in a stanza of *rime croisée** (crossed rhyme, patterned abab) from Malherbe's (elaborately named) 'Ode, Pour Le Roi allant châtier la rébellion des Rochelois, et chasser les Anglais, qui en leur faveur étaient descendus en île de Ré' ('Ode, For The King [Louis XIII] Going to Punish the Rebellion of the Rochelois, and Chase Out the English, who in Their Favor Had Landed on the Isle of Ré'). In the second line (which features diaeresis in "Louis and "lion"), the syntax and the punctuation impede us from linking the *e atone* to the next syllable:

Donc un nouveau/ labeur// à tes ar/mes s'apprête: (4+2+3+3)
Prends ta foudre,/ LOUIS,// et va/ comme un lion (4+2+2+4)
Donner/ le dernier coup// à la derniè/re tête (2+4+4+2)
    De la rébellion.[12] (6)

Thus a new trial for your arms is readying itself,
Take your thunder, LOUIS, and go like a lion
Give the last blow, to the last head
    Of the rebellion.

Finally, before the Renaissance, one also sees the case of a pronounced *e atone* falling after the caesura. This practice is called a *césure enjambante.** Here is an example in a decasyllable from Eustache Deschamps (1346–1407):

Que la victoi//re venait/ avec moi[13] (4+3+3)

That victory came with me

As with the *césures épiques* and *lyriques*, the *césure enjambante* is abolished from Classical verse, but the *coupe enjambante,** or measure-straddling *e atone*, is allowed to remain and is extremely common. We again find examples of these in Malherbe's stanza cited above. Since there is no reason for pause, the *coupes* dividing the measures naturally fall in the middle of the words "ar/mes" (in line 1) and "derniè/re" (in line 3). This enhances the general rhythmic effect of *enchaînement* characteristic of French verse.

For the ordinary student of French poetry, it is not essential to memorize every rule and convention proscribing or prohibiting alternative practices with respect to the *e atone*. It suffices to know that such conventions and rules exist and apply especially to the *coupes* (positions dividing accented measures) just as they do to the caesura. The strategies that pre-Classical and post-Classical prosody used for getting around the rhythmic complications presented by the *e atone* involved *apocope** (as in the *césure épique*), that is, the license to drop, or not pronounce, an unelided *e atone* at the end of a word, as well as *syncope,** the license to drop an undesirable *e atone* falling in the middle of a word. Though such free-wheeling practices were already waning in the middle of the sixteenth century, some will survive as *licences poétiques*: for example, the spelling of "encor" without e.

The first liberties modern poets took in composing free verse were often the last freedoms relinquished before the Classical period. Thus, Verlaine experimented with *césures lyriques* and *césures enjambantes*, and we find many examples of *césure épique* (by an *e atone apocopé*) in early twentieth-century poems, as in the following line by Guillaume Apollinaire:

Qu'un au/tre te condamn(e)// tu m'as/ ensorcelé[14] (2+4+2+4)

Let another condemn you you have bewitched me

As Apollinaire practiced both regularity and irregularity, sometimes in the same poem, we cannot always hear or scan his verses in accordance with such (pre-Classical) conventions, but the dropping of the *e atone* in the above example seems the most natural prosodic option.

To conclude with Malherbe, and return for a moment to the historical insistence on regularity, symmetry, and proportion, the lines of his hetero-metric stanzas manage to strike a balance between various types of metrical and syntactic sameness and difference, achieving a kind of massive equilib-rium. Similarly, by deploying a consistent pattern of silencing or articulating the *e muet*, and by separating or condensing contiguous vowels according to strict pre-set rules, his verse exemplifies the compromise Classical French prosody struck with the ever-evolving pronunciation of spoken French. It eliminated as much as possible the confusion that can arise from special prac-tices with respect to unelided *e atones* at the critical position of the caesura. At the same time it allowed flexibility with respect to the *coupes*. Most importantly perhaps, Malherbe and other Classical French poets insisted unconditionally on the pronunciation of the *e atone* in front of consonants. By making this choice, they solidified what often strikes French and non-French readers alike as an unnatural rule of pronunciation for verse, forcing that paradoxical sounding of the "silent e," which must be heard in the vast majority of French poems, and which marks, no doubt, the most audible, unmistakable difference between verse and prose.

Our next examples of Classical alexandrines will be taken from Racine, whose verse often reveals a subtle and flexible implementation of Classical rules, rather than illustrating, like our previous examples, either pre- or post-Classical exceptions, or straightforward application. Let us begin by considering the following lines, drawn from his 1667 tragedy *Andromaque:*

> Ce n'est pas/ les Troyens,// c'est Hector/ qu'on poursuit. (3+3+3+3)
> Oui,/les Grecs/ sur le Fils// persécu/tent le Père. (1+2+3+3+3)
> Il a /par trop de sang// acheté/ leur colère.[15] (2+4+3+3)

> *It is not the Trojans, but Hector who is being pursued.*
> *Yes, the Greeks through the Son are persecuting the Father.*
> *He has by too much blood bought their anger.*

In the first alexandrine, we see the same kind of parallelism and syntactic and metrical convergence that we saw in the stanzas by Malherbe. But in the second line, there is a divergence between the rhythm of the syntax and our expectations of the meter: an immediate complication, insofar as the first word of an alexandrine is not normally accented or followed by a pause. Within a general context of symmetry and parallelism, we thus see a principle of variation at work. It is this kind of variation, more than the relentless symmetries of Malherbe, that creates the shifting, phrasal rhythm especially beautiful in French verse. And it is for this kind of variation, which paradoxically recalls the ever-changing accentual patterns of prose, that Racine is especially admired, even by the most rule-conscious poets of his day.

Let us take a closer look at the prosody of the second line. The syntax and resulting punctuation of the first hemistich determine an extra internal accent on the word "Oui" (recall that we defined the alexandrine as having usually only two variable rhythmic accents, one within each hemistich). The offsetting and extraordinary accentuation of this term correspond very well to the meaning of the verse, which is one of emphatic affirmation. But they do not go so far as to break any rule of the alexandrine meter. We might be concerned that the line's principal pause falls after "Oui" instead of at the position of the caesura. However, we are accustomed to thinking of the caesura in terms of a pause only because it generally corresponds to the line's most prominent syntactical break, as occurs, for example, in each of Malherbe's alexandrines (whether or not the break is marked by a comma and a pause). In fact, the caesura does not have to coincide with the primary syntactic break of the line, though the alexandrine's syntax must be able to support the metrical emphasis on the sixth syllable. Thanks to the syntactical inversion* of the references to the Father and the Son, Racine's line accepts the caesura's emphasis beautifully, articulating a compelling binary structure. To put this another way, the natural prosaic order of this line would be: ". . . les Grecs persécutent le Père sur le Fils." But Racine upsets this order to several good effects. First, by performing a syntactical inversion that places "sur le Fils" at the end of the first hemistich, he manages to poetically recreate an inverted relationship between the Son and the Father that is both in accord with the line's meaning and supported by its metrical accents. At the same time, he avoids (by the same inversion) having the caesura fall in the middle of "persécutent" (an arrangement requiring a *césure enjambante*, which the rules of Classical prosody would not allow), by displacing this word to the less critical position of the *coupe*, and settling for a *coupe enjambante* (a measure-straddling word within the hemistich), which Classical prosody does allow. This operation repeats itself, moreover, in a parallel syntactical inversion in the very next line, since the phrase's natural syntax – "Il a acheté leur colère par trop de sang" – would be equally unsuited to a medial accent, while the accent on "sang" seems most appropriate. In Racine, and in French poetry generally, syntactic inversions often perform just this double function: they get around metrical difficulties and lend poetic emphasis by forging new subtle alliances between word order and obligatory metrical accentuation.

There are dramatic moments, however, where even Classical prosody exploits, rather then resolves, the tension created by discordances between meter and syntax. These can present themselves wherever the metrical accent seems denied or overriden by the rhythm of syntax. The most striking cases of metrical and syntactic discordance are not associated with the line-internal *coupes* or *césures enjambantes*, but are rather extrinsic, occurring from line to line. These are especially dramatic because they overreach not only the line's last metrical accent, but also the phonetic accent created by the rhyme, whereas French verse rhythm, normally tied to its end-line demarcation, is not inherently on-going as the rhythm of much English verse is. There are three basic types of discordances that override end-line demarcation: the *rejet*,* the *contre-rejet*,* and the *enjambement*.*

The *rejet* occurs when a brief element at the beginning of one line is both highlighted and strongly linked syntactically to the preceding line. One of the most famous examples of this takes place in Racine's *Phèdre*, where Aricie, speaking to her captor, the monster-slaying Thésée, suggests that Phèdre (his wife) is also a monster. Thanks to the *rejet*, she does this in a manner which is prosodically bold (emphatic because of the conflict between the meter and the syntax), yet semantically understated, or subtle:

> Mais tout/ n'est pas détruit. //Et vous/ en laissez vivre (2+4+2+4)
> Un . . . /Votre Fils,/ Seigneur,// me défend/ de poursuivre.[16]
> (1+3+2+3+3)
>
> *But all are not destroyed. And of these you are letting live*
> *One . . . Your Son, my Lord, will not allow me to go on.*

Used sparingly in Classical prosody, the *rejet* abounds in modern poetry, and often for its shock effect. Thus, one of the greatest scandals of Hugo's 1830 Romantic drama *Hernani*, which defied all conventions of Classical theater, was its deployment of a seemingly gratuitous *rejet* between the first and second lines, in the middle of a set, prosaic phrase:

> Serait-/ ce déjà lui?//
>   *(Un nouveau coup)*
>   C'est bien/ à l'escalier (3+3+2+4)
> Dérobé./
>   *(Un quatrième coup)*
>   Vite, ouvrons.//[17] (3+3 . . .)
>
> *Would that be him already?*
>   (Another knock)
>   *It is at the secret*
> *Stairway.*
>   (A fourth knock)
>   *Quick, let's open.*

In Rimbaud's 1870 sonnet 'Le Dormeur du val' ('The Sleeper in the Vale'), which implicitly criticizes the futility of the Franco-Prussian war, we find the use of multiple *rejets* building a cumulative effect of suspense and surprise. This culminates in a paradoxically shocking evocation of peacefulness in the final line of the poem. The syntactical run-on and metrical isolation of the term "Tranquille" (and the following destruction of the caesura) play an important part in underscoring the irony;* the young soldier's peaceful sleep, which the poem had first seemed to be describing idyllically, is in fact an eternal one, caused by a violent death:

> Les parfums /ne font pas (//) frissonner/ sa narine; (3+3+3+3)
> Il dort/ dans le soleil, // la main/ sur sa poitrine (2+4+2+4)
> Tranquille./ Il a/ deux trous (//) rou/ges au côté droit.[18] (2+2+3+5)

> *The perfumes don't make his nostrils flutter;*
> *He sleeps in the sun, his hand on his tranquil*
> *Chest. He has two red holes in the right side.*

In the *contre-rejet*, which is also far more common in modern than in Classical poetry, an element metrically highlighted at the end of one line is syntactically bound to the next one. We find an example of this in 'Le Lac' ('The Lake') a Romantic elegy by Alphonse de Lamartine (1790–1869), where "l'aurore" comes too quickly (even before the beginning of the next line), precisely at the moment when the lover asks for a longer night:

> Je dis/ à cette nuit://Sois plus len/te; et l'aurore (2+4+3+3)
>   Va dissiper/ la nuit.[19] (4+2)

> *I say to this night: Pass more slowly; and dawn*
> *Comes to dissipate the night.*

Though many writers on prosody refer to of all kinds of extrinsic discordances between meter and syntax as *enjambements* (including *rejets* and *contre-rejets*), Jean Mazaleyrat makes a useful distinction. He reserves this term for cases where the end of one line runs seamlessly into the next one, without especially accentuating any particular element at the end or beginning of either line. Often, as in these lines from Baudelaire, this kind of *enjambement* will reinforce a semantic reference to some other kind of crossing:

> Et quand /il s'en allait //sans rien voir,/ à travers (2+4+3+3)
> Les champs,/ sans distinguer// les étés/ des hivers,[20] (2+4+3+3)

> *And when he left without seeing anything, across*
> *The fields, without distinguishing the summers from the winters,*

Here, the relatively smooth run-on transition between the lines of verse corresponds to the character's blindness to other natural distinctions.

Thus, in regular verse, the interruptions of metrical norms amount to stylistic effects, which are more or less bold, frequent, and acceptable depending on the period in which the poetry is composed. And though it is within the Classical era on the whole that metrical stylistic effects were the least tolerated, we find extremes of regularity and irregularity even within this period. Because of the lightness and specificity of their genre, the *Fables** of Jean de La Fontaine (1621–1695) were, for example, widely admired in the seventeenth century, though they are composed of highly varied verses and rhyme schemes, showing metrical irregularity in many respects. However, since La Fontaine's irregular verses (examples of which we will see further) still rhyme and display a carefully patterned mixture of meters, contemporary prosodists generally refer to them as *vers mêlés** (mixed lines) as opposed to *vers libres,** to distinguish them from modern free verse.

At the other end of the Classical spectrum, Nicolas Boileau (1636–1711), the French Academy's first arbitrator of poetic taste, comes to incarnate the very notion of the all-powerful, monarchic poetic rule. Yet his dictates, far from presenting themselves as oppressive or arbitrary, tend to justify themselves as promoting only "natural," universally perceived expressions of beauty, taste, and reason. Thus, many of the norms of Classical prosody have been passed down to posterity through famous lines from his *Art poétique*, a long poem which overtly celebrates the progress in prosody achieved by Malherbe and Racine, and insists on the need to steer clear of previous poets' metrical, syntactic, and phonetic offenses:

> N'offrez rien/ au lecteur //que ce /qui peut lui plaire. (3+3+2+4)
> Ayez /pour la cadence// une orei/lle sévère: (2+4+3+3)
> Que toujours/ dans vos vers// le sens/ coupant les mots, (3+3+2+4)
> Suspen/de l'hémistiche,// en mar/que le repos. (2+4+2+4)
> Gardez /qu'une voyelle,// à courir/ trop hâtée, (2+4+3+3)
> Ne soit /d'une voyelle// en son chemin/ heurtée. (2+4+4+2)
> Il est/ un heureux choix// de mots harmonieux. (2+4+2+4)
> Fuyez /des mauvais sons// le concours/ odieux: (2+4+3+3)
> Le vers/ le mieux rempli,// la plus no/ble pensée (2+4+3+3)
> Ne peut plaire/ à l'esprit //quand l'oreille/ est blessée.[21] (3+3+3+3)

> *Offer nothing to the reader but that which can please him.*
> *Have for cadence a severe ear:*
> *Let always in your verse the meaning cutting the words*
> *Suspend the hemistich, and mark the pause.*
> *Make certain that no vowel, too hasty to run,*
> *Be knocked by another vowel in its way.*
> *There is a happy choice of harmonious words.*

> *Flee the odious concourse of ugly sounds:*
> *The fullest line of verse, the noblest thought*
> *Cannot please the mind, when the ear is hurt.*

As might be expected, Boileau takes pains in his verse to practice what he preaches. When he emphasizes (in lines 3 and 4) the necessary link between syntax and meter by pointing to the role that meaning plays in determining a line's accentuation, he places the word "sens" in a strategic, rhythmically accentuated position. A *coupe* falls, moreover, right before the word "coupant," referring to the line's cutting or division into measures. The next line similarly emphasizes the importance of binary division by placing the word "hémistiche" at the end of the hemistich. In lines 2, 4, 5, and 6, his verse achieves a kind of rhythmic balance by the repeated elision of the *e atone* at the caesura. In lines 5 and 6, he discourages hiatus* (the contact between articulated vowels, as in "j'ai acheté") and then avoids vowel collision (in lines 7 and 8) in a paradoxical way: the words "odieux" and "harmonieux," containing semi-vowels in spoken French, have their vowels neatly separated in *diérèses*. This slow and deliberate articulation cannot help, moreover, but to emphasize the value of the rhyme pair, which thanks to the semantic contrast (balancing the phonetic sameness) constitutes a Classical ideal.

But one does not have to be acquainted with Boileau's precepts to recognize a Classical alexandrine, just as one does not have to know much about French history to grasp the importance of Louis XIV's court at Versailles. So massively central and omnipresent is the even binary rhythm of this most regular French meter, and so familiar are the syntactic inversions that tend to accompany it, that many a native French speaker will recognize an alexandrine whether or not it is inscribed in a context of regular verse. And this rhythm, wherever it is recognized, communicates in and of itself a considerable measure of French worldliness, as well as signaling strictly regulated and highly refined poetry. Thus, in the twentieth-century comic book adventure *Astérix et Cléopâtre* (*Asterix and Cleopatra*), of the famous *Astérix* series by Uderzo and Goscinny, when an architect from Alexandria named Numérobis greets the Gallic druid Panoramix with the following line:

Je suis/ mon cher ami,// très heureux /de te voir.[22] (2+4+3+3)

I am my dear friend very happy to see you.

a greeting immediately seconded by Panoramix's explanation of the visitor's identity – "C'est un Alexandrin" (He/It is an Alexandrine) – most readers of the series are likely to get the joke. As there is no *e atone* here to complicate perception, a well-tuned French ear will simply hear the familiar meter's articulation of the line into symmetrical halves, as well as the noble poetic effect of the syntactic inversion. What analysis contributes is only awareness that the alexandrine in question is *created* by the inversion – the rearrangement of the prose-line: *Je suis très heureux de te voir, mon cher ami.* Such a string of syllables could never pass, on its own, for an alexandrine, owing to its asymmetrical structure, since an accent at the caesura would place an inappropriate emphasis on the word *de*. Iconoclastic poets of the late nineteenth and twentieth centuries will eventually compose twelve-syllable lines like these within alexandrine contexts. And we find the word *de* in the even more awkward position of the rhyme, for example, in the provocative lyrics of the songwriter Georges Brassens. Denis Roche (1937–), a member of the 1960s *Tel Quel* group,[23] often ends his verse (quite ironically) in the middle of a word ("passe/Relle") or other unbreakable unit, as in these twelve-syllable lines (if no *e muet* is counted) which include a famous indictment of poetry (repeated in eleven poems), and reduce the alexandrine to inexistence:

> *La poésie est inadmissibl(e). D'ailleurs ell(e) n'*
> *exist(e) pas*, mêm(e) devenu(e) familièr(e) comme il n'
> Est pas possibl(e) [. . .][24]
>
> Poetry is inadmissible. In fact it doesn't
> exist, *even having become familiar like you wouldn'*
> *T believe [. . .]*

Such radical conflicts between the accents of syntax and meter inevitably flaunt an overturning of Classical poetry's constraints, rather than signifying nobility, tradition, and respect.

One of the first generalized movements away from Classical norms was in the frequent recourse taken by Romantic poets to the *alexandrin ternaire**
(also called the *trimètre romantique*), a three-measure alexandrine where the traditional binary effect of the caesura is effaced. Although rare examples of it can be found in seventeenth-century dramatic verse, as in the following line from Pierre Corneille's *Suréna* (where the caesura, though weakened, is still perceptible),

> Toujours aimer, toujours souffrir, toujours mourir [25] (4+4+4)
>
> *To always love, always suffer, always die*

and in the light verse of La Fontaine, Hugo was the first to recast alexandrines in this way wherever it suited him in lyric poems. This was a defiant act, which, as often happens with Hugo, he did not hesitate to claim credit for and poetically dramatize, as in the following "vers manifeste":

J'ai disloqué/ ce grand niais/ d'alexandrin[26] (4+4+4)

I dislocated that great idiot the alexandrine

Note that the poet adds insult to his injury of the alexandrine by the mocking, very Classical sounding *diérèse* on the word "niais".

The *trimètre romantique*, however, while being a significant innovation, functions for the most part as a complement rather than as a competitor to the regular alexandrine. In fact, this ternary pattern, despite its name, does not even have the true value of a meter, since it was not used as the predominant type of verse in any Romantic poem. Rather, its metrical importance lay in undermining the alexandrine's structure from within. This transformative operation on a body that had come to be treated as sacred inaugurated a revolutionary process that would lead first to the reclaiming of pre-Classical liberties, and finally to the complete freeing of verse.

In emphasizing the alexandrine's importance, we must not however forget that a number of alternatives to this meter had always figured prominently in French verse. Indeed, the octosyllable and decasyllable were used more widely than the alexandrine before the mid-1550s, and enjoy an even longer and nobler lineage. The octosyllable is ubiquitous in medieval narrative and lyric poetry; shorter meters like two-, four-, and six-syllable verses also have a long tradition and play a complementary role in heterometric stanzas. During the first half of the sixteenth century, the (4//6) decasyllable, considered roughly equivalent to the Latin hexameter, was the verse of choice. Though the Classical alexandrine evolved from an old French form, before the Renaissance it struck poets as too long and prose-like in comparison to the decasyllable. In shifting from the ten- to the twelve-syllable line, the Pléiade poets played at first on this "prosy" effect, employing, for example, many *enjambements* in the *beau style bas* (the beautiful low [familiar] style) of collections such as Du Bellay's *Regrets* and Ronsard's *Amours de Marie* (*Love Poems for Marie*). This shows that it was not so much the alexandrine's symmetry that attracted them as its meandering length. In their hands, however, it rapidly structured, nourished, and balanced itself to become the dominant form of French verse. And today, poets such as Jacques Réda (1929–) are experimenting with fourteen-syllable lines just as the Pléiade did with the alexandrine.

Whatever their length, frequency, or accustomed use, even-numbered meters are privileged instruments of French verse. By contrast, imparisyllabic* (or odd-numbered) meters were traditionally granted a lesser status, and considered until the nineteenth century to play a subordinated role. Five- and seven-syllable lines, for example, are throughout the earlier periods traditionally reserved for song, although Renaissance and Classical poets also used the latter meter for unsung odes. Thus it is not surprising that a marked return to the appreciation of lyricism and of expressive musicality in nineteenth-century poetry was often expressed by the use of imparisyllabic lines. We find these, for example, in one of Baudelaire's most widely read poems, 'L'Invitation au voyage,' ('Invitation to the Voyage') which evokes the musical quality of Carl Maria Von Weber's 1819 *Invitation à la valse* (*Invitation to the Waltz*) by using heterometric stanzas of pentasyllables* and heptasyllables* along with a heptasyllabic refrain:

> Mon enfant, ma sœur,
> Songe à la douceur
> D'aller là-bas vivre ensemble!
> Aimer à loisir,
> Aimer et mourir
> Au pays qui te ressemble!
> Les soleils mouillés
> De ces ciels brouillés
> Pour mon esprit ont les charmes
> Si mystérieux
> De tes traîtres yeux,
> Brillant à travers leurs larmes.
>
> Là tout n'est qu'ordre et beauté,
> Luxe, calme, et volupté. [. . .]²⁷

> *My child, my sister,*
> *Dream of the sweetness*
> *Of going there to live together!*
> *To love at leisure,*
> *To love and to die*
> *In the country that resembles you!*
> *The wet suns*
> *Of those foggy skies*
> *For my spirit have the charms,*
> *So mysterious,*
> *Of your treacherous eyes*
> *Shining through their tears.*
>
> *There, all is but order and beauty,*
> *Luxury, calm, and voluptuousness. [. . .]*

Nine-syllable verses (enneasyllables*) were also, before the nineteenth century, generally reserved for song. Verlaine, however, reclaimed them for poetry, along with other odd-numbered lines in collections such as *Fêtes galantes* (*Gallant Fêtes*) and *Romances sans paroles* (*Romances without Words*). His 1874 'Art poétique,' a work which attacks several principles of Boileau's head on, begins by praising the light musicality of the *vers impair,** dismissing the heavily poised symmetrical structure of the alexandrine:

> De la musique avant toute chose,
> Et pour cela préfère l'Impair
> Plus vague et plus soluble dans l'air,
> Sans rien en lui qui pèse ou qui pose.[28]

> *Music before all else,*
> *And for that prefer the Uneven line*
> *More vague and more soluble in the air,*
> *With nothing within that weighs or poses.*

Similarly, one of the earliest modern uses of the hendecasyllable* (eleven-syllable) verse occurs in a poem entitled 'La Fileuse et l'enfant' ('The Spinning-woman and the Child') by Marceline Desbordes-Valmore (1786–1859). This poem also immediately invokes music:

> J'appris à chanter en allant à l'école:
> Les enfants joyeux aiment tant les chansons![29]

> *I learned to sing going to school:*
> *Joyful children love songs so!*

Written by one of the few Romantic women poets to be recognized by such contemporaries as Baudelaire, this poem's unusual meter seems appropriate not only to represent the distinctiveness of the poet's own feminine voice, but also to convey the subordinated status of the spinning woman's song.

Thus, by the mid-nineteenth century, whether by resorting to alternative meters or transforming the internal structure of the alexandrine, we find French poets consistently pushing the limits of regular verse from within.

The 1869 publication of Baudelaire's *Le Spleen de Paris (Petits poèmes en prose)* (*The Spleen of Paris* [*Little Poems in Prose*]) constituted, no doubt, the greatest onslaught on the power of regular verse from without, establishing for modernity the general viability of the prose poem. This was a genre marginally attempted during the Romantic period by Aloysius Bertrand (1807–1841) and others, and made known to Baudelaire by the posthumous 1842 publication of Bertrand's *Gaspard de la nuit* (*Gaspard of the Night*). But the Symbolist poets of the fin de siècle viewed Baudelaire himself to be the first to have realized the ambition set forth in *Le Spleen de Paris'* preface, which was to create a new form of lyricism (that is, of poetic expression at once subjective and musical) that could entirely do without the conventions of meter and rhyme: "Who among us has not, in his ambitious days, dreamed the miracle of a poetic prose, musical without rhythm and without rhyme, flexible enough and halting enough to adapt itself to the lyrical movements of the soul, to the undulations of rêverie, to the sudden starts of consciousness?"[30] We will look further at one of Baudelaire's prose poems; for the moment it suffices to underscore the role he played in opening poetry to prose.

Baudelaire's principal successors, Mallarmé, Verlaine, and Rimbaud, also waged war on French meters from without and within. Mallarmé, who was noted by his contemporaries for his prose poems, and notorious in his verse and prose for the contorsions of his syntax, definitively exploded the definitional boundaries of verse in his 1897 *Un coup de dés jamais n'abolira le hasard* (*A Throw of the Dice Will Never Abolish Chance*), where the text is typographically arranged accross double-pages in dispersed (high, middle, and low) fragments along the lines of a musical score. But the radical irregularity and musicality of this late work are also subtly anticipated in much of Mallarmé's earlier "classical" verse, as in the interrupted alexandrines of his 1876 *L'Après-midi d'un faune* (*The Afternoon of a Faun*), where the poet claimed he was aiming to create the effect of a musical accompaniment. His essay *Crise de vers* insisted, moreover, on each poet's freedom to modulate the rhythmic and acoustic patterns of verse on a wholly individual scale in the interest of music as much as of revolution, comparing, for example, free-verse lines to the melodies played by solo instruments, and the alexandrine to organ music, which expresses the orthodoxy of the church.

As for Verlaine, the extreme musicality of his verse is due in large part to the ease with which he varies accentual patterns in the measures of both odd- and even-numbered lines. In his poem 'L'Allée' ('The Lane'), for example, we find alexandrines (ternary or not) in which, beside the erasure of the caesura, the presence and uneven distribution of *coupes lyriques* give the impression of irregularity:

> Fardée et pein/te comme (//) au temps / des bergeries, (4+4+4)
> Frêle / parmi les nœuds (//) énor/mes de rubans, (2+4+2+4)
> Elle passe, / sous les (//) ramu/res assombries [. . .][31] (4+4+4)
>
> *Powdered and painted as in the age of pastoral paintings,*
> *Fragile amidst the enormous ribbon-bows,*
> *She passes, under the darkened boughs [. . .]*

In the early 1870s, Rimbaud's metrical irregularity was by far the most radical of any French poets. And contrary to that of Mallarmé and Verlaine, it most often created effects of rhythmic and syntactic rupture rather than continuity and smoothness. We already saw this in the *rejets* of 'Le dormeur du val.' In the sonnet 'Voyelles' ('Vowels'), where the *e atone* is associated with whiteness, an impression of chaos is created not only semantically and syntactically, by the sudden, seemingly nonsensical enumeration of juxtaposed vowels and colors (and the disordering of the *u* and *o*), but also rhythmically, since the serial structure of the first line creates a bizarrely even or binary dodecasyllable, but certainly not a regular alexandrine:

> A noir,/ E blanc,/ I rouge,/ U vert,/ O bleu:/ voyelles, (2+2+2+2+2+2)
> Je dirai/ quelque jour// vos naissan/ces latentes: (3+3+3+3)
> A,/ noir corset velu// des mou/ches éclatantes (1+5+2+4)
> Qui bombi/nent autour// des puanteurs/ cruelles, (3+3+4+2)
>
> Golfes d'om/bre; E, candeurs// des vapeurs/ et des tentes, (3+3+3+3)
> Lances / des glaciers fiers,// rois blancs,/ frissons d'ombelles[. . .][32]

> *A black, E white, I red, U green, O blue: vowels,*
> *I will one day declare your latent births:*
> *A, black hairy corset of exploding flies*
> *Which buzz around cruel stenches,*
>
> *Gulfs of shadow; E, candors of vapors and of tents,*
> *Lances of proud glaciers, white kings, shivering umbels:*

Along with the internal structure of the verse (which traditionally depends on the prosodic treatment of vowels, and especially on that of the mute *e*), Rimbaud disrupts the global structure of his poem. He does this from the outset not only by accumulating feminine rhymes (breaking the rule of rhyme gender alternation), but also by placing an especially shocking and awkward *rejet* at the beginning of the second stanza. The "Golfes d'ombre," placed in apposition to the "puanteurs cruelles" of the previous line, are supposed to be linked to the exploding flies and the black hairy corset of the letter A. However, the application of the normal rule concerning elision creates confusion and irony, since it results in the over-emphasis of an isolated *e*; the reader feels forced to phonetically overlay the dark sound and image of the word *ombre* on the blank space of the E. This seems paradoxically both appropriate and inappropriate since it tends to make the vowel's silent/white sound/image disappear.

The importance of the *e atone* to French prosody and to the French language generally can be gauged in a 1969 novel by Georges Perec (1936–1982), entitled *La Disparition* (*The Vanishing*). This 300-page text is written from beginning to end without the letter e. It tells the unsolved mystery of the disappearance of something crucial, whose identity remains hidden until the very end. The novel takes as its point of departure an e-less sonnet entitled 'La Disparition,' by the poet and mathematician Jacques Roubaud (1932–), and features parodical rewritings of 'Voyelles' and other nineteenth-century poems, by Perec himself. In these opening lines from 'Vocalisations,' note the telling *blanc* (whiteness or blank) in the position of the E; also note that the inevitable absence of feminine rhymes in this e-less version gives a heavily masculine inflection to Rimbaud's 'Voyelles,' which has often been interpreted as a *blason* (a poem of descriptive praise) celebrating a woman's body:

> A noir (Un blanc), I roux, U safran, O azur:
> Nous saurons au jour dit ta vocalisation [. . .][33]
>
> *A black (A white/blank), I russet, U saffron, O azure:*
> *On the said day we'll know your vocalization [. . .]*

Rimbaud's transgressions of the conventions of rhythm and rhyme in his first collection of *Poésies* prefigure the more radical departures of his last work, *Illuminations*, which marks a critical moment in the development of the prose poem in France, as well as the beginning of the *vers libre* with the poems 'Marine' ('Marine/Seascape') and 'Mouvement' ('Movement'). There is a sense of the interpenetration of verse and prose throughout the volume. We find, for example, metrical patterns highlighted by the positioning of sentences in several of the prose poems. 'Aube' ('Dawn'), one of the most accessible of these, recounting a child's wakening of a personified dawn, begins and ends with octosyllabic phrases:

> J'ai embrassé l'aube d'été. (4+4)
> [. . .]
> Au réveil il était midi.[34] (3+5)
>
> *I embraced the summer dawn.*
> *[. . .]*
> *On awakening it was noon.*

In other poems, such as 'Enfance (III)' ('Childhood [III]'), the typographical isolation of sentences suggests either highly irregular verses, or *versets*,* an intermediary line-structure between verse and prose, soon to be developed by Paul Claudel (1868–1955):

> Au bois il y a un oiseau, son chant vous arrête et vous fait rougir.
>
> Il y a une horloge qui ne sonne pas.
>
> Il y a une fondrière avec un nid de bêtes blanches.
>
> Il y a une cathédrale qui descend et un lac qui monte.[35]

> *In the woods there is a bird, his song stops you and makes you blush.*
> *There is a clock that does not strike.*
> *There is a bog with a nest of white beasts.*
> *There is a cathedral that descends and a lake that rises.*

'Marine,' however, is composed of what would soon be called *vers libres*: lines of poetry of variable lengths and rhythms, which are neither systematically rhymed nor accented (and thus lines in which each reader must choose whether and where to count the *e atones*):

> Les chars d'argent et de cuivre – (7)
> Les proues d'acier et d'argent – (7)
> Battent l'écume, –   (3 or 4)
> Soulèvent les souches des ronces.[36] (6, 7, or 8)

> *The chariots of silver and copper –*
> *The prows of steel and silver –*
> *Beat the froth, –*
> *Tear up the stumps of the brambles.*

In all of the *Illuminations* formal innovation accompanies a new poetic vision: strange prosaic rhythms carry the impassible description of an enchanted, composite universe, which a half-century later would come to be known as "surreal."

Following Rimbaud, it was the avant-garde poet Marie Krysinska (1864–1908) who first began to experiment with free verse in the early 1880s. However, her claims for priority were dismissed in her own time. This was, no doubt, because of her gender, but also, perhaps, because some of her irregular verse presented itself in a "light," humorous context evoking song or dance, and retained some metrical and rhyme patterns in the manner of *vers mêlés*. This happens, for example, in these lines from 'La Gigue' ('The Jig'):

> La danseuse exhibe ses bas noirs
>   Sur des jambes dures
>   Comme du bois.
>   Mais le visage reste coi
>   Et l'œil vert,
>   Comme les bois,
> Ne trahit nul émoi.[37]

> *The dancer exhibits her black stockings*
>   *On her legs hard*
>   *As wood.*

> But her face stays quiet
>   And her eye green
>   As woods
> Does not betray any emotion.

It was not until 1886 that the freeing of French verse became an official event with the publication of a Symbolist manifesto by Jean Moréas (1856–1910) in the September 18 edition of *Le Figaro*, and of Mallarmé's *Crise de vers*. Along with putting an end to any clear distinction between verse and prose, Mallarmé's essay praises the *faux vers* (or faltering verse) of Laforgue and Henri de Régnier (1864–1936), and mentions several other pioneers of free verse – such as Moréas, Gustave Kahn (1856–1936), the American-born Francis Viélé-Griffin (1863–1937), and the Belgian Émile Verhaeren (1855–1916) –, insisting on the polymorphousness of their rhythms, and on the fragmented harmony of their tonal (as opposed to metrical) compositions.[38] Important early free verse poems appearing this same year in *La Vogue* include those in Rimbaud's *Illuminations* (the greater part of which was first published at this time, though the collection had been composed and abandoned to Verlaine in the early 1870s); selected translations by Laforgue of Walt Whitman's *Leaves of Grass*; several poems from Kahn's 1887 *Palais nomades* (*Nomad Palaces*, the first collection of free verse poems published in France); and a number of Laforgue's *Derniers vers* (*Last Poems*), posthumously collected in 1890.

Laforgue often emerges as the poet canonically representing the invention of free verse. Perhaps this is because his work anticipates much of what would develop in the first decades of the twentieth century, with poets such as Apollinaire and Blaise Cendrars(1887–1961). Apollinaire's 1913 *Alcools* (*Alcohols*) – a collection which the poet purged of all punctuation – opens with 'Zone,' an explicitly modernist poem whose audacity in associating images matches its prosodic boldness, stretching meters and threatening the *e atone*. In the opening lines, for example, the Eiffel tower, an industrial tour de force and a symbol of modern international culture, is represented as a shepherdess:

> À la fin/ tu es las/ de ce mon/de ancien (11)
>
> Bergè/re ô tour Eiffel/ le troupeau des ponts/ bêl(e) ce matin (15)
>
> Tu en as assez/ de vivr(e)/ dans l'antiquité/ grecque et romaine (16)
>
> Ici/ mêm(e) les automobil(es)/ ont l'air/ d'être anciennes (13)
>
> La religion seule/ est restée/ tout(e) neuv(e)/ la religion (14)
>
> Est restée simpl(e)/ comm(e) les hangars/ de Port-Aviation (13)
>
> [. . .]

Tu lis les prospectus/ les catalog(ues)/ les affich(es) qui chant(ent) tout
  haut (17)
Voilà la poésie ce matin/ et pour la prose/ il y a les journaux (19)[39]

In the end you are tired of this ancient world
Shepherdess O Eiffel tower the herd of bridges is bleating this morning
You've had enough of living in Roman and Greek Antiquity
Here even the automobiles look ancient
Only religion has remained brand new religion
Has remained simple like the hangars at Port-Aviation
[. . .]
You read the prospectuses the catalogues the posters that sing out loud
That's poetry this morning and for prose there are the newspapers

The simultaneity of the old and the new in 'Zone' extends and sharpens
the convergence of modernism and decadence in Laforgue's 'L'Hiver qui
vient' ('Winter's Coming'), with its mixture of mournfulness and whimsy;
its parodical juxtapositions of high eloquence and everyday, urban language;
its constant interruptions of rhetorical flights; and finally, its multiple suspen-
sions and mocking, phantom-like recoveries of rhyme patterns and meters
(including alexandrines that can be counted with and without *syncope* and
apocope) – all of which were typical of the so-called "Decadent" inspiration
of the fin de siècle:

Blocus sentimental! Messag(e)ri(es) du Levant! . . .
Oh, tombée de la pluie! Oh! tombée de la nuit,
Oh! le vent! . . .
La Toussaint, la Noël et la Nouvelle Année,
Oh, dans les bruin(es), toutes mes cheminées! . . .
D'usines . . .

On ne peut plus s'asseoir, tous les bancs sont mouillés;
Crois-moi, c'est bien fini jusqu'à l'année prochaine,
Tant les bancs sont mouillés, tant les bois sont rouillés,
Et tant les cors ont fait ton ton, ont fait ton taine! . . .[40]

Sentimental blockade! Carriers from the Levant! . . .
Oh, rainfall! Oh! nightfall!
Oh! the wind! . . .
All Saints, Christmas and the New Year,
Oh, in the drizzles, all my chimneys! . . .
Of factories . . .

One can no longer sit, all the benches are wet;
Believe me, it's all over till next year,
Since the benches are so wet, and the woods are so rusted
And the horns have so much blown ton ton, blown ton taine! . . .

Note the *césure épique* or *lyrique* in line 5 (which can be read as a decasyllable or an alexandrine), and the *trimètre romantique* (line 13) that closes the second stanza's series of more or less regular alexandrines. These metrical details support the exaggerated melancholic lyricism of the poem (expressed in the multiple "Oh!"), and the nostalgic Romantic reference to the autumnal hunting season, whose onomatopoeic music, "ton ton [. . .] ton taine" expresses directly, albeit ironically, the earlier century's preoccupation with the *sentiment de la nature** (the projection of human feeling on the natural landscape). Here, as in much twentieth-century free verse, the upsetting of the structural balance generally epitomized by Classical verse and the disruption of metrical and rhyme patterns do not lean, as we might think, in the direction of prose understood as sequences of language lacking overtly perceptible rhythm and rhyme. Rather, we are faced with just the contrary: a disorderly rush of accents, and a flood of homophonies resulting from mutliple alliterations,* assonances* and internal rhymes.

This brings us back to the broader issue (which we will develop in further chapters) of rhythm and rhyme's interdependence in various types and periods of French poetry. As a general matter rhyme is, not surprisingly, discouraged in prose, though it does occur in the some of the most heavily cadenced varieties. In free verse, rhyme effects can be either weak or excessive, but rhyme in the strict sense is only intermittent and often displaced. Within the framework of regular verse, rhyme is not only a required structuring feature, it is often considered (and will sometimes be resented) as poetry's defining stylistic ornament. This is true whether the rhyme's value be judged according to the principles of accumulation and virtuosity, as happens in the Middle Ages and for much of the Renaissance, or whether it be judged from the Classical perspective of balance and discrimination, showing rigorous adherence to pre-set rules such as those earlier mentioned concerning gender, etymological origins, and derivation.

We have already seen examples of three prominent patterns of French rhyme: *rimes plates* (aabb), *rimes croisées* (abab), and *rimes embrassées* (abba), and we will focus on these in the next chapter. There are also, however, three degrees attributed to French rhyme, whose analytical description and categorization have changed over time. They are currently classified as follows: the *rime pauvre** (weak rhyme) has only one identical element, the tonic vowel, *bleu/feu*; the *rime suffisante** (sufficient rhyme) has two identical elements, the tonic vowel and a supporting consonant, *rire/maudire*; and the *rime riche** has more than two elements in the tonic syllable, *pleine/haleine*. A very rich rhyme that involves two syllables is called a *rime léonine** (*abolie/mélancolie*). Weaker in effect than the "poor" rhyme, the mere identity of like vowels within tonic syllables containing different consonants (*nu/dur*) is called assonance. While *assonance* and *rime pauvre* occur in the Middle Ages, as in the assonantal *laisses,** or Old French epic stanzas of *La Chanson de Roland*, there is a definite trend toward rhyme saturation in this period. This trend reaches its height in the ornamental *rimes équivoques** (equivocal rhymes, in which homophonous elements extend to entire words and beyond) of the *Grands Rhétoriqueurs* (a group of late fifteenth-/early sixteenth-century poets and historiographers, famous for their formal virtuosity), as in the following lines from an epistle by Guillaume Cretin (1460–1525):

> Me doibt on veoir en jeux esbanoyer,
> Quant par langueur voy ton esbat noyer
> En lac profond, plain de larmes et plainctz?[41]
>
> *Should I be seen enjoying myself in play*
> *When I see your joy drowned by sadness*
> *In a deep lake full of tears and cries?*

Such practices will be condemned by the Classical attention to keeping "rhyme" within the limits of "reason": "La rime est une esclave, et ne doit qu'obéir" [Rhyme is a slave, and must only obey], warned Boileau. In the nineteenth century, while the constraints of rhyme are being progressively weakened, we also find, paradoxically, a renewed taste for *rime riche* and extreme examples of *rime équivoque*, culminating in the exercises of fin-de-siècle humorists, as in the following lines from a 'Sonnet Olorime' ('All Rhyming Sonnet') by Jean Goudezki (1866–1934):

> Comme aux Dieux devisant, Hébé (c'est ma compagne). . .
> Commode, yeux de vice hantés, baissés, m'accompagne . . .[42]
>
> *As though conversing with the Gods, Hebe (that's my companion) . . .*
> *Easy-going, with lowered, vice-haunted eyes, accompanies me . . .*

This sonnet is an homage to Alphonse Allais (1854–1905), an inveterate punster who, in 1900, echoes Laforgue's "ton ton [. . .] ton taine" in the closing of a brief ditty entitled 'Le jeune homme sans soin, et de plus, irrespectueux' ('The Young Man Without Care, and Also Disrespectful'):

> Surveille mieux, fiston,
> Ton thon, ton Taine et ton ton.[43]
>
> *Better watch more carefully, son,*
> *Your tuna, your Taine, and your tone.*

But let us conclude our discussion of the relations between verse and prose on a more serious note. The varying effects and implications of these two basic modalities of poetry can be grasped at the deepest level through an unmediated experience of effective whole poems – poems with enough common features to make their textural difference stand out. To allow for this experience, I have chosen two powerful poems from different historical periods, which draw our attention to the different qualities associated with verse and prose. The synthetic self-containment of regular verse is underscored, for example, in the rich circularity of the first poem's rhymes, while the second poem, leaning toward prose, presents a more analytic form of reflexivity in the poet's *autocritique*, and the text's commentary on itself. Each of these poems responds to the death of a beloved woman, but their lines accomplish the work of mourning in opposite, if equally compelling ways.

The poem in regular verse is a well-known Renaissance sonnet, by Ronsard:

> Comme on voit sur la branche au mois de May la rose
> En sa belle jeunesse, en sa premiere fleur,
> Rendre le ciel jaloux de sa vive couleur,
> Quand l'Aube de ses pleurs au poinct du jour l'arrose:
>
> La grace dans sa fueille, et l'amour se repose,
> Embasmant les jardins et les arbres d'odeur:
> Mais batue ou de pluye, ou d'excessive ardeur,
> Languissante elle meurt fueille à fueille déclose.
>
> Ainsi en ta premiere et jeune nouveauté,
> Quand la terre et le ciel honoroient ta beauté,
> La Parque t'a tuee, et cendre tu reposes.
>
> Pour obsèques reçoy mes larmes et mes pleurs,
> Ce vase plein de laict, ce panier plein de fleurs,
> Afin que vif et mort ton corps ne soit que roses.[44]

> *As one sees on the branch in the month of May the rose*
> *In its beautiful youth, in its first flower,*
> *Render the sky jealous of its vivid color,*
> *When Dawn at first light sprinkles it with tears:*
>
> *Grace in its petal, and love reposes,*
> *Embalming the gardens and the trees with its scent:*
> *But beaten either by rain or excessive ardor,*
> *Languishing it dies, scattered petal by petal.*
>
> *Just so in your first and young newness,*
> *When the earth and sky were honoring your beauty,*
> *The Fates killed you, and in ashes you repose.*
>
> *For Obsequies accept my tears and my laments,*
> *This vase full of milk, this basket full of flowers,*
> *So that your body alive and dead will be but roses.*

The poem that leans toward prose, entitled 'Méditation de la comparaison' ('Meditation on Comparison'), is by the modern poet Roubaud :

Il pourrait me venir à l'esprit de te comparer à un corps noir, rayonnant d'une distance énorme, quasi infinie, une sombre lumière qui n'arrête pas de me parvenir.

Pénétrant mon sommeil comme les rayons X la chair, ma veille comme une couche de nuages est traversée d'innombrables et véloces radiations.

Je le pourrais mais je ne m'y résigne pas.

Je m'acharne à circonscrire *rien-toi* avec exactitude, ce bipôle impossible, à parcourir autour, de ceci, ces phrases de neuf que je nomme poèmes.

Avec tout le mécontentement formel dont je suis capable au regard de la poésie

Entre les mois de silence où je ne me prolongeais que muet.

Et le futur proche où je me tairai de ces poèmes avec absolue incompréhension.

Car pousser la moindre de ces lignes noires sur le papier jusqu'à son bout, son retour, veut dire que d'un instant à l'autre je vais me mettre à verser dans un second silence.

Et qu'entre ces limites étroites je dois essayer de me tendre et te dire, encore.[45]

It could come to my mind to compare you to a black body, shining from an enormous distance, almost infinite, a dark light which does not stop coming toward me.

Penetrating my sleep like X rays do flesh, my vigil like a layer of clouds is crossed by innumerable and fleeting radiations.

I could do this, but I don't resign myself to it.

I stick to circumscribing nothing-you *with exactness, that impossible bi-pole, to travelling around, (with) this, these new phrases that I name poems.*

With all the formal discontent I am capable of with regard to poetry

Between the months of silence when I just extended myself mute.

And the near future where I will become quiet about/shut out these poems with absolute incomprehension.

For to push the least of these black lines on the paper to its end, its return, means that momentarily I am going to start falling into a second silence.

And that between these narrow limits I should try to stretch myself and speak (to) you, once more.

Ronsard's sonnet – commemorating the death of Marie de Clèves, the King's mistress, within the context of a collection of earthly *Amours* (love poems) dedicated to the peasant girl Marie – shows the alexandrine's shift from a verse primarily associated with the *beau style bas* (beautiful low style) to an instrument capable of expressing the most noble register. Epitomizing a successful synthesis of the alexandrine's meandering breadth with traditional marks of high style – rich reflexive rhymes, mythological and Classical allusions,* and conventional, universalizing rhetorical figures – this sonnet has represented for centuries an apogee of Renaissance verse.

Closer to the *verset* and to prose in its composition than to free verse, 'Méditation de la comparaison' is from Roubaud's 1986 *Quelque chose noir* (*Some Thing Black*). Treating the poet's grief over the death of his own wife, these lines obstinately refuse the very rhetorical strategies that Ronsard's poem exploits, along with eschewing the support of meter and rhyme. In an attempt to keep the beloved near, they explicitly stave off the inevitable moment of her transformation into a poetic figure. By doing this, however, in a disjointed but deeply moving way, the poem does not escape performing its own kind of monumentalization, achieving a high point within the modern lyric – a lyric typically situated between verse and prose.

Chapter 2

Forms and genres

Just as effective poetry heightens our sensitivity to the texture and rhythm of its verse or prose, so do well-made poems draw our attention to their formal and generic framework. Defining what makes a poetic form involves the text's structural composition, its overall length and intrinsic proportions, and the manner of its division (or lack thereof) into stanzas (patterned units called in French *strophes*). In regular French verse, as in English verse, the division of a poem into stanzas is not merely a matter of the print's spatial arrangement on a page. Rather, stanzaic structure is determined by the number and meter of lines put together and by the organization of rhymes. We have already seen that French stanzas follow three main rhyme patterns, and that their lines may be all of one meter or heterometric. While the global structure of some poems varies with each new composition, the form of others is "fixed," or pre-set, by convention. Among the fixed forms to be examined here are the medieval *virelai*,* *rondeau*,* and *ballade*;* the *dizain*,* the sonnet* – the dominant short form of French and other European literatures from the Renaissance onward; and the *haiku*,* which twentieth-century French poets imported from Japan.

The definition of poetic genres is murkier than that of poetic forms, in part because the notions of form and genre have long been confused. During the Renaissance, the Pléiade poets continually mixed imitations of ancient Greek or Latin forms and genres to introduce new kinds of poetry that are often difficult to classify, such as the ode,* the elegy,* the *hymne*,* and the *discours*.* Some of Ronsard's *Odes*, for example, imitate the Greek poet Pindar, both in genre (Pindar composed heroic poems designed for publically singing the praise of glorious feats) and form (a strict, tripartite stanzaic structure). But others imitate the odes of the Latin poet Horace, more loosely structured and more contemplative in tone. Still others imitate the familiar, low-style odes attributed to the Greek poet Anacreon, which tend to be brief and flexible in structure, and to celebrate down-to-earth things such as erotic love and wine. Ronsard's *Hymnes* and *Discours* are by contrast genres largely of the poet's own invention; they share the same formal features (long poems composed of rhymed couplets of alexandrines), but the former are celebrations of cosmic forces, while the latter are political attacks triggered by contemporary events. In more general terms, the love poem, the descriptive poem, the poem celebrating or invoking nature, the fable, and the *art poétique** are types classified by their theme or function. We shall see that these can coincide with preferred formal patterns and pre-set genre expectations throughout the history of French poetry, but they cannot be structurally defined.

Deriving from the Latin term *genus* (Greek *genos*) indicating first a logical or biological category, the word genre can designate any type of thing. However, in European culture generally, there are specific notions of literary genres that originate in key texts of Greek philosophy. Plato's *Republic* performs the first basic distinction, dividing literary texts into three main types: a mimetic (or imitative type) which comes to be associated with drama; a descriptive type, which comes to be associated with narrative; and a third, mixed type combining both of these. Aristotle's *Poetics* further elaborates on Plato's ideas and subdivides his classifications into several new categories. Aristotle divides dramatic poetry, for example, into high and low registers – the tragic and the comic – and defines the aims and ideal stylistic and compositional qualites of each of these genres, along with establishing definitional norms for other kinds of poetry.

Subsequent refashionings of these categories led to the eventual development, in the Romantic period, of a new system of classification (proposed by the German philosopher G. F. W. Hegel, 1770–1831), which remains largely current today. This typology distinguishes three principal poetic genres: the epic,* the dramatic, and the lyric.* Epics are noble, or high-style, narrative poems, such as Homer's *Odyssey* and *Iliad*, or Virgil's *Aeneid*, or the medieval *Chanson de Roland*, telling the heroic exploits of a superior individual or people; dramas also tell a story, but do it through the direct speech of the characters themselves. What interests us here, for the most part, is lyric poetry, a large and flexible category that came to encompass, in the modern era, the entire genre of poetry itself, as the epic gave way to the novel – fictional narrative in prose – and theater also evolved into an autonomous genre (for which prose also became the medium of choice). Lyric poetry can be broadly defined as the musical-sounding expression of subjective emotions, experiences, and ideas. As a general matter, when there is an eclipse of this kind of poetry, as occurs in France in the eighteenth century, there is an impoverishment of poetry on the whole. By contrast, a renewed interest in lyricism such as that occurring in the Romantic era tends to lead to the enrichment of poetry and to the expansion of its cultural importance.

The etymology of the term "lyric," deriving from the term *lyre*, already suggests the inseparability of lyric poetry and music proper in Antiquity. However, to know that a poem was created to be put to music in this period, or in the medieval or Renaissance periods of European literature, is not to specify either the poem's particular structure or its stylistic register, or function, or theme. For example, the changing definitions and faces of the ode, which became one of the most important kinds of French poetry from the Renaissance forward, shows that the interweaving of form and genre is as central to the history of poetry as is the interpenetration of verse and prose.

When the term "*ode*" (deriving from a Greek word meaning a poem to be sung) first came into the French language, it was on the one hand associated with the fashion for all things Greek, and on the other equated (for example in Thomas Sébillet's 1548 *Art poëtique françois* [*Art of French Poetry*]) with the early sixteenth-century French *chanson*.*[1] This was a genre developed by Clément Marot and his disciples. Its major formal difference with earlier medieval lyric forms consisted in its stanzaic structure, which allowed far greater flexibility in the number and patterns of rhymes. In a manner characteristic of the Pléiade poets' self-aggrandizement, Du Bellay asserts in the *Deffence* that nothing like an ode had ever been heard in France, and calls for poets to imitate Ancient ones. However, the difficulty of pinning down precisely in what these new-fashioned odes would consist becomes apparent when we consider the diversity inherent in the Greek and Latin models, and the fact that their subject matter could range from "the praise of the Gods and of virtuous men" to "the concerns of young men, such as love, free wines, and the good life."[2] The sole continuity in Ronsard's and other Pléiade poets' project to resuscitate the ode lies in the fact that they (contrary to the poets who simply created *chansons*) set out to imitate the authentic odes of Antiquity, even as they granted themselves freedom to choose their own themes and to mix and match various aspects of their models' forms and genres.

Ronsard's most famous Pindaric ode, 'Ode à Michel de L'Hospital,' follows strictly, for example, the three-part pattern (including *strophe*, *antistrophe*, and *epode*), is high-style in tone, and was even set to music. Yet the heroic feat it celebrates is not a victory at the Olympic games, but rather the glory of the chancellor who in the early 1550s defended the honor of poetry at the court of the French King Henry II, so that the ultimate theme of this ode is the glory of poetry itself. In the late eighteenth century, the poet André Chénier (1762–1794), who was executed under the Terror by the order of Robespierre, used an adaptation of the Pindaric ode to celebrate his own spirit's "resistance" to the bloody excesses of the French Revolution, thus mixing traditional inspiration with urgent political attack:

> O mon esprit, au sein des cieux,
> Loin de tes noirs chagrins, une ardente allégresse
> Te transporte au banquet des Dieux,

Lorsque ta haine vengeresse,
Rallumée à l'aspect et du meurtre et du sang,
Ouvre de ton carquois l'inépuisable flanc.[3]

> *O my spirit! in the heart of the heavens,*
> *Far from your black troubles, a joy*
>   *Transports you to the banquet of the Gods,*
>   *When your vengeful hatred,*
> *Reignited at the sight of murder and blood,*
> *Opens the inexhaustible flank of your quiver.*

In the Romantic age, Hugo composed odes with much variety and invention, referring to this kind of poem's history only in the vaguest of terms. The most impressive work involving the genre in the twentieth century is perhaps Claudel's *Cinq grandes odes* (*Five Great Odes*, 1910). High-minded and celebratory, they extol the Catholic faith as the revelation of the true source of poetry and all things. Though these poems hail back in their tone and function to the original Pindaric ode (sometimes even implementing a triadic structure), Claudel, paradoxically, also develops therein his own particular poetic style (based on the *verset*), refusing the idea that he imitates anything other than the free and divine rhythms of nature. Hence, these lines in the 'Première ode' ('First Ode'):

O mon âme, il ne faut concerter aucun plan! ô mon âme sauvage, il faut nous tenir libres et prêts,
Comme les immenses bandes fragiles d'hirondelles quand sans voix retentit l'appel automnal!
O mon âme impatiente, pareille à l'aigle sans art! comment ferions-nous pour ajuster aucun vers? à l'aigle qui ne sait pas faire son nid même?[4]

> *O my soul, we must concert no plan! o my savage soul, we must remain free and ready,*
> *Like the immense fragile flocks of swallows when the voiceless autumnal call rings!*
> *O my impatient soul, like the artless eagle! how would we go about adjusting any verse? like the eagle who doesn't even know how to make his own nest?*

For Claudel, the essence of lyricism and of the ode is found in the music of nature, which also reveals itself in the Bible as the Word of God. This is a far cry from the poems of Classical erudition called for by Du Bellay, but retains the general ambition of sounding as high-minded as possible.

But the ode is only one form of lyricism. Most of the lyric poetry of the Middle Ages, which the Pléiade poets were reacting against, was also created to be sung. The first lyric poets, in the first half of the twelfth century, were *Troubadours* (singer-poet-composers) of southern France, such as Guillaume IX, duke of Aquitaine (1071–1127), and Bernard de Ventadour (*c*.1150), whose principal form and genre was the *canso** (song) exalting the values of *fin'amor** (courtly love) in the *langue d'oc*, or Provençal. Their art was imported into the northern provinces, where twelfth- and thirteenth-century *Trouvères* such as Gace Brulé (*c*.1200) and Thibaut de Champagne (*c*.1250) further elaborated this genre of poetry in the *langue d'oïl*, or Old French. Alongside songs of courtly love, there also developed during this period more popular lyric forms such as the anonymous *chanson de toile* (weaving song), singing of love from the woman's perspective, as well as dancing songs, which were at the origin of the *rondeau* and the *ballade*, the fixed forms that came to dominate French lyric poetry throughout the later centuries of the Middle Ages. Paradoxically, it was the great fourteenth-century composer Guillaume de Machaut (*c*.1300–1377) who contributed the most to the establishment of these forms, by articulating and performing in his own work a clean separation between the domains of music and poetry – composing certain poems to be set to music and others to stand on their own.

To begin our discussion of fixed forms, let us examine the structure of an early fifteenth-century *virelai* – a name that suggests, according to a popular etymology, a song (*lai*) that turns (*vire*) – by Christine de Pizan (*c*.1364–1431), one of the most prominent French women poets. The Italian-born Christine was a disciple of Machaut as well as of Eustache Deschamps, whose 1392 *Art de dictier* (*Art of Making Poetry*) is the first technical treatise on French poetry. The structure of Christine de Pizan's 'Virelay' does not correspond to the one presented in Deschamps' treatise: medieval "fixed" forms (contrary to Classical ones) in fact allow for a great deal of variation. The example we will consider features a one-line refrain in the manner of most *rondeaux* (whereas the refrain in most *virelais* consists of two lines or even a whole stanza); the first line of the poem, 'Je chante par cou-verture' ('I sing to feign'), is repeated in the middle of the poem and at the end. However, the poem takes its basic dimensions and meter from the general form of the *virelai*: twenty-one lines of seven-syllable verse in five stanzas. In this particular variant of the form, which is used in eight among the sixteen *virelais* collected by Christine de Pizan, the first, second and fourth stanzas are *quatrains** (four lines), and the third and fifth are *quintils** (five lines) composed of *rimes embrassées* and *croisées* structured according to the following pattern: a*bba cdcd abbaa* cdcd abbaa* (the asterisk here indicates a repeated line, or refrain). As should also be the case with the *virelai*, the poem plays on the dominant rhymes of the first stanza (*couverture/endure, oeil/traveil*) which are repeated three times, and then turns, or changes direction, on the rhymes of the second and fourths stanzas (*doulour/plour, pitié/amitié*). Masculine and feminine rhymes are alternating here – a century before the firm establishment of the rule. The refrain and the tightly structured, repetitive rhyme pattern converge with the seven-syllable meter, to give an impression of music which is circular, turning back on itself:

Je chante par couverture,
Mais mieulx plourassent mi oeil,
Ne nul ne scet le traveil
Que mon pouvre cuer endure.

Pour ce muce ma doulour
Qu'en nul je ne voy pitié,
Plus a l'en cause de plour
Mains treuve l'en d'amistié.

Pour ce plainte ne murmure
Ne fais de mon piteux dueil;
Ainçois ris quant plourer vueil,
Et sanz rime et sanz mesure,
Je chante par couverture.

Petit porte de valour
De soy monstrer dehaitié,
Ne le tiennent qu'a folour
Ceulz qui ont le cuer haitié.

Si n'ay de demonstrer cure
L'entencion de mon vueil,
Ains, tout ainsi com je sueil,
Pour celler ma peine obscure,
Je chante par couverture.[5]

I sing to feign,
But my eyes would better cry,
No one knows the torment
That my poor heart endures.

The reason I hide my pain
Is that I see no one has pity,
The more one has cause to cry,
The less one finds amity.

This is why I neither complain
Nor murmur about my piteous mourning;
I laugh when I wish to cry,
And without rhyme or measure
I sing to feign.

It is of little worth
To show oneself unhappy,
This is just taken for folly
By those with a happy heart.

Thus I have no care to show
The intention of my will,
And so, as always is my habit,
To hide my obscure pain,
I sing to feign.

This structural circularity ideally expresses the theme of the *virelai* –
the idea that the poet's singing is a dissimulating act – which is stated in
the first, middle and final line of the poem: "Je chante par couverture." The
Middle French word "couverture" designates not only a feigning or dissim-
ulation, but also that which is dissimulated, the secret thought held hidden
behind appearances. Consonantly, this particular song, which presents the
poet's singing from the outset as a sham, reveals insistently what it claims
its purpose is to hide: the poet's pitiful mourning ("piteux dueil"); her
desire to cry rather than to sing or laugh ("mieulx plourassent mi oeil,"
"ris quant plourer vueil"), the suffering of her poor heart ("le traveil que
mon pouvre cuer endure"); in short, her pain ("ma doulour"). The poet
is no more hiding her feelings in the process of singing than she is singing
"sanz rime et sanz mesure" (that is, literally "without rhyme and without measure," and figuratively "without rhyme or reason"), a claim which
the rigorously constructed poem also falsely advances at the end of stanza
three.

The poet's negation of the authenticity and value of her singing does
result in a kind of feigning. But is it of the kind she admits? Her opening
'Virelay' plays with our emotions, spins the paradoxes inherent in her poetic
stance to the extent that we wonder whether her laughing and singing self
or her crying, non-singing self is the true one. The ambivalence expressed
may be linked to the actual circumstances of Christine de Pizan's life, for
she was in fact left a widow with three children in an impoverished state,
and was among the first French writers to have to make a living by her pen.
At the same time, the poet shows herself to be not just any poor woman,
who is forced to put on a good show by singing. Rather, she sufficiently
masters the codes of *fin'amor* to turn them to her own ends and express
through a plaintive song – where she plays neither the conventional role of
l'amant (the lover), nor *la dame* (the beloved lady) – the authentic accent
of a lonely young woman's voice. Her first 'Virelay' is exemplary of how
she was able to use lyric poetry in general – the turning of its rhymes,
and the circularity of its forms – to subtly overturn literary conventions
concerning gender. This along with the strength and scope of her didactic
prose works – such as *La Cité des dames* (*The City of Ladies*, 1405) – helped to
establish her (even within her own lifetime) as an important writer exerting

considerable cultural influence, and as the first of a handful of women poets to be recognized within the French canon.

At the summit of the social and political world within which Christine de Pizan wrote (though a generation younger), was the poet-prince Charles d'Orléans (1391–1465), nephew of the French King Charles VI, and father of Louis XII. Charles d'Orléans holds a place in the history of medieval English poetry as well, because he lived and wrote in captivity for over twenty-five years in England, where he was taken and held hostage after the battle of Agincourt (1415). The following opening lines from a French *chanson*, 'Ma seule amour, ma joye, et ma maistresse,' for which the poet also composed an English version, show a more conventional approach than Christine de Pizan's 'Virelay' to singing of loss, love, and separation. They also give us a sense of Charles d'Orléans' style in both Middle French and Middle English:

> Ma seule amour, ma joye, et ma maistresse,
> Puisqu'il me fault loing de vous demorer,
> Je n'ay plus riens, a me reconforter,
> Qu'un souvenir pour retenir lyesse [. . .]
>
> *My love only, my ioy, and my maystres,*
> *Syn y may not ben longe with yow present,*
> *With discomfort y must ben resident,*
> *Save oon poore hope which doth to me gladnes [. . .]* [6]

Charles d'Orléans wrote extensively in the predominant fixed forms of his day: 123 *ballades* and 344 *rondeaux*. The latter form, which suited his poetry particularly well, presents the following stucture: twelve or thirteen lines constructed on two rhymes a*b*ba aba*(b*) abbaa* (the second line of the refrain is often not repeated). One of the best-known poems of the French Middle Ages is his *rondeau* 'Le temps a laissié son manteau.' It shows among other things that the *rondeau* can extend out of the domain of love (the original concern of much lyric poetry), to treat a variety of themes, even as it retains complex courtly metaphors from the tradition of *fin'amor*. Perhaps this poem, which displaces the traditional amorous theme of the "reverdie," or return of spring, has appealed to modern readers' sensibilities because it anticipates the Romantic penchant for *le sentiment de la nature*, what John Ruskin called the "pathetic fallacy": the projection of human feelings on to the natural world. But unlike Romantic poems, in which the sky, land, and waters often reflect the raw sentiment of an isolated individual, this poem has nature readily assuming the hierarchical order of medieval society as its clothing and ornament. "Le temps," moreover, (in this poem, a pun that can be translated as either time or weather), rather than being characterized as a mysterious enemy (as often occurs in nineteenth-century poetry), is presented as an adored regal figure, whose glory is joyfully reflected in the shining filigree of the river, fountain, and stream – his earthly servants:

> Le temps a laissié son manteau
> De vent, de froidure et de pluye,
> Et s'est vestu de brouderie
> De soleil luyant cler et beau.
>
> Il n'y a beste ne oyseau
> Qu'en son jargon ne chante ou crie:
> "Le temps a laissié son manteau
> De vent, de froidure et de pluye."
>
> Riviere, fontaine et ruisseau
> Portent, en livree jolie,
> Gouttes d'argent d'orfaverie;
> Chascun s'abille de nouveau:
> Le temps a laissié son manteau.[7]

> *Time has shed its cloak*
> *Of wind, cold, and rain,*
> *And has put on an embroidery*
> *Of clear and fair sun rays.*
>
> *There is no beast, nor bird*
> *That doesn't in its own tongue cry or sing:*
> *"Time has shed its cloak*
> *Of wind, cold, and rain."*
>
> *River, fountain, and stream*
> *Wear in pretty livery,*
> *Drops of silverwork;*
> *Each dresses fresh again:*
> *Time has shed its cloak.*

In Charles d'Orléans' *rondeau* as in Christine de Pizan's *virelai*, we note the convergence between formal circularity and self-reference, since the poet implicitly includes his own song in the universal singing referred to at the beginning of the second stanza. The *rondeau* seems, however, less concerned than the *virelai* with its own lyrical form. Similarly, its octosyllabic meter (which is typical for the *rondeau*) suggests a further remove from the domain of actual song. The gradual distancing of the *rondeau* from its original status as a song also becomes apparent in the reduction by later poets (notably Jean Marot and his son Clément) of the refrain to a *rentrement*,* an abbreviated form including only the first part of the line.

Though the *ballade* form is as deeply rooted in music and dance as are the *rondeau* and the *virelai*, its significant length (twenty-four to thirty-five lines) and the dimensions of its stanzas – first, in "*la petite ballade*" (the little *ballade*), typically three stanzas of eight octosyllables (patterned ababbcbc) with a four-line closing or *envoi** (bcbc*), then growing (in "*la grande ballade*") [the long ballade] to three stanzas of ten decasyllables (ababbccdcd*) with a five-line *envoi* (ccdcd*) – give more an impression of squareness, symmetry, and balance, than of roundness or musicality. The effect of the *ballade*'s refrain, which is repeated at the closing of each stanza, is often more rhetorical (persuasive or admonishing) than lyrical in nature. In fact, the *envoi*, which addresses the poem to a prince or other high figure, is a feature not present in the original musical form: it was borrowed from the longer, more massive *chant royal*,* a fixed form with five stanzas of eleven lines of variable length (patterned ababccddede*) with an *envoi* of five lines (ddede*),[8] a poem majestic in style and generally dedicated to a regal figure, as the name suggests (often, in the late fifteenth century, the Virgin Mary).

Villon, one of the greatest masters of the *ballade*, is for many the greatest lyric poet of the French Middle Ages. He is sometimes referred to as the "poet-pariah," since he occupied an opposite social position from that of the "poet-prince" Charles d'Orléans. While a student in Paris, Villon was repeatedly imprisoned for his involvement in various violent skirmishes and crimes, including robbery and manslaughter, for which he was condemned to death, reprieved, and sent into exile in 1463. Despite this unlawful agitation, he participated marginally in the poetic life of his day, writing a number of courtly pieces. He even engaged in a *ballade* contest held at Blois by Charles d'Orléans, which invited variations on a poetic theme given in the first line. His greatest works, however, including the *Testament* (a long satirical poem in the form of the author's testament, containing several famous *ballades*), were written outside the court.

Though Villon created an original poetic persona – that of the poor social outcast – which happens to be the contrary of the high-minded, melancholic figure created by Charles d'Orléans, he was not the first medieval poet to draw on rough or popular language and incorporate lowly images of himself and others within a lyrical style. This was also accomplished by Rutebeuf (active 1250–1280), whose satirical, autobiographical poems complained of poverty and other worldly problems. Still, Villon's poetry is remarkable for its combinations of stylistic registers, ranging, sometimes within the same poem, from sublime eloquence to grotesque vulgarity. These qualities are both obvious and effective in his most famous piece, later entitled 'L'Epitaphe,' where the poet, speaking for a group of hanged criminals, directly addresses not a worldly sovereign (as the *ballade* form customarily does), but rather all us readers, contemporary and future, as well as Jesus

Christ (the sovereign of all Christian kings), asking for forgiveness from a post-mortem perspective. Throughout the poem, depictions of hanging skeletons combine with prayer for divine intercession. From the first stanza, grotesque, macabre images create fear in the reader, helping to underscore the refrain's admonishment that all we mortals will finally depend on God's mercy:

> Freres humains, qui après nous vivez,
> N'ayez les cueurs contre nous endurcis,
> Car, se pitié de nous povres avez,
> Dieu en aura plus tost de vous mercis.
> Vous nous voiez cy attachez, cinq, six:
> Quant de la chair, que trop avons nourrie,
> El est pieçà devorée et pourrie,
> Et nous, les os, devenons cendre et pouldre.
> De nostre mal personne ne se rie;
> Mais priez Dieu que tous nous vueille absouldre.[9]

> *Human brothers, who live after us,*
> *Hold not your hearts hard against us,*
> *For if you take pity on poor us*
> *God will sooner have mercy on you.*
> *You see us here, five or six attached:*
> *As for the flesh which we fed too much,*
> *It has long ago been devoured and rotten,*
> *And we, the bones, are becoming ashes and dust.*
> *Let no one laugh at our bad fate;*
> *Rather pray that God will absolve us all.*

As the early Renaissance poet Clément Marot prepared one of the first printed editions of Villon's *Œuvres* (*Works*) (including the 'Epitaphe'), it is interesting to note the thematic connections between this poem and the culmination of Marot's own technical achievement in the *rondeau* form: the 'Rondeau parfaict à ses Amys après sa delivrance' ('Perfect Rondeau to His Friends after His Liberation', 1526), which announces and celebrates the poet's own release from prison (he was accused of heresy). Here are the opening lines:

> En liberté maintenant me pourmène,
> Mais en prison pourtant je fus cloué:
> Voilà comment Fortune me démène.
> C'est bien, et mal. Dieu soit de tout loué.[10]

> *Now I am going about freely*
> *However I was long stuck in prison:*
> *This is how Fortune treats me.*
> *It's good, and ill. God be praised for all.*

As in an ordinary *rondeau*, this idiosyncratic *"rondeau parfait"* is built on only two rhymes. However, each line of the first stanza becomes a refrain of sorts, being repeated in turn as the last line of the four subsequent stanzas. The poem then closes on the circle-breaking words "en liberté."[11]

Thus, while certain forms such as the *rondeau* or *ballade* may be originally associated with particular types or styles of poem, they often transcend this condition, lending themselves to a variety of genres. Conversely, a poet or movement's interest in developing a particular genre can also lead to the creation of new forms, which may be indigenous or transposed from other cultures, singularly adapted to an individual poem's subject matter or inherently open-ended. Two loosely defined Classical genres adopted by Renaissance poets in the first half of the sixteenth century are the *épître** (epistle) and the *épigramme.** The epistle is a letter in verse, whether fictitious − as in the *Epistres de l'Amant vert* (*Epistles of the Green Lover*, 1511) by Jean Lemaire de Belges (1473–1524), love letters supposedly sent to Margaret of Austria by her dead green parrot − or genuine, as in Clément Marot's 'Epistre au Roy, pour sa delivrance' ('Epistle to the King, for His Liberation,' 1527), sent to Francis I to plead the cause of the imprisoned poet. The epigram is a short verse "inscription," which builds toward a crucial last line, or *pointe,** with no special rules concerning the patterning of the verse. Marot also developed the *blason*, a kind of epigram dedicated to the detailed description of an object. In 1536, he organized a contest involving *blasons du corps féminin* (blasons of the female body), which was won by the Lyonnais poet Maurice Scève. Typically, these *blasons* extolled the details of a woman's body in a low or simple style, as in Marot's own 'Le beau tétin' ('The Beautiful Breast'), but they could also employ a high, noble style, as in Scève's winning poem 'Le sourcil' ('The Brow'):

> Sourcil tractif en vouste fleschissant
> Trop plus qu'hebene, ou jayet noircissant,
> Hault forgeté pour umbrager les yeulx,
> Quand ils font signe, ou de mort, ou de mieulx [. . .][12]

> *Well-made brow in an arching vault*
> *Much more than ebony or jet blackening,*
> *Projected high to shade the eyes,*
> *When they signal death, or something happier [. . .]*

The *contre-blason* uses a satirical vein, as in Marot's 'Le laid tetin' ('The Ugly Breast'). Some *blasons* also sing the praises of other natural objects, such as animals, or gems, as in the *Eschanges des pierres précieuses* ('Exchanges of Precious Gems') of Pléiade member Rémy Belleau (1528–1577).

In Rimbaud's earlier mentioned 'Voyelles' (*c*.1871), whose title has been interpreted as a play on words to be read "Vois-elles" (See-they), we see the *blason*'s evolving connections not only with disparate forms, since here the genre presents itself as a sonnet, but also with a dramatic mixture of styles. Rimbaud establishes correspondences between vulgar and refined stylistic registers and "low" and "high" parts of the body, as the description moves from associating the letter A with the shape of flies, the female sex, and "cruel stenches," to heavenly associations between the letter O, the Omega, the clarion of *Revelation*, and the Eyes of the beloved divinity.

In the twentieth century, the flexibility inherent in such unregulated forms as the prose poem allows poets to shape descriptive pieces in such a way as to evoke either abstractly or concretely whatever they represent, by establishing various kinds of correspondences between their objects and verbal signs. In the work of Francis Ponge (1899–1988), the precise manner in which the verbal substance of the poems unfolds seems in part motivated by properties inherent in words (etymologies, sonorities, double meanings, etc.) and in part decided by aspects of the material things the poems evoke. Thus 'Le Mimosa,' a burgeoning text which develops in several sequences multiple aspects of its object, begins with a theatrical comparison determined as much by verbal riches – built in the very word "mimosa" – as by natural ones – actually describing or metaphorically associated with the delicate Mediterranean flower:

> Sur fond d'azur le voici, comme un personnage de la comédie italienne, avec un rien d'histrionisme saugrenu, poudré comme Pierrot, dans son costume à pois jaunes, le mimosa.
> Mais ce n'est pas un arbuste lunaire: plutôt solaire, multisolaire . . .
> Un caractère d'une naïve gloriole, vite découragé.
> Chaque grain n'est aucunement lisse, mais, formé de poils soyeux, un astre si l'on veut, étoilé au maximum.
> Les feuilles ont l'air de grandes plumes, très légères et cependant très accablées d'elles-mêmes; [. . .]
> . . . Comme dans tamaris il y a tamis, dans mimosa il y a mima.[13]

> *On a background of azure, here it is, like a character from Italian comedy, with a touch of histrionic absurdity, powdered like Pierrot, in its yellow-dotted costume, the mimosa.*
> *But it is not a lunar shrub: solar instead, multisolar . . .*
> *Naïvely vainglorious by nature, quickly discouraged.*
> *Each grain is in no way smooth, but rather formed of silky hair, a celestial body, if you like, starred to the maximum.*
> *The leaves look like long feathers, so light / loose and yet overwhelmed by their own burden; [. . .]*
> *. . . Just as there is* tamis *(sieve) in tamarisk, there is* mima *(mimed) in mimosa.*

Pierrot, a melancholy character who came from the Italian *commedia dell'arte* to star in fin-de-siècle pantomimes, is called up by virtue of several distinct associations: the powdery face, the pom-pommed costume, the "plume" of a popular song, the naïveté and fragility – all ultimately motivated by the pun on "mime." Typical of Ponge's art is the way in which the initial seductive comparison is objected to (Pierrot is associated with the moon, and his colors are black and white), only to be transformed into an even more faithful – if fanciful – mimetic image: not the moon, but the sun, and many suns at that.

It may seem that a lack of specific formal requirements leads to the greatest possibilities for fusion between a poem's *signifiers** (its verbal material) and the *signifieds** (the words' meanings) or *referents** (what they refer to). And yet free-formed prose poems often depend less than regularly patterned verse on establishing direct relationships of this kind. 'Congé au vent' ('Leave to the Wind'), a prose poem by René Char (1907–1988), belongs, for example, to an ancient performative genre insofar as it *apostrophizes** (or addresses) and commands the complicity of a natural element. The poem seeks to influence the wind just like Du Bellay's imitation of a Latin rustic poem, 'D'un vanneur de blé aux vents' ('From a Wheat Winnower to the Winds'). But the ends and the means of Char's and Du Bellay's poems are diametrically opposed. Assuming the persona of a winnower, Du Bellay conjures up the wind's complicity in regularly patterned Renaissance verse – three stanzas of six hexasyllables (patterned aabccb ddeffe gghiih, more rhyme changes than would be tolerable in the Middle Ages) – and employs well-established rhetorical conventions. He calls on the winds directly,

> A vous troppe legere,
> Qui d'aele passagère
> Par le monde volez [. . .]
>
> *To you light troop,*
> *Who with fleeting wing*
> *Fly about the world [. . .]*

extends them an offering of flowers,

> J'offre ces violettes,
> Ces lis, & ces fleurettes [. . .]
>
> *I offer these violets,*
> *These lilies, & these flowerets [. . .]*

and finally articulates a *vœu* (vow) that makes their activity compensate for his own poetic work of winnowing:

> De vostre doulce halaine
> Eventez ceste plaine,

Eventez ce séjour:
Ce pendant que j'ahanne
A mon blé, que je vanne
A la chaleur du jour.[14]

With your sweet breath
Air out this plain
Air out this sojourn:
While I pant over
This wheat that I winnow
In the heat of day.

By contrast, 'Congé au vent,' instead of calling forth the wind, functions effectively to dispel it. And Char achieves the quietness which he simultaneously orders and depicts in a manner both suble and indirect. He does this by recreating around his poem an atmosphere of calm at once mysterious and stunning – a fragile, peaceful aura, which seems to emanate from the image it describes:

À flancs de coteau du village bivouaquent des champs fournis de mimosas. À l'époque de la cueillette, il arrive que, loin de leur endroit, on fasse la rencontre extrêmement odorante d'une fille dont les bras se sont occupés durant la journée aux fragiles branches. Pareille à une lampe dont l'auréole de clarté serait de parfum, elle s'en va, le dos tourné au soleil couchant.
Il serait sacrilège de lui adresser la parole.
L'espadrille foulant l'herbe, cédez-lui le pas du chemin. Peut-être aurez-vous la chance de distinguer sur ses lèvres la chimère de l'humidité de la Nuit?[15]

Flanking the village slopes fields filled with mimosas are bivouacking. At picking time, it happens that far from where they are, one can have an extremely fragrant encounter with a girl whose arms have been occupied during the day with the fragile branches. Like a lamp whose aureole of light would be perfume, she leaves, her back turned to the setting sun.
It would be sacrilegious to speak to her.
Espadrille trampling the grass, concede her the way. Perhaps you will have the good fortune to distinguish on her lips the chimaera of the Night's dew?

Divinity is attributed not to the wind (as is conventional with this genre and occurs in Du Bellay's poem), but rather to the young girl who has worked the harvest. The perfumed light she emits is not an obscure mystery (she turns her back to the sunset, and the dew on her lips, residue of Night, is only an illusion, a "chimère"), but simply the effect of the day's pick of mimosa in her arms. The young girl's mystery is thus that of a purely natural figure, but one whose sanctity is such that she can be neither directly addressed ("il serait sacrilège de lui adresser la parole"), nor physically approached ("cédez-lui le pas") by the poet or his accomplices: the readers and the wind. Accordingly, far from being mimetically "performative" in the sense that Du Bellay's *apostrophe* to the wind is – lifting up natural and rhetorical flowers, in exchange for measured gusts of air – 'Congé au vent' uses the more prosaic devices of narrative description, theoretical statement, and even hypothetical speculation to create a desired distance, a space of stillness between the poetic image that presents itself and any response or interfering disturbance that might be caused by its communication.

Poems that present themselves as adhering to the traditions of a certain genre or type of poetic function are not then necessarily restricted by tight formal constraints. Rather, they often manifest great freedom and variety of form. Nowhere is this more evident than with fables. The fable genre is generally easy for readers to recognize despite great formal variations, and its typology is simple to grasp. Deriving from the latin word *fabula*, meaning fictional narrative, or *apologue* (a story with a moral lesson), and from the works of Aesop in Greek Antiquity, and Phaedrus in Latin, the fable is an indirect representation which generally employs allegories (in the sense of complex yet coherent symbolic narratives) featuring plant and animal figures to teach moral lessons applicable to human life.

Jean de La Fontaine, the preeminent lyric poet of the French Classical age, wrote twelve books of *Fables* between 1668 and 1693, consisting predominantly of allegorical narratives set in nature. Written in a style which favors wit, irony, and brief notation over heavy-handed moralizing and lengthy description, his fables aim explicitly as much to "please" as to "be useful" to readers (including King Louis XIV's grandson) by confronting them with figures who incarnate their various foibles. The first books mostly feature simple, down-to-earth figures, drawn from the French countryside, while in the later books we also find supernatural figures drawn from Greek and Oriental mythology. At times La Fontaine's fables seem to paint universal beings – he described each fable as consisting of a body (the substance of the representation) and a soul (the moral message) – but more often they offer diverse portraits of contemporary French society, articulating "realistic" (some have said pessimistic) and potentially contradictory moral lessons that are apt to change from one fable to the next, or even within the same fable according to the reader's point of view. Most striking in the *Fables* is the rich formal mixture: of narrative, dramatic, and lyrical modes; of high and low stylistic registers; of stanzaic and structural design; and of different types of verse.

La Fontaine ingeniously exploited the formal freedom that the low genre of the fable afforded him to create correspondences between the "bodies" of his poems and their individual "souls." In certain cases, the moral is left unstated, or is only implicitly revealed. This formal choice, which occurs for example in 'La Cigale et la Fourmi' ('The Cicada and the Ant,' La Fontaine's version of Aesop's 'The Ant and the Grasshopper'), tends to leave readers plenty of room for interpretation, and leads to a kind of moral ambiguity, which the eighteenth-century philosopher Jean-Jacques Rousseau (1712–1778) severely criticized in his pedagogical novel *L'Émile* as dangerous for children. In ideological terms, there is indeed, in 'La Cigale et la Fourmi,' a certain lack of a positive moral message: the uncharitable Ant is as reprehensible in her hard-hearted stinginess as the unforeseeing, happy-go-lucky Cicada. But other fables unfold through the combined means of narrative and dialog, to end with explicitly stated morals, both definitive and universal in tone. This is the case with 'La Grenouille qui veut se faire aussi grosse que le Bœuf' ('The Frog who Wanted to Become as Big as an Ox'), where, after the Frog's explosion, a final, totalizing set of condemning analogies aims to expose (and thereby discourage) the ridiculousness of all social ambition:

> Le monde est plein de gens qui ne sont pas plus sages:
> Tout bourgeois veut bâtir comme les grands seigneurs,
>   Tout petit prince a des ambassadeurs;
>   Tout marquis veut avoir des pages.[16]

> *The world is full of people who are no wiser:*
> *Every bourgeois wishes to build like great lords,*
>   *Every little prince has ambassadors;*
>   *Every marquis wants pages.*

From a political perspective, this would seem to reflect a conservative world view, supportive of the absolute monarchy of Louis XIV, or even of an older, more rigid aristocratic social order. Yet, La Fontaine got into trouble on numerous occasions for the too thinly masked social and political critiques lurking in other fables, such as 'Les Animaux malades de la peste' ('The Animals Sick with the Plague') and 'Le Loup et l'Agneau' ('The Wolf and the Lamb'). In the latter, as is fitting in a regime where there is little room for discussion or possibility of change, the "moral" lesson is bitterly ironic and stated *a priori*:

> La raison du plus fort est toujours la meilleure,
>   Nous l'allons montrer tout à l'heure.

> *The reason of the strongest is always the best,*
>   *We are about to show this.*

The Lamb, doomed from the start, incarnates all the virtues, and speaks and reasons well to boot. But his innocence and truthfulness prove no more useful to him in front of the Wolf than do his courteous deference and well-argued defense:

Qui te rend si hardi de troubler mon breuvage?
    Dit cet animal plein de rage;
Tu seras châtié de ta témérité.
    Sire, répond l'Agneau, que Votre Majesté
        Ne se mette pas en colère;
        Mais plutôt qu'elle considère
        Que je me vas désaltérant
           Dans le courant,
Plus de vingt pas au-dessous d'Elle [. . .]

Who makes you dare to trouble my drink?
    Says that animal full of rage;
You will be punished for your temerity.
Sire, the Lamb answers, let Your Majesty
    Not be angered;
    Rather let Him consider
    That I am drinking
      In the current,
More than twenty steps below Him [. . .]

The Lamb has no access to any form of justice despite the Wolf's (weak and transparently self-serving) judicial rhetoric, which prevails only thanks to his own brute force. In the final lines, the creatures' conflict is resolved as predictably and unfairly as the opening moral leads us to expect:

Le Loup l'emporte, et puis le mange,
Sans autre forme de procès.[17]

The wolf carries him off, and eats him,
With no other form of trial.

Composed with a symbolic mixture of refined and brutish rhetorical tones, of alexandrines and octosyllables balanced by a pivotal four-syllable line, and of three different rhyme schemes – *plates*, *embrassées*, and *croisées* – 'Le Loup et l'Agneau' exemplifies the extreme formal virtuosity associated with La Fontaine. This diversity was possible, in the Classical age, only because of the fable genre's inherent limitations, that is, its relative lowliness and its clearly defined functional and thematic constraints.

In the Romantic period, as in the Renaissance, there is a general attempt to redefine genres against the conventions of the period immediately preceding. The subversion of Classical rules that occurs in Romanticism not only affects verse structure, but also strives to topple and abolish traditional types of poems, while privileging the general notion and absolute value of poetry as such. This does not mean that Romanticism rejects all previous forms and genres or that it fails to produce any new ones. Though the prose poem becomes fully established in the mid- to late nineteenth century, in its hybrid character it is both literally and quintessentially a Romantic invention. Nor should we think that Romantic poems, because of their vague contours and effusive lyricism, cannot be generically characterized and formally classified. Yet Romantic poetry's self-categorizations are often the result of odd mixtures and loose definitions; they should not be confused with previous categories, which tend to be more narrowly defined. The Romantic *ballade*, for example, as fashioned in Hugo's *Odes et ballades* (a revealing juxtaposition), though it originates in a nostalgic desire to return to medieval – as opposed to Classical – roots, has little to do with the fixed form practiced in the Middle Ages. Rather, it imitates the traditional story-song found throughout the nations of Europe: a narrative poem with real or simulated folkloric roots and a legendary theme. The treatment of the form can also turn to whimsy and parody in short-verse poems such as the 'Ballade à la lune' ('*Ballade* to the Moon') by Alfred de Musset (1810–1857), where instead of a refrain we have a final return, with minor variations, of the first stanza:

> C'était, dans la nuit brune,
> Sur le clocher jauni,
>   La lune
> Comme un point sur un i.[18]

> *There was, in the dusky night,*
> *On the yellowing steeple,*
>   *The moon*
> *Like a dot on an i.*

Perhaps the kind of poem most associated with Romanticism is the elegy (which generic term comes from the Greek *elegos*, lament). In Antiquity, the elegy was a plaintive song or poem often dealing with love, composed in a particular meter – dactylic hexameter couplets – following a fixed form. French elegies from the Renaissance forward ignore this form, but retain the mournful tone, some poems, such as Chénier's late eighteenth-century 'La Jeune Tarentine' ('The Young Tarentine') and 'La Jeune captive' ('The Young Captive'), even presenting themselves, in one way or another, as songs of mourning. Typically, however, the Romantic elegy is a rather long heterometric poem treating love nostalgically in a natural setting, as in Lamartine's 1820 'Le Lac' ('The Lake') or Hugo's 1837 'Tristesse d'Olympio' ('Olympio's Sadness'). These two pieces represent equally well the Romantic *sentiment de la nature*, but from different angles. 'Le Lac' rhetorically establishes a complicity between the scene of nature and the poet's sentiments, while Hugo's poem, representing a later stage of Romanticism, complains of a failure of this union between the poet and nature, turning Romantic poetry in the general direction of introspective Symbolism. In the third stanza from 'Le Lac,' Lamartine repeatedly addresses the lake as the faithful witness who shares his pain:

> Tu mugissais ainsi sous ces roches profondes,
> Ainsi tu te brisais sur leurs flancs déchirés,
> Ainsi le vent jetait l'écume de tes ondes
>   Sur ses pieds adorés.[19]

> *You moaned thus under those deep rocks;*
> *Thus you broke against their torn flanks:*
> *Thus the wind threw the froth of your waves*
>   *On her adored feet.*

In the first stanza from 'Tristesse d'Olympio,' Hugo affirms instead, and with equal hyperbolic force, the natural setting's indifference to the lover's feelings:

> Les champs n'étaient point noirs, les cieux n'étaient pas mornes;
> Non, le jour rayonnait dans un azur sans bornes
>   Sur la terre étendu,
> L'air était plein d'encens et les prés de verdures
> Quand il revit ces lieux où par tant de blessures
>   Son cœur s'est répandu![20]

> *The fields were not black, the skies were not bleak;*
> *No, the day shone forth in an endless blue*
>   *Stretched over the earth,*
> *The air was full of incense and the prairies with greenery*
> *When he saw again those places where through so many wounds*
>   *His heart had spilt!*

In a third version of the same theme, Musset's 1841 elegy 'Souvenir' ('Memory') evokes the Fontainebleau landscape in which he had spent time with his lover George Sand: inspired by the beauty of the forest, the poet refuses to regret the past moment, focusing instead on memory's bliss.

Just as some poetic periods and movements will tend to refuse formal definition and constraint, some poetic forms, in turn, will resist being tied to any particular theme or generic function. This is first and foremost the case with the most enduring and popular of all short forms, the sonnet. Though it was created in thirteenth-century Sicily and developed by Dante (1265–1321) and Petrarch (1304–1374) in connection with love poetry (in *La Vita Nuova* [*The New Life*] and the *Canzoniere* respectively), in the French context this association is rapidly outgrown: the sonnet can be satirical or political, for example, as well as amorous. And, as also occurs in England, some of the form's basic prosodic features become transformed. For example, the French sonnet, like the Italian, consists of fourteen lines of regular verse divided into a *huitain** (an eight-line group composed of two *quatrains*) and a *sizain** (a six-line group composed of two three-line stanzas, or *tercets**), but its typical rhyme schemes vary significantly from those of the Petrarchan model (as do English ones in a different way).[21]

How does the sonnet define and situate itself in French poetics? In the words of the Parnassian poet Théodore de Banville (1823–1891), "the Sonnet resembles a figure whose bust would seem too long and whose legs would seem too thin and too short."[22] This description from his *Petit traité de poésie française* (*Little Treatise on French Poetry*, 1872) betrays the endurance, into the late nineteenth century, of a tenacious Classical French taste for proportion and symmetry. Banville sees the sonnet as an ill-formed body, which the poet must reshape and redress. But this does not discourage him. Rather, formal difficulties inspire him, as they did his mentor, the Romantic turned Parnassian Théophile Gautier (1811–1872), whose *art poétique* (a long heterometric poem entitled 'L'Art' ['Art']) defined the aesthetics of the "Parnasse" school, dedicated to "l'art pour l'art" (art for art's sake). The poem urges poets to use formal materials that are hard (in every sense) and tirelessly rework their verse in order to capture their dreams in stone:

> Oui, l'œuvre sort plus belle
> D'une forme au travail
>   Rebelle,
> Vers, marbre, onyx, émail.
> [. . .]
> Sculpte, lime, cisèle;
> Que ton rêve flottant
>   Se scelle
> Dans le bloc résistant![23]

> *Yes, the work emerges more beautiful*
> *From a form against our labor*
>   *Rebelling,*
> *Verse, marble, onyx, enamel.*
> *[. . .]*
> *Sculpt, file, chisel;*
> *Let your floating dream*
>   *Become fixed*
> *In the resisting block!*

Thus, Banville comes to represent the "magnificence," the "prodigious beauty" of the sonnet as inseparable from its inherent "infirmity" – its division into uneven parts: two quatrains, rhythmically "pompous" and "slow" by nature, and two tercets producing a "lively" and "quick" effect. To restore the form's "good order," he recommends a typically Parnassian "artifice": the ennobling of the sense and sound of the tercets, and the granting of special weight to the last line, as in the *pointe* of the traditional epigram.

Banville's comments, consistent with their time as they appear, also echo Boileau's ambivalent view of the form (which he deemed too difficult for the mediocrity of countless practitioners), and Renaissance critiques, made at the time the sonnet first came to France from Italy. Sébillet's *Art poëtique françois* describes the newly fashionable sonnet as being nothing other than "the perfect Italian epigram," which he claimed the ten-line *dizain** was for the French, and deems its uneven structure "a little trying."[24] Despite the fervent Petrarchism of their patron Francis I, early French Renaissance poets preferred the more symmetrical and tightly constructed stanzas of the old circular French forms (*rondeau, ballade, chant royal*), and saw no special advantage to the sonnet over their own imitations of Ancient epigrams. Clément Marot, who was the first to translate some of Petrarch's sonnets into French, published one of his own few sonnet compositions in a collection of *Épigrammes*. And Scève, who was the first to imitate the Petrarchan *Canzoniere* in his 1544 *Delie, object de plus haulte vertu* (*Delie, Object of the Highest Virtue*), chose not to embrace the sonnet (which Petrarch had used among other forms), but rather to transpose its uneven stanzas into the perfectly square decasyllabic *dizain* (a unity of verse sharing the proportions, though not the rhyme scheme, of the ballad stanza – such as the one used in Villon's 'Epitaphe'). One of the most shocking aspects of the sonnet for French Renaissance poets was the license to use five rhymes in so short a form. That is why Marot chose to enhance the unity of the rhymes in his translations: he did this by patterning the tercets with *rime plates* – ccd eed – as opposed to *croisées* in the Petrarchan way – cde cde or cdc ede. This variation gave a more circular, rhyme-saturated quality to the sonnet, drawing it closer to what would be the rhyme scheme of Scève's *dizains* (ababb+ccdcd).[25] In sum, the sonnet did not really succeed in France before the late 1540s, even though Petrarchism permeated the rhetoric of French love poetry. Before considering the sonnet form further, let us then look at Petrarchan rhetoric, as it was set forth in the *dizains* of *Delie*.

There are many formal and thematic similarities linking the opening sonnet from Petrarch's *Canzoniere* – 'Voi ch'ascoltate in rime sparse' ('You Who Listen in These Scattered Rhymes')[26] – and Scève's first *dizain*:

> L'Œil trop ardent en mes jeunes erreurs
> Girouettoit, mal cault, a l'impourveue:
> Voicy (ô paour d'agreables terreurs)

Mon Basilisque avec sa poingnant' veue
Perçant Corps, Cœur, et Raison despourveue
Vint penetrer en l'Ame de mon Ame.
    Grand fut le coup, qui sans tranchante lame
Fait, que vivant le Corps, l'Esprit desvie,
Piteuse hostie au conspect de toy, Dame,
Constituée Idole de ma vie.[27]

My Eye too ardent in my youthful errings
Was turning, misguided, unawares:
Whence suddenly (o fear of pleasurable terrors)
My Basilisk with her poignant gaze
Piercing Body, Heart, and Reason unarmed,
Came to penetrate the Soul of my Soul.
    Great was the blow, which using no cutting blade
Makes it so that, while my Body lives, my Spirit dies / deviates,
Pitiful host upon beholding your image, Lady,
Constituted Idol of my life.

In portraying love with a mixture of Classical and Christian symbols (the beloved is a "basilisk," a mythological lizard-like monster, and the lover a "host," or victim) as opposed to mainly Christian ones, and in abandoning the social and political model of courtly love in favor of a more exalted Platonic-religious framework,[28] Scève's *dizain* clearly emulates Petrarch. An avid admirer of the Tuscan poet, Scève believed that he had found the tomb of Laura, the woman celebrated in the *Canzoniere*. Like the name Laura, which recalls Daphné's transformation into Apollo's Laurel (the tree that also symbolizes poetic inspiration), Délie, the symbolic name of Scève's beloved muse, combines reference to an actual woman, Pernette du Guillet,[29] with a mythological allusion: it refers to Artemis (or Diana) born in Délos, the unattainable Goddess of the moon, who also visits earth as the virgin hunter.

Delie also retains from the Petrarchan *Canzoniere* the fundamental inaccessibility of the beloved, the consequence that her beauty inflicts on the lover enormous suffering and desire, and the further effect that this unquenchable, maddening desire extracts from him a form of poetic devotion comparable only to religious adoration. However, the two poets situate their poetry in relation to the divine and religion in opposing ways. Petrarch represents himself as becoming, through the very process of writing his love poetry, a faithful, repentant, and devoted lover of Christ, who has been led astray only temporarily by the corporeal beauty of his lover. Scève presents himself, on the contrary, as hopelessly trapped by the beauty of his Lady (which is at once corporeal and mystical), as imprisoned in a world that does not open up to the Christian God, but rather remains proudly closed on its own beautiful forms.

In the first *dizain*, for example, the poet/lover admits to having been taken by surprise in his erring youth by a false, painful, and misguided love. This also happens in Petrarch's first sonnet. However, the precise manner in which each poet chooses to represent this love is quite different. In Petrarch's poem, there are no concrete descriptions of the effects of Laura's beauty or of its terrible powers. The wound that explains the *Canzoniere*'s very existence is explained simply by the mention of love. In Scève's poem, by contrast, the sweet madness and destruction that love wreaks are rhetorically loaded, portrayed through apostrophe, hyperbole* and oxymorons* ("ô paour d'agréables terreurs"). What is more, the enemy is not described as a mischievous interloper (as can happen elsewhere in the *Canzoniere* with the intervention of the god "Amor"), but as the beauteous presence of the beloved herself, who by virtue of her poignant gaze is antithetically characterized as the "Basilisk" of deadly glance and breath. And there is another crucial difference. Petrarch, purified by the suffering and confession of his love for Laura, claims from the start to have been ultimately cured of the illusory carnal desire the ensuing poems will recount. The last line of his sonnet gives all readers notice "che quanto piace al mondo è breve sogno" [that what pleases in the world is only a brief dream]. Scève emphasizes instead the impossibility of his (and thus perhaps also our) ever escaping worship of his beloved's beauty, by representing himself as a Body with a Spirit that is dead or wandering. This is what makes him a piteous "host," a figure committed to adoring the bodily symbol of his untouchable Lady, whom he invokes directly and consecrates his Idol for life.

Thus Scève does not hesitate to subvert the Petrarchan (and Platonic) representation of love that he admires and imitates. And his thematic celebration of the supremacy of Délie's beauty and power (which is conveyed in the title's phrase "object de plus haulte vertu") is communicated through the tight formal beauty of his hermetic poems. His first *dizain* neither addresses us directly nor invites us to read further as Petrarch's first sonnet does, and as is customary with introductory poems. Rather, it rivets our attention on its own formal presence and aesthetic details, by using such techniques as the symmetrical, mirror-like construction of the poem's rhyme pattern (ababb+ccdcd); the richness of the initial rhymes (*erreurs/terreurs, impourveue/despourveue*); the inherent duplicity of certain words ("poignante" means "sharp" in a concrete sense, but also emotionally touching or heart-gripping, while "tranchante" means cutting, but also, in a moral sense, decisive); and the word-play that underscores semantic similarities and differences relating other key terms, as in the rhyming of *Ame-lame-Dame*, of *impourvue-veue-despourveue-veue*, and of *desvie-vie*.

Many of the poems in *Delie* paraphrase or even translate lines from Petrarch's *Canzoniere*. The first line of our *dizain*, "L'Œil trop ardent en mes jeunes erreurs," appears, for example, to transpose a phrase from Petrarch's first sonnet: "in sul mio primo giovenile errore" (in the first error of my youth). But this very visible imitation (Renaissance poets transplant not only themes and forms, but also words and phrases from their Classical and Italian models) in no way implies servile copying. In fact Scève's *dizain* is highly "original," departing from its model in its overall style, sense, and shape (it concludes quite differently from Petrarch's poem and does not even use the sonnet form). So is the structuring of *Delie* on the whole. Indeed, one of the collection's most mysterious aspects is its rigorously constructed arrangement of 449 *dizains* divided by fifty *emblèmes* (word-captioned engraved images). This creates a hermetic verbal-visual structure, about which scholars are still in debate.

Hermeticism, which implies at once formal and thematic impenetrability – obscurity and closure – is the most striking quality of Scève's poetry. This is a salient quality in many of France's greatest poets. Scève's first *dizain* is important not only because it opens the first French *canzoniere*. Rather, the poem's insistent hardness, in the double sense of its emphasis on matter (the image of the idol) and its formal and thematic impenetrability, appears also to add to Petrarchism a distinctively French twist, one that we will also observe affecting the sonnet in late Romanticism and in the Parnassian and Symbolist schools. These movements variously privilege poetic difficulty, as well as formal and material perfection, as we saw above in the *traité* and *art poétique* of Banville and Gautier. It is paradoxical that the sonnet's structure, which was initially found wanting, came to embody many French poets' plastic ideal.

We have already encountered one of the most celebrated French Renaissance sonnets, Ronsard's 'Sur la mort de Marie' ('On the Death of Marie'). The sonnet form has become fully gallicized in this poem, owing in part to Ronsard's masterful renewal of the alexandrine (which, we saw, achieved the formal "high" style previously associated with decasyllable verse within the initially looser, structure of the twelve-syllable line): Ronsard manages to fill or fit the imported form with a custom-made kind of French verse. Moreover, the very rich and restricted three-rhyme pattern of this sonnet (abba abba cca bba), though highly irregular, appears hyperbolically French insofar as it exaggerates the importance of the rhyme. It should also be noted that if, during the Renaissance, the sonnet is appropriated by the French as a universal fixed form, this is precisely thanks to the abundance of experiments that the Pléiade poets undertook. The particular use of the alexandrine in 'Sur la mort de Marie' represents just one among many moments in these poets' experimentation with high and low stylistic registers in the sonnet.

The 182 sonnets of Ronsard's first cycle of *Amours* (*Love Poems*, 1552), dedicated to the young aristocrat of Italian origin Cassandre Salviati, are his most Petrarchan in inspiration, and are written in syntactically contained decasyllable verse. However, his *Continuation des amours* (1555) and his *Nouvelle continuation* (*New Continuation*, 1556) abandon the Petrarchan construction of love to sing the praises of an accessible peasant girl, Marie, in a *beau style bas* (beautiful low style) made of supple alexandrines with many run-on lines. 'Sur la mort de Marie,' which was added to this collection much later, was written at the time (1578) when Ronsard published his last *Amours* – very Petrarchan, but also very ironic – entitled *Sonnets pour Hélène* (*Sonnets for Hélène*).

It is in Du Bellay's *Regrets* (1558) that the French sonnet becomes most forcefully unmoored from the theme of love. The title of this collection would lead one to expect love poems, especially after the publication of the poet's *L'Olive* (1549–1550), the first French *canzoniere* to be composed in decasyllable sonnets. But readers found instead a series of poems mixing satire and elegy to express the poet's lost inspiration and nostalgia for his homeland (as he had spent four years working in Rome), his sense of poetic exile and failure. What is more, in alternating sonnets written in decasyllables and alexandrines in his second Roman collection, *Les Antiquités de Rome* (*The Antiquities of Rome*, 1558), the same Du Bellay was engaging the sonnet's rhythms within a visually compelling structure. Embracing a form of discontinuity within continuity, the collection created a harmonious framework for the form, comparable to an architectural object.[30] This is an especially interesting strategy of appropriation insofar as the sonnet's own formal harmony, the secret to its success as the preeminent fixed form among all European cultures, no doubt stems in part, as François Jost has put it, from "la loi de de l'asymétrie dans la symétrie" (the law of asymmetry in symmetry).[31]

The many metrical, lexical, and syntactic means by which French poets have attempted to highlight or offset the sonnet's difficult structural equilibrium would be impossible to summarize here. But the quality of the form that they came to appreciate the most was precisely the paradoxical *bascule*, or see-saw balance-in-imbalance, created by the form's uneven proportions, which, we saw, they also resisted in principle. By the end of the Renaissance the sonnet is the short form of French poetry *par excellence*, to be employed in the later centuries for every possible thematic and stylistic register within the lyric: sonnets deal, for example, with matters as diverse as pornography, faith, and death (as in the haunting 'Sonnets sur la mort' ['Sonnets on Death'] by the Protestant Baroque poet Jean de Sponde, 1557–1595). The importance of the sonnet and the passion invested in defining its proper nature and use are reflected in one of the innumerable "querelles" (heated and extensive literary debates) that animated the seventeenth century.[32] However controversial, it is this very domination within Classical poetry that explains the form's temporary wane among the first Romantics. Their refusal or neglect of the sonnet makes sense, as they set out to render lyricism infinite by detaching it from previous conventions, definitions, and constraints. Hugo, the most prolific practitioner (with Ronsard) of most of the genres and forms of French poetry, wrote only a few sonnets, as did the other Romantics. But the form had a dramatic resurgence among the mid-nineteenth-century moderns, a renewal that began with a nostalgic return to the medieval and Renaissance roots of poetry.

This is evident in 'El Desdichado,' the first of a short collection of notoriously obscure sonnets entitled *Les Chimères* (*The Chimeras*), by Gérard de Nerval, the ultimate Romantic poet, who was touched and then destroyed by madness. This poem prefigures Symbolism by virtue of its confusion of dream, memory, and the evocation of previous lives. It also has a subversive rhyme scheme – abab abab cdd cee – which reappears in two of the many irregular, or "false," sonnets in Baudelaire's 1857 *Les Fleurs du mal* (*The Flowers of Evil*). It begins by underscoring the mourning of the "Disinherited One" for his lost love – that is, his lady/inspiration, symbolized as a star – and by suggesting magical ties between himself and historical or mythological poetic personae from by-gone days.

> Je suis le ténébreux, – le veuf, – l'inconsolé,
> Le prince d'Aquitaine à la tour abolie:
> Ma seule *étoile* est morte, – et mon luth constellé
> Porte le *Soleil noir* de la *Mélancolie.*
>
> Dans la nuit du tombeau, toi qui m'as consolé,
> Rends-moi le Pausilippe et la mer d'Italie,
> La *fleur* qui plaisait tant à mon cœur désolé,
> Et la treille où le pampre à la rose s'allie.
>
> Suis-je Amour ou Phébus? . . . Lusignan ou Biron?
> Mon front est rouge encor du baiser de la reine;
> J'ai rêvé dans la grotte où nage la syrène . . .
>
> Et j'ai deux fois vainqueur traversé l'Achéron:
> Modulant tour à tour sur la lyre d'Orphée
> Les soupirs de la sainte et les cris de la fée.[33]

> *I am the dark one, – the widower, – the unconsoled,*
> *The Prince of Aquitaine of the abolished tower:*
> *My only* star *is dead, – and my spangled lute*
> *Carries the* black Sun *of* Melancholy.
>
> *In the night of the tomb, you who consoled me,*
> *Give me back Posilippo and the Italian sea,*
> *The* flower *that so pleased my desolate heart,*
> *And the vine where the leaf joins with the rose.*

Am I Love or Phoebus? . . . Lusignan or Biron?
My brow is still red from the kiss of the queen;
I have dreamed in the grotto where the siren swims . . .

And I have twice victorious crossed the Acheron:
Modulating in turn on Orpheus' lyre
The sighs of the saint and the fairy's cries.

In the first stanza, the poet presents himself as a desolate widowed prince and a star-crossed lute player (a reverie on one of his ancestors, or perhaps the *Troubadour* Guillaume IX). This declaration turns to reminiscence of a past love (Posilippo is a hill in Naples), then to self-questioning ("Suis-je Amour ou Phébus? . . . Lusignan ou Biron?"), as the poet invokes the disjointed figures of Eros, Apollo, a descendant of the fairy Mélusine, and a sixteenth-century admiral, beheaded in 1602 (or perhaps Lord Byron). But the poem ends on a happier – if no less hallucinatory – note. As Rae Beth Gordon has shown, the last stanza affirms the poet's ability to recover not only his lost love, but also his own fragmented identity, modeled on that of Orpheus. The antagonistic desires, disparate rhythms, voices, and selves, which make "the sonnet a vertiginous place of movement, metamorphosis and infinite expansion,"[34] are not resolved, but reorganized by the lyric voice's mastery of its own singing.

Indeed, Nerval's mastery of the ancient lyre appears to reinstate the sonnet as a privileged vehicle for a variety of French poets to follow, who often hold little else in common. At the same time the sonnet has no doubt endured, in recent as in earlier times, because it lends itself to all kinds of stylistic transformations. Its resilient structure seems to offer poets of every ilk an ultimate test, condemning them, in the words of Paul Valéry, "to perfection."[35]

Valéry and other modern poets have often attributed poetic perfection – the theme, the ambition, and even the achievement – to Mallarmé. He, who defended both the alexandrine and free verse in *Crise de vers*, has been as regarded for his classically constructed sonnets (which have been compared to architectural monuments),[36] as for his invention of a new kind of verbal-visual poetry. In particular, his poem 'Le vierge, le vivace et le bel aujourd'hui' has been held out as a perfect sonnet. It has been "rearranged" in several twentieth-century poems and it has also been quoted, for example by Jean-Joseph Rabéarivelo (1904–1937), a poet from Madagascar, in a piece from his 1928 collection *Volumes*.[37] Because of the sonnet's harmonic sonorities, critics have compared it to a "symphony." However, its alternating masculine and feminine rhyme scheme (abba abba ccd ede) corresponds precisely to what Banville and others describe as the "regular" structure:

Le vierge, le vivace et le bel aujourd'hui
Va-t-il nous déchirer avec un coup d'aile ivre
Ce lac dur oublié que hante sous le givre
Le transparent glacier des vols qui n'ont pas fui!

Un cygne d'autrefois se souvient que c'est lui
Magnifique mais qui sans espoir se délivre
Pour n'avoir pas chanté la région où vivre
Quand du stérile hiver a resplendi l'ennui.

Tout son col secouera cette blanche agonie
Par l'espace infligée à l'oiseau qui le nie,
Mais non l'horreur du sol où le plumage est pris.

Fantôme qu'à ce lieu son pur éclat assigne,
Il s'immobilise au songe froid de mépris
Que vêt parmi l'exil inutile le Cygne.[38]

The virgin, vibrant, beautiful today
Will it tear for us with a drunken wing stroke
This hard forgotten lake which beneath the frost is haunted
By the transparent glacier of flights not flown!

A swan of another time remembers that it is he
Magnificent but who without hope delivers himself
For not having sung of a region in which to live
When the boredom of sterile winter showed its splendor.

His whole neck will shake off this white agony
Inflicted by space on the bird who denies it,
But not the horror of the ground where his feathers are caught.

Phantom assigned to this place by his pure brilliance,
He becomes still in the cold dream of disdain
Which the Swan dons in his useless exile.

Despite this poem's marked difficulty – caused by its syntactical inversions and the *mise en abîme**(or self-mirroring effect) of its images – we notice that it links, like Nerval's poem, the theme of melancholy and despair with the production of lyrical song (especially in the second quatrain). What is more, the figure of the poet, *le cygne* (the swan) – which is itself a symbol, rendering tangible a conflict between abstract and concrete, temporal and metaphysical forms of presence (the beautiful present day caught in the frozen lake haunted by a glacier of "flights never flown") – recalls in its multiple ghostly apparitions the contrary avatars and loves of Nerval's disparate lyric personæ, who also were caught, in a sense, between earth and sky, life and death, desire and remembrance. But unlike in 'El Desdichado,' there is no victory or transcendence in Mallarmé's poem. And what divides the lyric subject is not a conflict of differences, though there are many diametrical oppositions in the sonnet. The problem for Mallarmé's swan is the separation of the self-same from itself: in metaphysical terms, the structure of representation, or identity-in-difference, that appears to constitute all presence.

Mallarmé's dying swan, especially in its final appearance as a capitalized, allegorical *Cygne*, alludes to a mythological, cosmic kind of presence, the mourning singer Cygnos, whom Apollo transforms into a constellation (a supreme image of the poet, previously invoked by Ronsard, which may also factor into Nerval's "luth constellé"). But it also refers, through punning on the word "cygne" (which is a homonym for "signe") to its own verbal apotheosis, that is, to its poetic bringing into being of the ideal Sign. However, what the swan finally sings is simply the full assumption of responsibility for his own dying song; he admits his unwillingness to save himself, and vainly girds himself in his commitment to useless exile.

When we understand that Mallarmé's swan is caught in the ice because of his refusal to go to a warmer place, and because of his own pure brilliance – which shines through the reflective power of his (poetic) purity and the cold dream of his disdain – the poem begins to recall the "resistant block" where dream becomes fixed in Gautier's *L'Art*. Even more, though more narcissistically, the lyric dilemma brings to mind the reflexive idolatry of Scève's *Delie*, where the poet commits himself, from the outset, to entrapment in a world of beautiful forms.

Most strikingly modern in this sonnet is the poetic sign's reflexivity, and the degree to which it points to a world of philosophical closure. There is no love, no real other, no transcendence, no animated presence even, except for the ghosts which arise from the process of the swan/sign's own auto-negation. What makes the poem so beautiful, so hauntingly moving, however, is the rich integrity of means by which Mallarmé suggests this pure poetic negation. The images are made of nothing but variations of white on white (in homage perhaps to Gautier's *Symphonie en blanc majeur* [*Symphony in White Major*]), just as the sonorities, with their alliterative and assonantal (or harmonic) dispersement of the words "cygne" and "hiver," seem to compose a winter "symphony in i."

Though the sonnet has remained vital throughout twentieth-century French poetry (witness Guy Goffette's 'Montée au sonnet' ['Climb to the Sonnet'] in his 1991 collection, *La Vie promise* [*The Promised Life*]), its fixed character has naturally held little appeal for certain types of poets, from Dada and Surrealism forward, whose iconoclastic, exploratory, or liberating objectives, in some ways similar to those of the Romantics, have shunned poetic traditions of all sorts. While Aragon and others returned, as we shall see, to older French verse forms during the Resistance for political effect, the majority of mid-twentieth-century poets opted for free verse. The widely popular Jacques Prévert (1900–1977) generally chose very simple free verse forms to convey the beauty of everyday life. Yet other poets, explicitly drawn to formal constraint and experimentation – such as Raymond Queneau (1903–1976), who in 1960 created the group OuLiPo (Ouvroir de Littérature Potentielle [Workroom for Potential Literature]) – remained especially engaged with the sonnet and continued to revive it. In 1967 OuLiPo member Jacques Roubaud published an important collection of sonnets (including some "shortened," some "in prose") under the mathematical sign ε; he has commented on his "sonettomania" in his most recent work *Poésie: (récit)* (Poetry: [Narrative]).[39] The most extreme example of innovation is perhaps Queneau's 1961 *Cent mille milliards de poèmes* (*One Hundred Thousand Billion Poems*), which, by affording the reader the possibility to systematically combine the individual lines of ten regular sonnets, offers, in a slim collection, what is no doubt the vastest sonnet cycle ever known.[40]

Given this constrained yet expansive project, it is interesting that Queneau, in an early 1960s essay entitled *Littérature potentielle*, both praises and lightly mocks the formal perfection of Mallarmé's sonnets, stating that they are made of "choice material like the drosophila [fruit-fly] in genetics." He describes each line of verse as "a little world, a unit whose meaning accumulates, in effect, in the rhyming section," and draws our attention to the sonnet's phonetic and semantic repetitiveness, subjecting it to what he calls a "haikuization" (after the brief, seventeen-syllable Japanese form), an operation demonstrating that the sonnet's essential sounds and meaning are effectively condensed, not in the last line as Banville would have wanted, but rather in the rhymes:

> Aujourd'hui
> Ivre,
> le givre
> pas fui!
>
> Lui
> se délivre . . .
> où vivre?
> L'ennui . . .
>
> Agonie
> le nie,
> pris,
>
> assigne
> mépris,
> le Cygne.[41]
>
> *Today*
> *Drunk,*
> *the frost*
> *not flown!*

He
delivers himself . . .
where to live?
Boredom . . .

Agony
denies it,
caught,

assigns
disdain,
the Swan.

Queneau claims that his transformation has the added values of creating a beautiful new poem (the punctuation is his own personal touch), and of clarifying the meaning of the original sonnet: by paring out "redundancy," it demonstrates that this poem's sounds and images are but reflections or echoes of one another.

When we know the context and spirit of Queneau's "haikuization," we are not surprised to find an actual *haiku** of Mallarmé's sonnet in the 1997 *Poèmes fondus* (*Melted Poems*) by Michelle Grangaud (1941–), an Oulipian writer of the next generation:

C'est l'hiver. Le lac
est pris sous le givre du
glacier magnifique.

It is winter. The lake
is caught under the frost of
the magnificent glacier.[42]

Taken by itself, this rewriting achieves much more than the reduction and clarification of the sonnet's original repetitiveness. It also negates its elegiac quality and the particular character of its "Symbolism." That is, in simply seeming to designate the elements of a natural scene, as is appropriate with the *haiku* genre (although there is something strange in the notion of a lake caught under a glacier), Grangaud not only eliminates the central figure of the swan, but also negates the first principle of Mallarmé's poetics, which is not to name things, but to suggest them, or more precisely to evoke the effect of things in their absence. In one decisive stroke, she transforms Mallarmé's complex, rhyme-saturated, figurative construction – with its hermetic mirroring effects – into a contemporary scene of Japanese-style French art.

But this haiku ought not to be read in isolation, as it is evenly strung in Grangaud's collection of *Poèmes fondus* among many other "haikuized" sonnets by Mallarmé and other French masters of the form: Du Bellay, José-Maria de Hérédia (1842–1905), Baudelaire, and Nerval; each recreation having its own individual character. Grangaud's purpose, moreover, is no more to produce orientalist poetry than it is to simplify the works of Mallarmé or her other predecessors. Rather, by transposing the most canonical sonnets of her literary tradition into the strict confines of the *haiku* – a form which remains from the French perspective relatively foreign and new – her stated goal is to undertake "translations of French into French," or to experience "translating a poem into its own language."[43]

By implementing a change in genre that operates also a change of form in a melt-down of great model poems, Grangaud, like her Renaissance forefathers, creates a new poetic world, one which is at the same time traditionally determined, and yet wholly her own. She proceeds in a manner that strikes one as typically French in at least two ways. On the one hand, her work presents itself as the realization of an explicit poetic program and unfolds with the same harmonious rigor we have seen in many of her predecessors; the collection moves from the "fondus" of the sonnets to a final "*fondu de fondus*," a poem composed of one-line "meltings" of the previous melted poems. On the other hand, Grangaud's way of engaging us and herself within this poetic process is at once playful, parodical, and subversively "feminine." To place her laboring with fixed forms under the sign (or title) of soft cooking as opposed to that of hard sculpture, architecture, or mathematics, as we have seen her compatriots consistently do, is to poke fun at their own rigid representations of what poetry is and how it is made.

An untranslatable pun in Grangaud's final prefatory remark underscores this conventionally gendered difference, while also heralding her efforts to recreate the special flavor of her forebears' poems: "finalement, il ne reste plus qu'à fondre aussi les poèmes fondus, en s'appliquant pour les faire bien revenir" (finally, all that is needed is to melt also the melted poems, applying oneself to properly brown them [that is, to bring out their taste by gentle cooking/to make them come back again]). Culturally French, of course, in its culinary emphasis, Grangaud's ambivalent wordplay and deceptively humble self-representation are also characteristic of a tendency among French women poets (which we have already seen in Christine de Pizan) to cast their work in a mold ostensibly different from that of their male counterparts – often in an intimate, self-effacing, flexible, and domestic mode. Thus we see, from the most recent developments of French poetry as from its beginnings, how culturally complex and inseparable are matters of genre and form.

Chapter 3

Words and figures

Verse and prose, forms and genres, the fundamental contours of poetry are themselves made up of building blocks: words and figures. So crucial are these elements that whatever we say about a poem ultimately arises out of their analysis and interpretation. The traditional French exercise of *explication de texte* (text explication) which is a line-by-line, often word-by-word, and sometimes sound-by-sound or letter-by-letter unfolding of a text's meaning, has the advantage of revealing how much our understanding of poetry depends on the attention we pay to its words, and to the stylistic devices that are used to select and combine words: figures.

We have seen that the classification of French poetry often involves consideration of high, low, and middle style. This distinction of stylistic levels has its origins in Classical rhetoric (the art of persuasion through public speaking). It became increasingly rigid in late Antiquity, as the practice of oratory was adapted to Christian preaching, and throughout the Middle Ages, which tended to understand style levels in terms of social hierarchy (high style was used to address or discuss nobles, low style peasants, and so forth). As a general matter, rhetoric used high style to move or overwhelm the audience; low or simple style, to teach or inform; and middle style, to please or to bring together the audience, notably in speeches conferring praise or blame. High style was rich in powerful, expressive figures, but these were not meant to be noticed or valued for their own sake, only to trigger passions in the audience; low style, by contrast, was deliberately poor in figurative effects, seeking precision and clarity; middle style allowed a more abundant and self-conscious use of verbal ornaments. Lyric poetry was most often associated with this last style and the celebration of persons, objects, and events.

French poets from the Middle Ages to the nineteenth century were solidly grounded in rhetoric's teachings. But the notion of levels of style was also connected to linguistic ideology, to ever-changing considerations concerning the French language, often determining which kinds of words were supposed to be used in which social contexts. Indeed, one of the most striking characteristics of French poetry is that it repeatedly involves itself in polemics over the state and evolution of the French language. Hence a continual shifting in the designation and aims of rhetorical registers, in which poets alternatively challenge or abide by normative definitions of language and of the place and role of poetry within it. We will refrain therefore from artificially fixing or stabilizing what constitutes high or low poetic style, but we will nevertheless recognize that words and figures, like other aspects of poetry, are often used and judged with reference to these criteria.

Just as some meters and genres have historically been deemed higher in their rhetorical register than others – in the seventeenth century, the alexandrine is nobler than the heptasyllable, and in the Renaissance, the *hymne* is higher than the *discours* – certain words have been generally considered to be higher in style than others, though such hierarchies evolve, like the rest, over time. Whether a word is deemed to be high or low in style often depends on how it falls into various other lexical categories. In its historical context, is the word that captures attention in a poem rare or common, familiar or erudite? Is it an archaism,* an old-fashioned word, or a word whose particular use has become more or less obsolete, such as the word "coi" (quiet) from Krysinska's 'La Gigue,' or "parmi" (used in the sense of in, rather than among) in Mallarmé's 'Le vierge, le vivace . . .'? Or is it a neologism,* a newly coined word, as with the word "bombinent" (buzz) in 'Voyelles,' which Rimbaud created from the rare Latin verb *bombino*?

What type or family is the word associated with in the dictionary? Is it a word that presents itself as inherently "poetical," for example "onde" (for a pool or wave of water) or "aurore" in Lamartine's 'Le Lac,' or as generically associated with poetry, as with "rime" in Christine de Pizan's 'Virelay'? Or does it rather bring to mind some other domain, as with the reference to "musique" in Verlaine's 'Art poétique,' or with the scientific and technological terms "rayon x" and "bipôle" in Roubaud's 'Méditation de la comparaison'?

Does a word or group of words seem especially refined, or *précieux*,* suitable for an inside group of elite readers, as with the convoluted speech and poetry of early seventeenth-century salons, where a mirror, for example, was called a "conseiller des grâces" (counselor of the graces)? Conversely, does a word or expression seem especially vulgar, as with "puanteurs" in Rimbaud's 'Voyelles,' or the familiar word "fiston" in Alphonse Allais' humorous verses? Or does it come from a group of "outsiders," as with slang poetry, which became popular in the avant-garde cabaret culture of fin-de-siècle Paris?

Is the word we notice actually French, or is it foreign, as with the Spanish title 'El Desdichado' of Nerval's poem, or from a French-derived dialect, as with the *créole* words one can find in Caribbean poetry (the poems of Gilbert Gratiant (1895–1985) are often composed entirely in Martiniquan *patois*) or the *joual* terms sometimes used by poets from Québec? Without necessarily referring us to the reality of another culture, does the vocabulary of a poem sound exotic? In Perec's Oulipian parody of Rimbaud, the "e-less" 'Vocalisations,' there are, understandably, several exotic terms borrowed from other languages, such as "fjord" and "Khan," as well as *barbarismes*,* that is, incorrectly formed French words. The word "nidoral," for example, does not appear in French dictionaries; but improper as the word is, we can deduce its sense insofar as it makes a noun equivalent in meaning to Rimbaud's "puanteurs," out of the proper French word "nidoreux," an adjective describing the odor of something rotting. Finally, do we hear onomatopoeias, words that sound like what they refer to, as with "becqueté" in Villon's 'Epitaphe,' or "ahanne" in Du Bellay's 'D'un vanneur de blé aux vents,' or the series "ton ton . . . ton taine" in Laforgue's 'L'hiver qui vient'?

While there is no need to be exhaustive in one's research concerning the values and categories associated with a poem's words, all of the above questions may be pertinent to consider. It would be convenient to assume we could find rare or refined words and figures in high-style poems, and vulgar or familiar words and figures in low ones. Sometimes we can; but the equation is not that simple. Rather, the history of French poetry can be seen to revolve around changing mixtures of "high" and "low" words and diverse uses of figures within the context of genres which are themselves unstable. What is more, the "levels" of words and figures can change radically even within particular poems.

Still, it is possible to paint some tendencies regarding the treatment of words and figures within certain periods of French poetry, and to see connections between these stylistic features and other aspects of French culture. It should be no surprise by now, for example, that the Classical era, with its strong political, prosodic, and generic rules, will have the most restrictive ideas about what kinds of words belong in what kinds of poetry (if they are deemed suitable for poetry at all), as well as the most clear-cut rules about what kinds of figures are appropriate. Nor should we be surprised to find that in the nineteenth century, in the domains of both words and figures, liberation from Classical constraints gets started in earnest with Hugo.

In the following excerpts from 'Réponse à un acte d'accusation' ('Response to an Act of Accusation'), a long verse manifesto that presents itself as a self-defense, Hugo claims, for instance, to have revolutionized the French lexicon in the strongest possible sense, and to have upset, as a consequence of his egalitarian language, a number of Classical customs regarding figures:

Je fis souffler un vent révolutionnaire.
Je mis un bonnet rouge au vieux dictionnaire.
Plus de mot sénateur! plus de mot roturier!
[. . .]
Discours affreux! – Syllepse, hypallage, litote,
Frémirent; je montai sur la borne Aristote,
Et déclarai les mots égaux, libres, majeurs.
[. . .]
Oui, je suis ce Danton! je suis ce Robespierre!
J'ai, contre le mot noble à la longue rapière,
Insurgé le vocable ignoble, son valet,
Et j'ai, sur Dangeau mort, égorgé Richelet.
[. . .]
J'ai de la périphrase écrasé les spirales,
Et mêlé, confondu, nivelé sous le ciel
L'alphabet, sombre tour qui naquit de Babel;
Et je n'ignorais pas que la main courroucée
Qui délivre le mot, délivre la pensée.
[. . .]
J'ai dit à la narine: Eh mais! tu n'es qu'un nez!
J'ai dit au long fruit d'or: Mais tu n'es qu'une poire!
J'ai dit à Vaugelas: Tu n'es qu'une mâchoire!¹
[. . .]

I made a revolutionary wind blow.
I put a red bonnet on the dictionary.
No more senatorial words! no more commoners!
[. . .]
Dreadful discourse! – Syllepsis, hypallage, litotes,
Trembled: I climbed up on Aristotle's stump
And declared words equal, free, of full age.
[. . .]
Yes, I am that Danton! I am that Robespierre!
I have, against the noble word with the long rapier,
Insurrected the ignoble vocable, his valet,
And I have, on Dangeau dead, slit the throat of Richelet.
[. . .]
I have of the periphrasis crushed the spirals,
And mixed, confused, leveled under the sky
The alphabet, somber tower born of Babel;
And I was not unaware that the angry hand
That delivers words, delivers thought.
[. . .]
I said to the nostril: So! You are just a nose!
I said to the long fruit of gold: But you are just a pear!
I said to Vaugelas: You are just a jaw!
[. . .]

To fully grasp these verses, which animate technical terms in a dramatic way, we need to know that Dangeau and Richelet were grammarians and lexicographers, and that Vaugelas was in the seventeenth century the main legislator of linguistic correctness. We also must be familiar with some of the rhetorical figures Hugo threatens. Broadly defined, syllepsis,* the first figure mentioned, allows any part of speech to perform simultaneously two different functions: to grammatically link two disparate subjects, or to convey at the same time two different meanings, literal and figurative. This occurs in the following lines of Pyrrhus from Racine's *Andromaque*, where the words "maux" and "feux" must be taken both literally and metaphorically:

> Je souffre tous les *maux* que *j'ai faits* devant Troie.
> Vaincu, chargé de fers, de regrets consumé,
> Brûlé de plus de *feux* que je n'en allumai [. . .]²
>
> *I suffer from all the* evils/pain *that* I inflicted *at Troy*
> *Conquered, charged with irons, consumed with regrets,*
> *I burn with more* fires *than I there lit [. . .]*

Periphrasis⁺ (from the Greek *peri*, "around," and *phrasis*, "expression"), the figure whose spirals Hugo claims to have crushed, circuitously describes an object rather than naming it. A good example, dismantled in the poem, is "long fruit d'or" (long fruit of gold), which indirectly designates the pear through aspects of its shape and color, creating a delicate phrasing.

These and other rhetorical terms, which Hugo represents as nobles trembling with fear in front of his lexical revolution, designate stylistic devices that allow poets to either privilege or avoid certain words and to change the weight or importance of others. This is what Pierre Fontanier, a rhetorician contemporary to Hugo, defines as figures in his treatise *Les Figures du discours* (*The Figures of Speech*), insisting on the difference between these kinds of expressions and simple, common language:

> Figures of speech are the more or less remarkable and aptly effective traits, forms, or turns by which discourse in the expression of ideas, thoughts and sentiments, more or less distances itself from that which would have been simple and common expression.³

As the multiple personifications and other images of his 'Réponse' amply show, Hugo, however, does not hesitate to use rhetorical figures himself. He often in fact uses more of them than Classical poets do. Nevertheless, his attack on some traditional figures makes sense insofar as these were used to exclude or separate various kinds or levels of speech. Hugo is dramatizing his own role in liberating, for the Romantic generation, more egalitarian, direct forms of discourse in poetry.

The process of defining and classifying figures is complex, partly because there is a significant list and changing history of terms that have been used from Antiquity onward to describe their various types, and partly because the effects of figures cannot really be evaluated or appreciated out of context. However, there are several basic figures that can be presented in a general way. Among those to be discussed here are metaphor, metonymy,* and synechdoche:* the fundamental tropes.* These are figures that either change or extend the literal meaning of a word to a figurative one.

More ambiguous than the simile,* which explicitly designates a similarity between two terms, metaphor makes an implicit comparison; it either associates a figurative word with a literal one on the basis of resemblance, or substitutes the former for the latter ("feu" for "amour"). When Malherbe says of the world "sa lumière est un verre et sa faveur une onde" (its light is a glass and its favor a wave), he is assimilating the fragility and unreliability of what we see through glass to the natural light of this world, and the inconstant, momentary movement of the water to its favor. Similarly, when Rimbaud, in a much more original and unexpected metaphor, says "A, noir corset velu des mouches éclatantes," he is positing a basic identity between the shape of the letter A and that of the black, hairy corset of a fly.

By contrast to metaphor, which creates figurative links between things on the basis of their similarity, metonymy establishes a relation on the basis of contiguity; a word stands for another which designates something distinct but featuring some form of connection or association. Many kinds of relationships produce metonymies. In the expression "the White House issued a statement today," the relationship between the president, or whoever issued the statement, and "the White House" is one of a contiguity of place, or physical proximity, while in Charles d'Orléans' 'Le temps a laissié son manteau,' the cloak stands for wintery weather because it is under these climactic temporal conditions that we wear one. Like metonymy, synecdoche depends on a connection between a figurative word and the thing it represents, but rather than representing one thing by another which is separate but related (as metonymy does), this figure designates the whole of something by referring to a part, or vice-versa. When Malherbe's 'Ode' to Louis XIII, for example, encourages the King to "Donner le dernier coup à la dernière tête / De la rébellion" (Strike the last blow to the last head / Of the rebellion), the poet does not necessarily mean that his master should deliver only one "final blow" to stop the rebellion. Rather, the King, leading his forces, is being incited through verbal drama to crush by any and all means the entire rebel army.

Since figures can be interpreted in more than one way, they are also subject to multiple categorization (metonymy and synecdoche are especially apt to overlap). The figurative expression *Un cœur simple* (*A Simple Heart*) for example, forms the title of a famous tale by Gustave Flaubert. As it refers to Félicité, the tale's heroine, it can be understood as a metonymy insofar as it designates her simple feelings, and as a synecdoche, insofar as her whole being is represented by this part of her body: Félicité is "all heart." Moreover, a poet can easily combine many different kinds of figures within one phrase. If Malherbe's "dernière tête de la rebellion" is understood, for example, as an allusion (an extrinsic cultural reference) to the Hydra of Greek mythology, then it must be understood as a metaphor, as well as a synecdoche, and could also be defined as a syllepsis in the broad sense outlined earlier, where a word retains a figurative and metaphorical sense simultaneously. The effectiveness of Malherbe's line also depends, moreover, on the presence of a catachresis,* an expression whose original figurative power has become "dead," because fully integrated into ordinary language. To refer to the "head" of a rebellion is to employ a "dead metaphor" since it is normal to call the leader of a group its "head." But to speak of the head of a rebellion as an implicit image of the multi-headed Hydra is to bring this dead figure back to life in the most compelling way.

As the last example has shown, the analytical categorization of rhetorical figures in context can be a mind-boggling exercise. Fortunately, for most readers, problems of classification are not of primary concern. What matters is that we learn to appreciate the ways in which figurative language transforms the meaning of poetic texts, and poetic texts play on the figurativeness of language. Beyond the tropes, some figures of importance that have already come up are: hyperbole (the figure of exaggeration), and its opposite, understatement – litotes* or euphemism;* apostrophe (the figure of address); antithesis* and oxymoron (two basic figures of contrast); inversion (a figure of syntax); and finally rhyme, assonance, alliteration, and onomatopoeia (the figures of sound).

The pages that follow will not develop or refine the above lists. Rather, they will try to convey the kinds of interaction that can take place in a poem between words and figures, and the effects they can have on creating or subverting conventions associated with high or low stylistic registers. While it is true that there is a regime of restrictiveness in the Classical era, and a leveling of distinctions in the Romantic and modern eras, it is also important to avoid the impression that choices of lexical and figurative resources are relevant only to contextualizing poems within historical periods.

Let us begin then by taking a synchronic, or ahistorical, approach to looking at the interplay between words and figures. We will consider a poem from the dawn of modernity that presents itself in two different versions:

Baudelaire's previously cited 'L'Invitation au voyage' in verse (first published in 1855), and a rewriting of the same poem in prose (initially appearing in 1857), which is included in the 1869 collection of "Petits poèmes en prose" entitled *Le Spleen de Paris*. The prose poem is quite long; let us first cite its opening paragraphs and compare them to the opening stanzas of the verse poem (quoted in Chapter One).

Il est un pays superbe, un pays de Cocagne, dit-on, que je rêve de visiter avec une vieille amie. Pays singulier, noyé dans les brumes de notre Nord, et qu'on pourrait appeler l'Orient de l'Occident, la Chine de l'Europe, tant la chaude et capricieuse fantaisie s'y est donné carrière, tant elle l'a patiemment et opiniâtrement illustré de ses savantes et délicates végétations.

Un vrai pays de Cocagne, où tout est beau, riche, tranquille, honnête; où le luxe a plaisir à se mirer dans l'ordre; où la vie est grasse et douce à respirer; d'où le désordre, la turbulence et l'imprévu sont exclus; où le bonheur est marié au silence; où la cuisine elle-même est poétique, grasse et excitante à la fois; où tout vous ressemble, mon cher ange.

Tu connais cette maladie fiévreuse qui s'empare de nous dans les froides misères, cette nostalgie du pays qu'on ignore, cette angoisse de la curiosité? Il est une contrée qui te ressemble, où tout est beau, riche, tranquille et honnête, où la fantaisie a bâti et décoré une Chine occidentale, où la vie est douce à respirer, où le bonheur est marié au silence. C'est là qu'il faut aller vivre, c'est là qu'il faut aller mourir!

Oui, c'est là qu'il faut aller respirer, rêver et allonger les heures par l'infini des sensations [. . .]

Oui, c'est dans cette atmosphère qu'il ferait bon vivre [. . .][4]

There is a superb country, a land of Cockayne, they say, that I dream to visit with an old friend. Singular country drowned in the mists of our North, and that could be called the Orient of the Occident, the China of Europe, so much has warm and capricious fantasy been given free rein there, so much has it been patiently and obstinately adorned with skilful and delicate vegetations.

A true land of Cockayne, where all is beautiful, rich, tranquil, honest; where luxury takes pleasure admiring itself in order; where life is lush and sweet to breathe; where disorder, turbulence and the unexpected are excluded; where happiness is married to silence; where cooking itself is poetic, at once rich and exciting; where everything resembles you, my dear angel.

You know that feverish illness that seizes us in our cold worries, that nostalgia for the unknown country, that anxiety of curiosity? There is a country which resembles you, where everything is beautiful, rich, tranquil and honest, where fantasy has built and decorated an occidental China, where life is sweet to breathe, where happiness is married to silence. That is where we must go to live, that is where we must go to die!

Yes, that is where we must go to breathe, dream and lengthen the hours by infinite sensations [. . .]

Yes, it is in that atmosphere that it would be good to live [. . .]

What are the similarities and differences between the verse and prose versions of this poem? Does the change from verse to prose, which obviously implements a change in form, also entail a change of the poem's degree of figurativeness, its level of rhetorical style, or its purpose? To what extent can the global changes we perceive in the poem be attributed to precise changes in words and figures? Conversely, to what extent might certain changes in words and figures ensure a certain identity between the two versions? Let us briefly address some of these questions.[5]

Along with the passage from verse to prose, what changes most evidently, in formal terms, is the work's general dimensions. The prose poem has many more lines than the verse poem, and contains many more words. In addition to this verbal abundance, we also find in the prose poem a variety of types of words that are not found in the verse. Among these are the impersonal expressions "Il est" and "dit-on," which are more appropriate to third-person narrative than to any kind of poetry; the phrase "vieille amie," which is a rather impersonal (if familiar) way to refer to a lover (especially in comparison with the more tender "mon enfant, ma sœur" used in the verse poem); the pedantic adverb "opiniâtrement," which sounds at once scholarly and satirical, and the semi-scientific word "végétations." All of these impersonal or objective words subvert the subjective, lyrical quality of the original poem, and draw our attention to the fact that the prose poem, in its opening at least, appears to be describing an "invitation" to a voyage, rather than actually making one.

In the second paragraph, we find a different type of undermining. Despite Hugo's lexical revolution, in Baudelaire's time it was still abnormal to find such vulgar words as "cuisine" and "grasse" in the language of poetry. However, the "prosaic" inappropriateness of these words is rhetorically underscored in the prose poem so as to redeem their use for poetry, or render them "poetic." First, the reference to cooking occurs within an oxymoron, a figure that realizes, as it were, a contradiction in terms. Secondly, the poetic quality of cooking in this context is, paradoxically, developed and emphasized in the rhetorical repetition of the word "grasse," which is used twice, once toward the beginning and once toward the end of the paragraph. In its first appearance, the word functions, figuratively, as a synecdoche (or perhaps as a metonymy), signifying either a general abundance of life or the excess of riches that life naturally produces (as in the English expression "the fat of the earth"); while in its second occurrence it denotes literally the fattiness of the ideal country's food. Qualified, moreover, by the adjective "excitante," which means stimulating in a culinary context and carries strong sexual connotations − referring to a certain "spiciness" − the term "grasse" helps to turn the poem in a more personal direction, conjuring up the poet's lover directly in the all-embracing comparison: "où tout vous ressemble, mon cher ange." This comparison sets up an elaborate analogy in the prose poem (which is also swiftly brushed in in the verse) between the (oxymoronic) familiar exoticism of the poem's addressee (a woman whose hybrid identity appears to be modeled on Baudelaire's actual lover, the mulatto Jeanne Duval) and every aspect of the ideal country resembling her.

While the prose poem strikes us as generally more literal and down-to-earth than the verse version, one should also note that the very words conveying exactitude and straightforwardness are often themselves figures. The most striking example of this may be in the prose poem's description of the idyllic country, which is only vaguely evoked in the impressionistic images of the verse poem. While the latter seems to paint a purely symbolic tableau of some ideal place, the prose poem indicates that this shining utopia paradoxically corresponds to a place that is both actual and unique: a "pays singulier." Along with the the initial mention of "delicate vegetations," further references to "horticulture," to the Dutch "florin," and to specific picturesque flowers – the poet's beloved *"tulipe noire"* and *"dahlia bleu"* – lead us unmistakably to Amsterdam: that is, not surprisingly in this new, low-style lyrical context, to the heart of the *Pays-Bas*.

The fact that these exotic flowers also have a figurative function – "ma tulipe retrouvée," "mon allégorique dahlia" – referring to earlier Romantic texts and symbolizing the poet's lover, like the whole of the ideal country that he associates with her, in no way cancels out the effect of real, "local" color they also convey. Returning to the opening of the poem, a process which the circular development of poetry always invites us to do, we realize that Amsterdam was from the beginning revealed as the poet's desired destination, for this is the only city "in the mists" of Europe's North that fits the descriptive details provided in both the verse and prose poems. In this first paragraph, it is (again paradoxically) through a series of figurative expressions beginning with the oxymorons "l'Orient de l'Occident" and "la Chine de l'Europe" that the real and specific existence of this ideal country is most forcefully conveyed.

Once we understand this, it does not surprise us that the closing paragraph of the prose poem presents the poem in its entirety, as an allegory (a complex, multifaceted symbolic representation) of the relationship between the lovers and the poem, and simultaneously explains the poem's genesis, or the realities behind the allegory. We also learn that all the aspects of the ideal country elaborated in the poet's tableau, which at first seemed to represent his lady only metaphorically (or by resemblance), also represent her metonymically (or through a correspondence), since it is his desire for her familiar yet exotic being that has created this realistic/figurative "tableau." The poetic evocation of Amsterdam is thus the expression of so many thoughts inspired by the poet's lover, which he offers in turn both as an invitation and a gift:

[. . .] Vivrons-nous jamais, passerons-nous jamais dans ce tableau qu'a peint mon esprit, ce tableau qui te ressemble?

Ces trésors, ces meubles, ce luxe, cet ordre, ces parfums, ces fleurs mirac-uleuses, c'est toi. C'est encore toi, ces grands fleuves et ces canaux tran-quilles. Ces énormes navires qu'ils charrient, tout chargés de richesses [. . .] ce sont mes pensées qui dorment ou qui roulent sur ton sein. Tu les con-duis doucement vers la mer qui est l'Infini [. . .] – et quand, fatigués par la houle et gorgés des produits de l'Orient, ils rentrent au port natal, ce sont encore mes pensées enrichies qui reviennent de l'Infini vers toi.[6]

[. . .] Will we ever live, will we ever enter this tableau that my mind has painted, this tableau that resembles you?

These treasures, these furnishings, this luxury, this order, these perfumes, these miraculous flowers are you. You again are these great rivers and tranquil canals. Those enormous ships that they carry, all loaded up with riches [. . .] those are my thoughts that sleep or roll along on your breast. You guide them sweetly toward the sea which is the Infinite [. . .] – and when, tired from the surge and stuffed with products from the Orient, they return to their native port, those are again my enriched thoughts that come back from the Infinite toward you.

Thus what appears most "prosaic" in Baudelaire's prose poetry still signi-fies figuratively. The poem's prosaic qualities expose what Barbara Johnson has described as "the conflict" and the reciprocal "work of mutilation and correction" of linguistic and cultural codes that poetry in general presupposes.[7] Baudelaire's prose poems are poetic precisely by virtue of their inclusion of the traditionally "non-poetic" within them, by virtue of their capacity to render the familiar strange and (to paraphrase Ezra Pound) "make it new." But this modern, paradoxical poetics is equally at play in much of Baudelaire's verse, since it too frequently draws, as Carol de Dobay Rifelj has shown, on prosaic words and on ostensibly realistic figures to make mud ("boue") into gold ("or") or conversely gold into mud.[8]

But before leaving our two 'Invitations,' let us also examine how the transposition of certain figures into others can paradoxically ensure a certain unity of poetry – in this case, a unity that transcends poetry's division into verse and prose. The Russian structuralist linguist and poetician Roman Jakobson attributes to all kinds of poetry and to poetic language in general the marked feature of repetitiveness; this is what separates it from ordi-nary language and communication: "at all levels of language, the essence, in poetry, of artistic technique resides in reiterated repetitions."[9] In his essay *Linguistics and Poetics*, Jakobson explains that the "poetic function" of lan-guage operates through "the projection of the principle of resemblance from the axis of selection onto the axis of combination."[10] This means that words belonging to a certain group or paradigm because of their common features (whether semantic or phonetic) tend to be used alongside each other in poetry, whereas they would normally substitute for one another in other kinds of discourse. The result of this transfer is that sequences of poetic language tend to be made up of words that are semantically and phonetically equivalent to one another.

Though Baudelaire's 'Invitation' in prose appears less repetitive or structurally circular than its verse counterpart, by virtue of its lack of meter and rhyme (as well as its sheer mass), there are many exaggerated forms of repetition in the prose that conserve a measure of the verses' lyricism, both in the harmonic and the rhythmic sense. The refrain, for example, which is perhaps the greatest marker of the verse poem's musicality, is transposed into another form of blatant repetition in the prose version. The first line of the latter, "Il est un pays superbe, un pays de Cocagne," is, for example, repeated with a variation at the beginning of the second paragraph: "Un vrai pays de Cocagne, où tout est beau, riche, tranquille, honnête." In addition, the ending of this phrase is itself repeated in the middle of the third paragraph: "Il est une contrée qui te ressemble, où tout est beau, riche, tranquille et honnête," and so on. The structuring of the prose remains thus essentially "musical" by virtue of these repetitions, which both highlight identity-in-difference through variation and mark the importance of structural parallelism at crucial starting points, as happens, for example, in the first lines of paragraphs one and two, as well as four and five.

When a repetition in this beginning position is exact, as occurs in the first two words of paragraphs four and five: "Oui, c'est là qu'il faut aller respirer . . ." and "Oui, c'est dans cette atmosphère qu'il ferait bon vivre . . . ," the poet is using the rhetorical figure of anaphora,* the repetition of a word or word-group at the beginning of a verbal sequence. The internal construction of these paragraphs also reveals several examples of anaphora within them; together they constitute a kind of phonetic accent contributing to the overall rhythmic quality of the prose. The most striking example is the repetition of the word "où," conjoining all of the clauses in paragraph two (as well as several of the clauses in paragraph three), creating an echo effect that reaches its climax in the assonance of "où tout vous ressemble, mon cher ange."

Another striking internal repetition involves the demonstrative adjective "cette" in the first sentence of the third paragraph. In each instance, the adjective introduces an alternative negative feeling, "maladie . . . nostalgie . . . angoisse. . . ." These are terms showing the kind of semantic equivalences Jakobson describes as constitutive of poetic sequences. The semantic similarity of "maladie" and "nostalgie" is moreover underscored by the terms' inherent phonetic similarity, while the parity of the last two terms is embraced within a larger rhythmic structure that cultivates syntactic parallelism even as it avoids verse-like regularity: "cette nostalgie du pays qu'on ignore, cette angoisse de la curiosité" (a ten-syllable phrase followed by a nine-syllable one). In a similar manner, the anaphora occurring in the last sentence of the paragraph creates a compelling antithesis (a symmetrical rhetorical opposition), which is strengthened not only by the parallelism of the construction – "C'est là qu'il faut aller vivre / C'est là qu'il faut aller mourir" – but also by the phrases' rhythmic near-parity (and progression from seven to eight syllables).

To conclude, the refrain and the rhyme of the verse poem are transposed in the prose version into contrary types of repetitive figures to produce a similar effect. The prose poem's varied repetitions and anaphoras simply transpose the principal homophonies of the verse poem from the end to the beginning of poetic sequences, reproducing alternatively marked forms of sameness and difference. The prose's anaphoras are exact repetitions, while the verses' rhymes are only partial ones; conversely, the verses' refrain is an exact repetition, while the prose's repeated phrases introduce an element of difference.

The dramatic intertwining and identification of contraries and the striking variations in vocabulary and figures that characterize Hugo and Baudelaire's poetics are in many ways at loggerheads with the restrictive evenness that Classicism demands. The Classical aesthetic promotes an idea of unity that links grammatical, semantic, syntactic, and phonetic clarity with reason, and presupposes that individual expression be ruled and regulated by self-criticism, moderation, and restraint. The poet's passions and imagination must be checked and brought into line with his public's (generally the Court's) sense of rationality, propriety, and good taste. As with Classical ideals concerning prosodic structure, this period's normative approach to determining what is properly poetic in the domain of words and figures finds its most compelling formulation in Boileau's *Art poétique*. We saw that alongside the dramatic works of Racine, this treatise often holds up the early seventeenth-century poetry of Malherbe – whose main disciples were François Maynard (1582–1646) and Honorat de Racan (1589–1670) – as exemplary of clarity and balance. It also criticizes the free-wheeling words and the imaginative excesses it deemed characteristic of Ronsard and his successors – notably Philippe Desportes (1546–1606) – as well as the strange, hybrid figures of the later Baroque poets Théophile de Viau (1596–1626) and Marc-Antoine de Saint-Amant (1594–1661). While Boileau aims many barbs at these and other un-Classical poets, his central charge against them tends to be obscurity:

Il est certains esprits dont les sombres pensées
Sont d'un nuage épais toujours embarrassées;
Le jour de la raison ne le saurait percer.
Avant donc que d'écrire apprenez à penser.
Selon que notre idée est plus ou moins obscure,
L'expression la suit, ou moins nette, ou plus pure.
Ce que l'on conçoit bien s'énonce clairement,
Et les mots pour le dire arrivent aisément.
  Surtout, qu'en vos écrits la langue révérée
Dans vos plus grands excès vous soit toujours sacrée.
En vain vous me frappez d'un son mélodieux,
Si le terme est impropre, ou le tour vicieux;
Mon esprit n'admet point un pompeux barbarisme,
Ni d'un vers ampoulé l'orgueilleux solécisme.[11]

There are certain minds whose somber thoughts
Are by a thick cloud always blocked;
The daylight of reason never could shine through.
Thus before learning to write, learn to think.
Depending on whether our idea is more or less obscure
The expression following it is less neat or more pure.
That which is well conceived is set forth clearly,
And the words to say it come easily.
  Above all make sure that in your writings the revered language
Will remain sacred to you in your greatest excesses.
In vain you strike me with a melodious sound,
If the term is improper or the formulation vicious;
My mind will not accept a pompous barbarism,
Nor of a swollen verse the proud solecism.

Boileau's insistence on the need to revere the French language – his call for the sacrifice of improper terms and phrases (even when they sound melodious) – is targeted first and foremost against the Pléiade poets' tradition of directly importing Greek and Latin terms (or even syntax) into the language of French poetry in order to render it more "illustrious." Boileau could not bear the pedantic lexicon of Ronsard, "sa muse en français parlant grec et latin" (his muse speaking Greek and Latin in French), his tendency to create neologisms or to forge at will a "pompeux barbarisme." But Boileau's criticism did not limit itself to pedantic language. Rather, it sought to eliminate a variety of lexical quirks, or anomalies, in relation to a restrictive idea of proper French, a standard which the French Academy's grammarian and dictionary editor Vaugelas arbitrated, basing his 1647 *Remarques sur la langue française* (*Remarks on the French Language*) largely on contemporary usage in Paris salons and at Court.

In a number of respects, Boileau's normative formulations in his 1674 *Art poétique*, and his endless attacks on contemporary Court poets in his *Satires*, simply systematize points made in Malherbe's 1609 critique of Ronsard's successor, the Petrarchan Desportes. This commentary, which presents itself in the form of marginal notes on an edition of Desportes' collected works, relentlessly chides the poet not only for his importation of foreign words, but for a number of other linguistic sins – examples of which he underscores and then follows up with a note. These faults include archaisms: "Tout le verbe *ardre* est hors d'usage" (The whole verb *ardre* is out of usage);[12] the use of improper or excessively poetical terms such as "*doléance*," "Mal pour: 'douleur'" (Not good for "pain");[13] technicisms such as "*léniment*" – "langage de médecins; encore je crois qu'ils disent *liniment*" (the language of doctors; although I think they actually say liniment);[14] provincialisms: "*Fier*, en cette signification de *joyeux*, est peu reçu hors de Normandie" (*Proud* in this sense of *joyful* is hardly accepted outside Normandy);[15] vulgar expressions, as in a reference to a "valet," which Malherbe deems "Plébée" (Plebean);[16] Latinisms, such as the word "fère" (beast) borrowed from Ronsard ("Ce mot se trouve assez en Ronsard, mais ni là ni ici il ne vaut rien" [This word is found a lot in Ronsard, but there or here it's worthless]);[17] and various other irregularities in grammar and spelling, which Malherbe tends to describe as (unintended) errors.

Alongside these criticisms of Desportes' language, other notes complain of his prosodic technique. Desportes' rhymes are often considered poor, but this can be either because their terms are too similar, as with "gendarmes/armes" (armed men/arms), which essentially pairs the same word with itself: "cette rime ne vaut rien" (this rhyme is worthless);[18] or because there is, conversely, too much difference between the terms, as with "contenance/sentence" (countenence/sentence), whose disparity in spelling troubles the eye, making the pair rhyme "comme un four et un moulin" (like an oven and a mill).[19] Several instances of alliteration and assonance in Desportes are presented by Malherbe as cacophonous: "Madame, Amour, Fortune, et tous les Eléments" [Madame, Love, Fortune, and all the Elements] . . . "*ma, da, ma, mou*"; and his internal rhymes are considered negligent: "Et ne *sens* pas souv*ent* ton doux allège*ment* . . . Rime au milieu" (And I don't often feel your sweet comforting . . . rhyme in the middle).[20]

Most interesting are the criticisms that Malherbe aims at Desportes' figures. On the one hand he makes fun of such hackneyed, illogical imitations of Petrarch as "Sans yeux je vois ma perte, et sans langue je crie" (Without eyes I see my loss, and without a tongue I cry out), and other facile redundancies or oppositions. On the other hand he also balks at images that strike him as too bold or unusual, as in the following comment: "Etrange imagination: le sommeil le retire des fers du feu, de l'air, de l'eau et de la terre" (Strange imagination: sleep takes him away from the irons of fire, air, water, and earth). One especially telling requirement concerns the mixing of figurative and literal language: in the line "D'ennui, de désespoir, de tempête, et d'orage," (Of trouble, desperation, tempest, and storm): "Il fallait que tout fût ou propre ou figuré, et non moitié propre, comme sont *ennui* et *désespoir*, et moitié figuré, comme *tempête* et *orage*" (Everything should have been either literal or figurative, and not half literal, as *trouble* and *desperation* are, and half figurative, like *tempest* and *storm*).[21]

Malherbe's indictment of Renaissance verse was fought, notably by Desportes' nephew, the satirist Mathurin Régnier (1573–1613), who attacked the censor's formalism and deplored what he viewed as the decadence of poetry under his yoke:

> Car on n'a plus le goust comme on l'eut autrefois;
> Apollon est gené par de sauvages loix
> Qui retiennent sous l'art sa nature offusquée
> Et de mainte figure est sa beauté masquée [. . .][22]
>
> *For taste is no longer what it was of old;*
> *Apollo is being tortured by savage laws*
> *Which keep his nature obscured under art*
> *And by so many figures his beauty masked [. . .]*

What Malherbe deemed natural, Régnier considered artificial or made-up; what Régnier deemed inspired, Malherbe judged motley and incoherent. The latter's critique prevailed, however, inaugurating the general aversion we find in Classicism for mixture, whether the elements be drawn from disparate types of images, levels of style, genres, or descriptive codes.

This rejection of mixture becomes entrenched (in the seventeenth and eighteenth centuries) before being finally overturned. Hugo's 'Réponse' contains many grotesque (or hybrid, incongruent) features, and the preface he wrote for his drama *Cromwell* theorizes the truth and beauty of this aesthetic, announcing a poetic and theatrical revolution that will be implemented from Romanticism to Surrealism with increasing force. Hugo's *Préface* and the various manifestoes of these later movements tend to promote, contrary to Classicism, the aesthetic value of mixture, of extremes, and of difference over evenness, identity, and unity, in every aspect and at every level of poetic expression.

Some of Boileau's criticisms of the Baroque poets Viau and Saint-Amant help to clarify the grounds on which Classical taste refuses rhetorical mixtures. In his 1701 *Préface* to his collected works, Boileau takes Viau to task for what he considers an extravagant, artificial (and therefore ineffective) metaphor that comes at the end of his tragedy *Pyrame et Thisbé* (*Pyramus and Thisbe*). Thisbé, who is about to kill herself with the very sword that has just killed her lover Pyrame, personifies the weapon as follows:

Ah! voici le poignard qui du sang de son maître
S'est souillé lâchement. Il en rougit, le traître!

Ah! here is the dagger which has shamefully stained itself / himself
With the blood of his master. He is blushing, the traitor!

What offends Boileau most in this figure is not the personification itself, but the "cold" and "false" idea that at this tragic moment, Thisbé (or her creator) would confuse or synthesize the delicate moral redness of blushing with the violent image of an actual blood-stained knife: "All the ices of the North put together are not, in my view, any colder than this thought. What extravagance, good God! to intend that the redness of blood staining the dagger of a man who has just killed himself with it, would itself be an effect of the shame this dagger feels for having killed him." What Boileau abhors, then, is the combination of the figurative and the proper in this hybrid figure, which surreptitiously mixes metaphor and metonymy to create an affective contrast. While Viau and Baroque taste revel in the dramatic power of this contrast, Boileau deems it absurd and far-fetched. For him, the most ingenious expression of an idea is not the most "original" or surprising one:

> What is a new, brilliant, extraordinary thought? It is not at all, as some ignorant people persuade themselves, a thought that no one has ever had, or should have ever had; it is on the contrary a thought that must have come to everyone, and that someone thinks to first express. An ingenious remark is only ingenious insofar as it expresses something that everyone has thought and does this in a manner that is fresh, lively, and refined.[23]

For Viau and his followers, on the contrary, much of poetry's power depends on the singularity of the poet's conception, and on his ability to use wit, equivocation, and unexpected reversals to take readers by surprise. These qualities are obvious not only in Viau's predilection for strange, grotesque figures, but also in his tendency to create striking changes in the meaning of words at crucial moments. One example is the witty metaphorical opposition that opens and closes the famous *épître* ('Lettre de Théophile à son frère' ['Letter from Théophile to his Brother']) in which he asks his brother to help him get out of prison:

> Achève de me secourir;
> Il faudra qu'on me laisse vivre
> Après m'avoir fait tant mourir.[24]
>
> *Finish rescuing me:*
> *I must be allowed to live*
> *Now that I have so long been made to die.*

Théophile's reference, in the last line, to his jailers having made him "die" strikes a desperate note, but it also, simultaneously, strikes the reader as funny, since it can only be interpreted as a hyperbole for the prisoner's suffering. Given this choice of expression, it is a tragic irony that Viau in fact died shortly after his release (he had been detained for his alleged composition of a blasphemous, obscene poem that appeared in the 1621 anthology *Le Parnasse des poètes satyriques* [*The Parnassus of Satyrical Poets*]).

Saint-Amant is another Baroque poet who delights in oppositions and paradoxes, and in mixing humor with seriousness. A friend of Viau's, he was also a prime target of Boileau's *Art poétique*. There he is sharply criticized, but not so much for writing such low-style pieces as 'La Pipe,' 'Le Paresseux' ('The Sluggard'), and 'Les Goinfres' ('The Gobblers'), texts anticipating the celebration of vulgar vices, concrete objects, and everyday states of being in Baudelaire, Tristan Corbière (1845–1875), and other moderns. Rather, he is taken to task for including both bizarre, fantastic images and picturesque details within sublime poetic contexts. The latter sin against Classicism occurs in the biblical epic *Moyse sauvé* (*Moses Saved*), when the poet, for example, indulges in concrete, dynamic descriptions of plants and animals (oxen and sheep replacing dolphins and whales) within his narration of the Hebrews' crossing of the Red Sea. He even inserts a moment of child's play:

> Là, l'enfant esveillé, courant sous la licence
> Que permet à son âge une libre innocence,
> Va, revient, tourne, saute, et par maint cri joyeux
> Temoignant le plaisir que reçoivent ses yeux,
> D'un estrange caillou, qu'à ses pieds il rencontre,
> Fait au premier venu la precieuse montre,
> Ramasse une cocquille, et, d'aise transporté
> La presente à sa mère avec naïveté [. . .][25]

> *There, the sharp-eyed child, running with the leave*
> *That is granted to his age by free innocence,*
> *Goes, comes back, turns, jumps, and with myriad joyous shouts*
> *Testifying to the pleasure his eyes take*
> *In a strange pebble that he discovers at his feet,*
> *Shows the precious find to the first passer-by,*
> *Gathers up a shell, and, transported with delight,*
> *Naïvely presents it to his mother [. . .]*

Boileau treats Saint-Amant as a "fou" (madman) for presenting such a "basse circonstance" within this sacred context, and for clouding the reader's perception with "de trop vains objets." He also warns other poets not to imitate him, recommending that they remain "riche(s) et pompeux" in their descriptions. However, it is not exactly, as we have seen, verbal richness and "pompousness" that Boileau is ultimately after. Rather, he seeks aesthetic unity, evenness, and balance (recall the charges he brings against the pomposity of Ronsard's lexicon). What is more, Boileau's attacks on the linguistic refinements of the *précieux* movement – which, launched from the Marquise de Rambouillet's salon, exalted the role and rights of women through elaborate conversation and intellectual debate – were at least as trenchant as on the vulgarisms of Saint-Amant, echoing, in many ways, Molière's mockery of the group in his 1659 comedy *Les Précieuses ridicules* (*The Ridiculous Précieuses*).

In seventeenth-century poetry the *précieux* movement is most directly represented by the light verse of Vincent Voiture (1597–1648), who cleverly incorporated precious periphrases and other techniques of avoiding "mauvais mots" (bad language) into entertaining poems – which he himself did not bother to publish, considering them nothing more than witty mundane exercises. That Boileau should have condemned with equal force the vulgarisms and refinements of certain poets is only logical, for within the frequent practice of equivocation* (the ambiguous combination of two different meanings within one word, a device that Classical poetics also generally rejects), these two extremes of language often prove reversible.

Thus, we find a *rondeau* by Voiture where the meaning of the refrain (occurring in the abridged form of the *rentrement*) radically changes from the beginning to the end of the poem:

> Ou vous savez tromper bien finement,
> Ou vous m'aimez assez fidèlement:
> Lequel des deux, je ne le saurais dire,
> [. . .]
> Pour votre amour j'ai quitté franchement
> Ce que j'avais acquis bien sûrement;
> Car on m'aimait, et j'avais quelque empire
>   Où vous savez.
>
> Je n'attends pas tout le contentement
> Qu'on peut donner aux peines d'un amant,
> [. . .]
> Mais laissez-moi vous toucher seulement
>   Où vous savez.[26]

> *Either you know how to betray me elegantly,*
> *Or you love me faithfully enough:*
> *Which of the two, I could not say,*
> *[. . .]*

For your love I cleanly left
That which I had solidly acquired;
For I was loved, and had power
          You know where.

I do not expect all the contentment
That one can give to a lover's pains,
[. . .]
But at least let me touch you
          You know where.

The opening phrase merely introduces the euphemistic formulation of a treacherous possibility ("Ou [. . .] / Ou") on the lady's part. But in its second occurrence the meaning of the word is dramatically transformed, through a pun exchanging the conjunction "ou" [or] for the relative pronoun "où" (where). This in turn prepares the word's third appearance, in the last line, where the poet asks only to be allowed to touch his lady "Où vous savez" (you know where). This equivocation drastically alters the stylistic and figurative level of the poem, converting an ostensibly polite love poem into a vulgar, insolent one. It also shows that even circumlocution can have an effect that is unambiguous, concrete, and direct.

The proximity of refined and vulgar forms of expression can also be seen in an overarching similarity that links precious language and slang and sets them both apart from "normal" kinds of language. It is interesting, for example, that slang poetry, developing in the cabaret culture of fin-de-siècle Paris, continues to define itself against the grain of Classical principles, inverting also many of the linguistic mannerisms of seventeenth-century salons. While many realist and naturalist writers, following the novelist Émile Zola (1840–1902), insist on the need to use slang in creating a faithful representation of the working class, authors of slang dictionaries and poetry spend more energy contrasting its peculiar aesthetic with the universalizing principles of Classical diction. Slang enthusiasts also tend to emphasize the uniqueness of their chosen language and celebrate the "club"-like superiority of those who use it properly, extolling slang expression in a manner that paradoxically recalls the elitism of high-society *précieux* (in fact, the word *argot* referred originally, in the twelfth century, to the code-like language of a group of outlaws).

Thus, in their introduction to an 1897 *Dictionnaire thématique argot* (*Thematic Slang Dictionary*), Jules Lermina and Henri Levêque insist that slang, by constrast to ordinary and academic language, cannot be subjected to rules or taught by the book: "slang is elusive, unconquerable, unteachable, without rules, without laws, a child of fantasy or of necessity; like the biblical spirit, it blows where it wills. Each minute of Parisian life sees a new word bloom."[27] Along with attributing slang's volatility to a spiritual, fantastic origin, they also admit that it has to change continually, to protect its speakers from capture by the cops. Hence, on the one hand, Lermina and Levêque pridefully attach the colorful language to a tradition of imaginative lyric poets, which includes Saint-Amant and Villon. To do this they emphasize, in a Romantic vein, both slang's originality – "In slang especially, it is crucial not to imitate anyone" – and its individualistic character, demanding that the speaker should "bend his tongue to his own nature." Yet they also offer, on the other hand, a number of rules and guidelines for "correct" slang usage, and claim that their dictionary can teach people not only how to read works such as Zola's 1877 novel *L'Assommoir* (*The Bludgeon*, name of a pub) but also how to proceed to create proper slang out of ordinary language.

Though the rules set forth by Lermina and Levêque consistently prove opposite to the letter of seventeenth-century poetics, they are supposed to be applied with the same spirit of reason, perspicuity, and restraint associated with Classicism. As an informal, oral language, slang has, for example, the opposite of Classical poetry's regulatory predisposition in front of the *e muet*; while the latter tends to conserve its pronunciation as much as is reasonably possible, slang tends to elide it. But the principle of the *e muet*'s elision cannot be implemented any less carefully in slang than in Classical poetry. A Classical scientific argument is enlisted to make this point: "Just as it was said of old that nature abhors the void, slang abhors the silent e and elides it tenaciously. And yet one must still apply this rule only with the greatest circumspection." One would say, for example, in proper slang: "J'vas gober un'prune" (I are goin to glub a plum), eliding the two "internal" *e atones*, but in the expression "Je l'gobe" (I glub it), the initial one would be left intact.

Slang deformations of ordinary language often take on a parodically *savant* air. Among the most common slang forms presented (more or less equivalent to what is known in English as "Pig Latin") is, for example, *le javanais*, which inserts the morpheme *av* within the beginning of a word, generating *P-av-ain* for *Pain* (bread), and *b-av-on* for *bon* (good). In performing this and other systematic operations on slang words as well as ordinary ones, the authors recommend that their readers follow the example of the poet Jean Richepin (1849–1926); the goal is to put "a double lock" on language;[28] this increases its degree of figurativeness and removes it from the commonplace. Richepin's collection of slang poetry *La Chanson des gueux* (*The Wretches' Song*, 1876) well exemplifies these paradoxes. His preface inscribes his work within the realist and naturalist traditions of Baudelaire, Flaubert, and Zola, and some of his poems mimic authentic working-class language. But others are so arcane, so out of reach (as were, in the fifteenth century, Villon's "Ballades en jargon" [Jargon ballades]) that they cannot be deciphered without a slang glossary, which Richepin provides in an appendix. The most impenetrable poem of the collection is the 'Sonnet bigorne' ('Who Cares / Whatever Sonnet') in "Argot Classique," a love sonnet which is juxtaposed to a slightly more accessible 'Autre sonnet bigorne,' in "Argot Moderne." The latter begins and ends as follows:

> J'ai fait chibis. J'avais la frousse
> Des préfectanciers de Pantin.
> À Pantin, mince de potin!
> On y connaît ma gargarousse,
> [. . .]
> Je me camoufle en pélican.
> J'ai du pellard à la tignasse,
> Vive la lampagne du cam![29]

> *I split. I was scared*
> *Of the Pantin cops.*
> *In Pantin, what a hassle!*
> *They know my mug there,*
> *[. . .]*
> *I'm camouflaging myself as a bumpkin*
> *I've got hay in my hair,*
> *Long live the ountry-ce!*

That slang poetry, despite many claims to the contrary, was not so much intended for the common people as for an "in" group of "outsiders," can finally also be deduced from socio-historical considerations on the culture within which it flowered. Richepin, like many other slang poets, was a member of such an elite. Indeed, in 1876 he was a co-founder of the *Vivants*, one of the first groups of "marginal" poets, musicians, and artists, which steadily grew in importance in fin-de-siècle Paris, forming the prototypes of Dada and Surrealism. Two among these groups, the original *Zutistes* and the *Vilains bonshommes*, had convened in the early 1870s around Charles Cros (1842–1888) and Verlaine, whose 1874 'Art poétique' inverts many Classical principles. Along with favoring the impair, it attacks the ideals of lexical and figurative clarity and precision; but Verlaine also mimicks Boileau, even as he offends his precepts by mixing, in the tradition of the Baroque, refined and crude words or figures. What is more, he warns against a poetics which is, in fact, less typical of Classicism than of what Boileau himself would have considered its corruption (in the hands of the *précieux* or of such eighteenth-century neo-Classicists as Voltaire (1694–1778) or Jean-Baptiste Rousseau (1671–1741), who created lots of rhetorical, witty verse cultivating the *"pointe"* or punchline):

Fuis du plus loin la Pointe assassine,
L'Esprit cruel et le Rire impur,
Qui font pleurer les yeux de l'Azur,
Et tout cet ail de basse cuisine![30]

Flee as far as possible the murderous Point,
Cruel Wit and impure Laughter,
Who make the Azure's eyes cry,
And all this low-cuisine garlic!

Verlaine's 'Art poétique' also mocks the plastic, hollow technique of mid-nineteenth century Parnassians such as Banville and Charles Leconte de Lisle (1818–1894), who were apt to waste their energy on over-polishing rhymes (Boileau too had complained of the tyranny of rhyme – but over reason, not music):

Prend l'éloquence et tords-lui son cou!
Tu feras bien, en train d'énergie,
De rendre un peu la Rime assagie.
Si l'on n'y veille, elle ira jusqu'où?

Ô qui dira les torts de la Rime?
Quel enfant sourd ou quel nègre fou
Nous a forgé ce bijou d'un sou
Qui sonne creux et faux sous la lime?[31]

Take eloquence and wring its neck!
You'll also do well, while you're at it,
To tame Rhyme just a little bit.
If we don't watch over it, how far will it go?

Oh who will say the wrongs of Rhyme!
What deaf child or what crazy negro
Has forged us this two-bit jewel
That sounds fake and hollow under the chisel?

In these parodical lines, Verlaine's fondness for delicate tones is expressed through vulgar and bizarre images, which are not characteristic of all "Symbolist" poets: Mallarmé's language, for example, tends toward refinement ("Donner un sens plus pur aux mots de la tribu" [Give a purer sense to the words of the tribe][32]); so does the language of his followers in the official Symbolist school. But the contrasts drawn here recall those already observed in Hugo and Baudelaire, and practiced to tremendous effect by Rimbaud – who was in fact discovered by Verlaine (with whom he had a scandalous and ill-fated liaison), and participated in the subversive communities that revolved around him.

In *Une saison en enfer* (*A Season in Hell*), where he sums up his poetic experience (which he renounced at the age of twenty-one), Rimbaud describes his 'Alchimie du verbe' ('Alchemy of the Word'):

> Je réglai la forme et le mouvement de chaque consonne, et, avec des rhythmes instinctifs, je me flattai d'inventer un verbe poétique accessible, un jour ou l'autre, à tous les sens. [. . .]
>
> Je m'habituai à l'hallucination simple: je voyais très franchement une mosquée à la place d'une usine, une école de tambours faite par des anges [. . .]; un titre de vaudeville dressait des épouvantes devant moi.
>
> Puis j'expliquai mes sophismes magiques avec l'hallucination des mots![33]

> *I adjusted the form and and movement of each consonant, and, with instinctive rhythms, I flattered myself with having invented a poetic language that would be accessible, one day or another, to all the senses. [. . .]*
>
> *I got used to simple hallucination: I really saw a mosque instead of a factory, a drumming school composed of angels [. . .]; a vaudeville title conjured up horrors in front of me.*
>
> *Then I explained my magical sophisms through the hallucination of words!*

In the same section, the poet evokes his fascination with "peintures idiotes" (idiotic paintings), "refrains niais" (stupid refrains), "rhythmes naïfs," and a drunken fly in a "pissotière," along with his attempts at writing down "silences" and noting "l'inexprimable."

But to appreciate the importance of such unsettling contrasts for Rimbaud's poetics, we do not need to explore his most extreme works. They are central to all of his poems, creating everywhere an effect of shock that jolts the reader out of complacency. In 'Le Dormeur du val,' which surprises us prosodically with multiple *enjambements*, we also note a marked contrast and alternation between elevated and crude language. The word "val" (vale) is conspicuously poetic, suggesting idyllic charm; Rimbaud threatens this effect when he refers again to the place in the first line, calling it a "trou de verdure" (green hole). And this prosaic periphrasis for the vale, especially against the delicate diction which dominates the verse, plays a crucial role in structuring the poem, preparing the brutal image of the young man's death in the last line: "deux trous rouges au côté droit" (two red holes in the right side).

The effects of contrast in Rimbaud's images and the unexpected verbal-visual logic of many of his metaphors (in which the literal meaning is often hard to distinguish from the figurative one) become commonplace in late nineteenth- and early twentieth-century French poetry. This is especially true for the Dadaists and Surrealists, who from different perspectives take

Rimbaud, his contemporary Lautréamont, and the fin-de-siècle poet Alfred Jarry (1873–1907), along with Nerval and Mallarmé, as their principal precursors. Lautréamont died virtually unknown at the age of twenty-four, but his epic prose poem *Les Chants de Maldoror*, first published in its entirety in 1890, was treated as a revelation by the Surrealists because of its radical revolt against all moral, aesthetic, and formal constraints. In his hallucinatory visions, Maldoror takes on himself all the evil, suffering, and cruelty of the world, and rebels (contrary to Christ) against God. A monstrous hero, he incarnates a form of the beautiful that is hyperbolically carnal and identified with the deformed, the horrible, and the ugly:

> Je me suis aperçu que je n'avais qu'un œil au milieu du front! [. . .] Aujourd'hui, sous l'impression des blessures que mon corps a reçues dans diverses circonstances, soit par la fatalité de ma naissance, soit par le fait de ma propre faute; [. . .] je jette un long regard de satisfaction sur la dualité qui me compose . . . et je me trouve beau! Beau comme le vice de conformation congénital des organes sexuels de l'homme [. . .]; ou encore, comme la caroncule charnue, de forme conique, sillonnée par des rides transversales assez profondes, qui s'élève sur la base du bec supérieur du dindon [. . .][34]
>
> *I saw that I had only one eye in the middle of my forehead! [. . .] Today, under the impression of wounds that my body has received in various circumstances, either by the fatality of my birth or by the fact of my own fault; [. . .] I take a long look of satisfaction at the duality that composes me . . . and I find myself beautiful! Beautiful like the congenital conformation vice in man's sexual organs [. . .]; or again, like the fleshy caroncola, of conic form, furrowed by rather deep transversal wrinkles, that rises on the base of the turkey's upper beak [. . .]*

Here a grotesque figure is brought to life through the use of precise, scientific language to exalt what is base and lowly in the incoherent self. Above all, Lautréamont uses the elaborate syntax and rhetorical devices of high Classical style (in this case, comparison) to frame unwieldy and cruel images, creating a thoroughly perverse effect.

Like Lautréamont, though in a lighter vein, Jarry is also noted for the invention of a monstrous character, le Père Ubu, hailed by Breton as his creator's single greatest poetic accomplishment – originally a caricature of the poet's high school physics teacher, who embodied "all that was grotesque in the world."[35] His farcical evil exploits are recounted in a cycle of plays in prose that opens with *Ubu Roi* (*Ubu Rex*), performed in 1896 in the distinguished setting of the Symbolist Théâtre de l'Œuvre, and closes with *Ubu sur la butte* (*Ubu on the Mount*), a puppet version of the same play performed in 1902 at the Quat'z'arts Cabaret in Montmartre. As with

Hugo's *Hernani*, the scandal of *Ubu Roi*'s opening followed as much from formal issues as from its content; in this instance, from outrageous combinations of incongruent stylistic registers (within the ostensibly serious context of a high-culture theatrical performance). The *barbarisme* of the play's infamous opening cry: "Merdre!" (Pshit!), introducing one of its most prevalent symbols, already reveals this, since the addition of the letter r comically veils and poeticizes "l'innommable" [the unnamable].[36]

Dada, an international group of anarchical, anticultural artists founded in Zurich, in 1916, by the Romanian-born poet Tristan Tzara (1896–1963), often develops the iconoclastic playfulness of Jarry, which itself grew from a late nineteenth-century brand of humor called *fumisme* (spreading through such groups as the *Hirsutes*, *Hydropathes*, and *Incohérents*): a blend of artistic practice and social comportment that blasted all seriousness and gleefully transgressed categorical boundaries, including the difference between art and life. Consider the utter flexibility of the term "dada" itself, which in Tzara's 1918 *Manifeste* is at the same time defined as meaning "nothing" and associated with an endless explosion of things. Dada's *fumiste* roots, its refusal to adopt any particular logical or aesthetic order of representation, and its rejection of stylistic distinctions are all visible enough in the nonsensical, simplistic diversity of terms that make up the first part of Tzara's 'Chanson Dada' ('Dada Song'), even as its shape reminds us of medieval forms:

> la chanson d'un dadaïste
> qui avait dada au cœur
> fatiguait trop son moteur
> qui avait dada au cœur
>
> l'ascenseur portait un roi
> lourd fragile autonome
> il coupa son grand bras droit
> l'envoya au pape à rome
>
> c'est pourquoi
> l'ascenseur
> n'avait plus dada au coeur
>
> mangez du chocolat
> lavez votre cerveau
> dada
> dada
> buvez de l'eau[37]
>
> *the song of a dadaist*
> *who had dada in his heart*
> *tired his motor too much*
> *which had dada in its heart*

the elevator carried a king
heavy fragile autonomous
he cut off his big right arm
sent it to the pope in rome

that is why
the elevator
had no more dada in its heart

eat chocolate
wash your brain
dada
dada
drink water

In fact, the disregard for reason and semantic unity expressed by the logical incoherence of this poem often goes further in Dada, sometimes resulting in the dissolution of words themselves. This happens in the nonsensical "verse without words," a form of pure "sound" poetry performed by the German poet Hugo Ball in 1916, during Dada's earliest collective performances at the Cabaret Voltaire in Zurich; it would take another thirty years, however, for such experiments to take root in France, with the "Lettrisme" of another Romanian, Isidore Isou (1925–).

Surrealism, though it officially holds up childhood as an ideal state and produces a myriad of games, tends to be more serious. Its origins lie, moreover, as much within the high-minded experimentation of individual modern writers and artists as within the subversive manifestations of marginal avant-gardes. The term "surrealism," we saw, was in fact coined by Apollinaire, the early twentieth century's most prominent poet and art critic, who used it first to describe the new approach to representation and the new alliance of the arts achieved in the 1917 Ballets Russes production *Parade*.

Contrary to Dada, Surrealism was the deliberate outgrowth of a centralized group of writers and artists who, like organized circles of Symbolist, Romantic, Classical and Renaissance poets before them, generated a wealth of theoretical writings blending commonly shared aesthetic doctrine with collective self-promotion. Indeed, despite its emphasis on freedom, Surrealism – perhaps because of the magnetic personality of its leader, André Breton – presents itself in many ways as the most dogmatic and tightly controlled movement in the history of French poetry. In his 1924 *Manifeste*, Breton systematically denies, for example, the role of reason, rules, and autoregulation within poetic creation, in favor of chance-determined word-play and unchecked explorations of the unconscious. And yet he insists on a rigorously formal approach to producing incoherence, through automatic-writing compositions and other Surrealist techniques. Breton's idea of what constitutes poetic freedom is generally more extreme than the models held up by nineteenth-century poets, and his principles are antithetical to Classical doctrine in most respects. But the authority of his tone and the absolute character of his precepts often bring to mind a kind of reverse Boileau.

The brilliant Surrealist idea, for example, far from having occurred to everyone, like Boileau's "new," "extraordinary" thought, will never have been thought before by anyone, not even the poet himself. And the poet (who for Breton, following Lautréamont, should be everyone: "Poetry should be made by all. Not by one"[38]) has neither any special claim to, nor any control over his own creations. Madness, childhood, dreams, and other states of being unfettered by reason, moral censorship, and aesthetic guidelines are set forth by Breton as the only authentic fields for cultivating Surrealist work. Yet his articulations of what Surrealism is, how its images can be created, and who may be considered properly Surrealist are paradoxically rigid. They are wide open yet inflexible, definite (in their superlative formulation) and yet imprecise. Breton defines Surrealism, for example, in terms of the purity of psychic automatism – a purity that implies not only the truthfulness of the psyche's revelations, but also their integrity, since they are defined as independent from all conscious thought processes:

> SURREALISM, n. Psychic automatism in its pure state, by which one proposes to express – verbally, by means of the written word, or in any other manner – the actual functioning of thought. Dictated by thought, in the absence of any control exercised by reason, exempt from any aesthetic or moral concern.[39]

In explaining the genesis of his ideas concerning automatic writing, Breton cites and praises the poet Pierre Reverdy (1889–1060), whose definition of the poetic image valorizes figurative contrasts and encourages originality and spontaneity by insisting on the mind's "pure creation" – its inherent capacity to juxtapose, or bring together, very disparate things:

> The image is a pure creation of the mind.
> It cannot be born from a comparison but from a juxtaposition of two more or less distant realities.
> The more the relationship between the two juxtaposed realities is distant and true, the stronger the image will be – the greater its emotional power and poetic reality [. . .][40]

Not only are the two things juxtaposed very distant, they are both equally considered "realities" that the mind puts in contact. Here the rhetorical notion of figure (as defined, for example, by Fontanier in the above quote), which supposes a clear distinction and hierarchy between "simple expression" and deviation from it, and thus, in the case of a simile or metaphor, between the comparison's tenor* (or *comparé*, the thing which is being compared) and its vehicle* (*comparant*, the thing to which the tenor is being compared), appears to be dissolved. The image stands only for itself.

Breton pushes Reverdy's conception of poetic purity even further, rewriting it so as to arrest any control that the poet might have on his artistic creations, giving the power of his images wholly over to physical forces and chance-determined psychological connections:

> It is, as it were, from the fortuitous juxtaposition of the two terms that a particular light has sprung, *the light of the image*, to which we are infinitely sensitive. The value of the image depends upon the beauty of the spark obtained; it is, consequently, a function of the difference of potential between the two conductors. When the difference exists only slightly, as in a comparison, the spark is lacking.[41]

Breton's own poetry manifests this predilection for startling, light-generating images created by "free associations," as in these lines from 'Dernière levée' ('Last Collection / Levying') in *Le Revolver à cheveux blancs* (*The White-haired Revolver*):

> Les mots jamais entendus prendront le large
> Ils seront de paille enflammée et luiront dans une cage d'amiante
> Suspendue à l'arbre à devinettes[42]
>
> *Words never heard will set to sea*
> *They will be made of inflamed straw and will glow in an asbestos cage*
> *Hung from the riddle tree*

and in these opening lines from a famous *blason*, allegorically entitled 'L'Union libre' ('Free Union'):

> Ma femme à la chevelure de feu de bois
> Aux pensées d'éclairs de chaleur
> À la taille de sablier
> Ma femme à la taille de loutre entre les dents du tigre
> Ma femme à la bouche de cocarde et de bouquet d'étoiles de
>   dernière grandeur
> Aux dents d'empreintes de souris blanche sur la terre blanche[43]
>
> *My woman of the wood-fire hair*
> *Of thoughts of heat flashes*
> *Of the hourglass waist*
> *My woman of the otter's waist between the tiger's teeth*
> *My woman of the cocade mouth and of the bouquet-of-stars-of-the-last-*
>   *magnitude mouth*
> *Of the white-mouse-track teeth on white earth*

Yet, as we see from both the range and the unity of the figures in these lines, Breton's images are not always as unexpected or a-rhetorical as his poetic theory might lead us to anticipate, nor does their fortuitous "juxtaposition" always depend on "the difference in potential between the two conductors." Rather, his images, like those of other poets, appear also partially governed by a variety of factors that we have consistently seen at work: the weight of poetic conventions. We see this in the *topos** (the universal subject matter or motif) of the beloved woman's beauty, as well as in its privileging of metaphor; in the repetitiveness of the poem's language (the several recurrences in both particular words and types of images); and even in the conscious will (clearly signaled in the title 'L'Union libre') to represent reality, to renew pre-set patterns of thinking and speaking through an inventive recycling of words and figures.

Collective thinking is a key feature of the Surrealist movement, whether this be in the uncontrolled, open mode of Breton's first automatic writings, *Les Champs magnétiques* (*The Magnetic Fields*), co-authored with Philippe Soupault (1897–1990), or in the movement's socio-political orientation, in its ambition to change life itself, which became increasingly defined over time and attached, as we shall see, to communism. Thus, many strongly individualistic poets, who at some point worked within the movement, eventually broke their ties with it. Char is an example of a major poet who evolved through but far away from Surrealism, as is Antonin Artaud (1896–1948), the theorist and practitioner of the ritual "Theater of Cruelty." The poet, anthropologist, and relentless autobiographer Michel Leiris (1901–1990) is another case, whose intensely subjective poetic dictionary, *Glossaire, j'y serre mes gloses* (*Glossary, I there enclose my glosses*), combines word-play with self-analysis and lexicographical study. So is Max Jacob (1876–1944), who traveled from Brittany to Montmartre and converted from Judaism to Catholicism, all the while developing an extreme kind of absurd humor which had much in common with Surrealism but never merged with it. The Egyptian-born Jew Edmond Jabès (1912–1991), whom Jacob mentored, was close to many Surrealists but refused to belong to the group: "La poésie ne change pas la vie, elle l'échange," he would later write (Poetry does not change life, it exchanges it).[44] Further afield, Jules Supervielle (1884–1960), born and raised in Uruguay, practiced a deceptive simplicity which was deeply attuned to the world's strangeness but did not engage in the Surrealist rhetoric of revolution or supreme discovery.

Finally, the work of Henri Michaux (1899–1984), considered by many the most unclassifiable of twentieth-century French poets, is at the same time unthinkable without Surrealism and wholly autonomous from it. Unconcerned with party lines, Michaux's poetic voice moves freely through ever-changing modalities of verse and prose, in an endless variety of forms

and genres, and in a style that critics hesitate to qualify, insisting on its inim-
itable originality. And yet it could be argued that Michaux's utter "uniqueness" arises from the flexible, chameleon-like character of his poetry, which
integrates seamlessly many of the most important stylistic features and tenets
of nineteenth- and twentieth-century aesthetics.

Thus, 'Glu et gli' ('Glu and gli'), a key poem in Michaux's first, 1927
collection (entitled *Qui je fus* [Who I Was]), synthesizes many of the principles and attitudes we have been discussing in connection with avant-garde
modernity's use of words and figures. The opacity of this poem threatens
the referential function of language, focusing our attention on the sheer
materiality of words through numerous "sound" effects, while mimicking
the violence of a meaningless, God-forsaken world. At the same time, as
these first stanzas show, it carries on a quintessentially French tradition in
mocking the mockery of Boileau:

> et glo
> et glu
> et déglutit sa bru
> gli et glo
> et déglutit son pied
> glu et gli
> et s'englugliglolera
>
> les glous glous
> les sales rats
> tape dans le tas!
> il n'y a que le premier pas!
> il n'y a que ça!
> dans le tas!
>
> le rire est dans ma . . .
> un pleur est dans mon . . .
> et le mal Dieu sait où
> on en est tous là
> vous êtes l'ordure de la terre
> si l'ordure vient à se salir
> qu'est-ce qui adviendra
> il adviendra ce qui adviendra
> l'ordure n'est pas faite pour la démonstration
> un homme qui n'aurait que son pet pour s'exprimer . . .
> pas de rire
> pas d'ordure
> pas de turlururu
> et pas se relire surtout Messieurs les écrivains
> Ah! que je te hais Boileau
> Boiteux, Boignetière, Boiloux, Boigermain,
> Boirops, Boitel, Boivéry,

Boicamille, Boit de travers
Bois ça[45]

and glo
and glu
and degluts his daughter-in-law
gli and glo
and degluts his foot
glu and gli
and will engloglugliate itself

the glug glugs
the dirty rats
give it to them!
only the first step!
only that!
to them!

the laugh is in my . . .
a cry is in my . . .
and the pain God knows where
we've all come to that
you are the rubbish of the earth
if the rubbish comes to dirty itself
what will happen
what will happen will happen
rubbish is not made for demonstration
a man who would only have his fart to express himself . . .
no laugh
no rubbish
no fiddlesmicks
and no rereading yourselves especially Messrs. writers
Ah! how I hate you Boileau
Boiteux, Boignetière, Boiloux, Boigermain,
Boirops, Boitel, Boivéry
Boicamille, Drinks askew
Drink that

A cacophonous frenzy of *barbarismes*, this obscure and biting yet playful poem makes parodical old- and new-fashioned literary recommenda-
tions by way of crude words and syntax ("l'ordure n'est pas faite pour la
démonstration," "pas se relire surtout Messieurs les écrivains"), mixing diametrically opposed stylistic registers. It combines pedantry and archaisms,
such as "bru," with vulgarisms such as "pet" or "tape dans le tas," as well as
truncated colloquialisms ("il n'y a que le premier pas") and a subversion of
the biblical phrase "You are the salt of the earth." And yet, the verse derives
its unity from the very source that it attacks, for what lends it coherence is first
and foremost a play on the name Boileau, an erudite joke depending of the

implicit pun *bois l'eau* (drink water). The ostensibly incoherent physiological sounds with which the poem begins are onomatopoeias evoking drinking (of the same "glug glug" variety as in English), while the mention of the name Boileau, followed by a proliferation of allusive literary-historical plays on it ("Boignetière," for example, is an allusion to the nineteenth-century critic Brunetière), explicitly culminates in the command "bois ça" (drink that). This creates a circular closure to the poem's first stanzas which brings us directly back to the initial idea and sound. Far from coming out of nowhere, then, this poem presents strong links with a long tradition of French *arts poétiques* and also elaborates on a well-developed poetics of drinking, one notable, for example, in Baudelaire's "wine" poems in *Les Fleurs du mal*, numerous fin-de-siècle ditties from the *Hydropathes* (a group of heavy- but non-water-drinking poets founded by Émile Goudeau [1849–1906] a.k.a. *Goût d'eau* [Taste for Water]), and Apollinaire's 1913 *Alcools*.

A number of poets left Surrealism behind to strengthen their commitments to other kinds of movements. This was the case, for example, with Thérèse Plantier (1911–1989), who broke her ties with the group to become "in her own words, 'strictly feminist and express [. . .] it in lyric poetry.' "[46] The beginning of 'Hommes po hommes à lunettes' conveys this perspective, even as it recasts, in a byzantine fashion, familiar approaches to forming (and deforming) poetic figures in a world dominated by men:

> hommes po hommes à lunettes
> hommes politi
> méphipolitimemphi
> > limemphi
> > > tiques
> vous êtes de farce pleins
> de mère-patrie dans vos nombreux trous[47]

> *men po men with glasses*
> *men politi*
> *mephipolitimemphi*
> > *limemphi*
> > > *tics*
> *you are stuffed full with farce*
> *with the mother-land in your many holes*

Similarly, Francophone poets touched by Surrealism, from Martinique's Aimé Césaire (1913–) to Québec's Gaston Miron (1928–1996), have often defined their work politically, in order to establish for themselves and their compatriots the very possibility of free expression, through an authentic lyric voice at once personal and indigenous. When writing outside France, and where other native languages and dialects have been options, what has it meant for French-speaking poets to use (or not) French (or non-French) words? In relation to which or to whose cultural traditions have they chosen to build their figures? And within France itself, to what extent has poetry been presented as formative of or subordinated to the cultural conventions of what Plantier calls "mère-patrie?" These are some of the questions to which we shall now turn as, armed with some experience in reading poetry in French, we move toward investigating its relations with the wider world of French culture.

Chapter 4

Poetry and politics

Poetry, insofar as it is an emotionally charged mode of language, cannot help but be rooted in politics and perform politics in a profound way. This could hardly be otherwise, since language is the primary instrument of human expression and communication, and politics, stripped bare, is the play of power relations within or amongst groups of people. Though political underpinnings and implications of French poetry's development have come up time and again in our analyses of metrical, formal, and stylistic features, the link between poetry and politics may come to some readers as a surprise. We think of poetry as far removed from the "*rapports de forces*," social, economic, and other mundane struggles that are politics' domain. Indeed poetry (and above all lyric poetry) tends to do politics from a distance – one that it is crucial not to reduce or forget. We shall see, however, that poetry's recurrent detachment from the world can be as politically significant or effective as its engagement, often reinforcing, in paradoxical ways, a poem's underlying connection with the body politic as a potent conduit of expressive language.

Poetry's distant yet unseverable relation with politics is hardly limited to a French context; and in French and Francophone poems, we find as much variety in direct and indirect political statement as in the poetry of other nations and cultures. Nonetheless, there is an interesting parallel between the apparent apolitical stance characteristic of much lyric poetry and the particular way that France, for centuries, has attempted to situate itself culturally and politically in the world. As Francophone writers from around the world have helped bring to the fore, one of the peculiarities of French culture has been the consistent determination to pass itself off as universal. And the singular "universality" of French culture has formed the premise of many cultural critiques undertaken from a variety of perspectives by French and non-French writers alike.

Thus, Léopold Sédar Senghor's ground-breaking *Anthologie de la nouvelle poésie nègre et malgache de langue française* (*Anthology of New Negro and Malagasy Poetry in French*, 1948), published in the context of a centennial celebration of the 1848 revolution, insists on the global importance of that political event in French history, which decreed an end to slavery and the beginning of free, mandatory education in the colonies. Senghor (1906–2001), one of the founding poets of the Négritude movement, a deputy of the French government during the colonial period, and then the first president of Sénégal, played a key role in the acquisition of independence for his country, and in the promotion of its particular culture. Yet his own belief in the "universality" of French ideas and in the cultural exemplarity of French acts is quite explicit when he amplifies the legacy of the 1848 decrees: "This is how men of color, particularly Negroes, were able to accede not only to the citizen's freedom, but also, and especially, to that personal life which culture alone gives [. . .];" and when he presents these vast gifts as allowing "people of color" to help expand French culture in turn: "this is how they were able, in spite of the regression constituted by the Second Empire and Third Republic, to bring their contribution to today's French humanism, which is making itself truly universal because fecundated by the saps of all the races of the earth."[1]

The association of French culture with universality can be explained to a certain extent by the nation's history as a melting pot, not so much through its blending of multiple immigrant races and far-flung ethnicities from around the world (as in America), but by virtue of the thoroughness with which the distinct elements of its own internal cultural heritage have over centuries been subordinated and assimilated into one hegemonic ideal. The French provinces, from Burgundy to Brittany and from Normandy to Provence, though often distinct (linguistically and otherwise), were yoked together to form a nation much earlier than the regional counterparts of most other European countries. And it is unlikely that this can be attributed to any natural, or intrinsic, unity characterizing these provinces' inhabitants. Rather, the political forces of French history appear to have systematically downplayed the importance of their own and others' ethnic origins in favor of consolidating the strength of a centrally controlled and unified culture.

Given these historical circumstances, the insistence on Gallic ancestral roots that often crops up in French culture is somewhat paradoxical. We find this expressed not only in dramatically different types of poems, but also in broader manifestations of culture, as in the strictly normative curriculum of French elementary education – where children in the hexagon and colonies alike, regardless of their ethnic origins, were required to recite their filiation to "our ancestors the Gauls." *Astérix*, the highly popular comic book series, is another example, where a mythic core of Gallic resistance to the Roman Empire, located in a small village on the northern coast of Brittany, anachronistically represents not Breton culture but, rather, stereotypical aspects of the French national character. The construction of the French identity appears thus to veer back and forth between an expansive movement which overlooks, transcends, or displaces the ethnic roots and geographic boundaries separating particular communities, and the contrary impulse to attach this abstract, universal stance to the foundation of a natural homeland and mythic ancestral roots. We find these two impulses suggested by a wide body of French and Francophone poems.

'Nuit blanche' ('White/sleepless night'), a short lyric poem from a 1937 collection entitled *Pigments* by the Guyanese poet Léon-G. Damas (1912–1978), points to the potential absurdity and danger in this paradoxical cultural stance, especially for the black lyric poet of African origins, whose calling is to freely express the different rhythms and feelings of his innermost self. In stanzas which both recall and undercut the triadic rhythms of the Viennese waltz, Damas' elliptical turning lines suggest how readily he, conditioned by his own French education – whose Gallic foundation is ironically invoked – appropriates for himself not only a "French" heritage, but also one that includes other European lands and traditions:

> Mes amis j'ai valsé
> valsé comme jamais mes ancêtres
> les Gaulois
> au point que j'ai le sang
> qui tourne encore
> à la viennoise
>
> Mes amis j'ai valsé
> valsé toute mon enfance vagabondant
> sur quelques Danube bleu
> Danube blanc
> Danube rouge
> Danube vert
> Danube rose
> Danube bleu blanc rouge vert rose
> au choix
>
> Mes amis j'ai valsé
> valsé follement au point que souvent
> souvent
> j'ai cru tenir la taille
> de tonton Gobineau
> ou de cousin Hitler
> ou du bon aryen
> qui mâchonne sa vieillesse sur quelque banc de square.[2]

> *My friends I waltzed*
> *waltzed like never did my ancestors*
> *the Gauls*
> *to the point that my blood*
> *is still turning*
> *Viennese-style*

My friends I waltzed
waltzed my entire youth wandering
on some blue Danube
white Danube
red Danube
green Danube
pink Danube
blue white red green pink Danube
all one price / as you please

My friends I waltzed
waltzed madly to the point that often
often
I believed I was holding the waist
of uncle Gobineau
or cousin Hitler
or the good Aryan
chewing his old age on some bench on the square.

The first and second stanzas' insistence on the dizzying effects of danc-ing and on the poet's youthful wanderings on some indifferently colored "Danubes" under the sign of the tricolor flag, may appear to highlight the political and poetic freedom offered to the black Caribbean poet who assumes this ostensibly color-blind, trans-European cultural stance. Since "vagabondage" in modern French lyric poetry applies conventionally as much to imaginary as to physical wandering, and "vert" and "rose" are as traditional poetic colors as "bleu blanc rouge" are political ones, we can assume, for example, that the poet's incessant "waltzing" has afforded him wide-ranging, unconstrained poetic and worldly experiences. But the third stanza stumbles upon the threat inherent in this kind of dance, since the poet recognizes that its frenzy has (often) led him to embrace his own worst enemies. It is no accident that the first of these mentioned, Gobineau, a fin-de-siècle theorist of race difference, is ironically referred to (insofar as he is French) as an intimate family member, with the affectionate appellation "tonton"(uncle); in 1937 "le cousin Hitler" can be seen as the symbolic child of this French intellectual, and their kinship as the common cultural heritage of any old "good Aryan" that the poet might encounter on any of the Continent's squares.

While the opposite representations of French culture's "universality" fea-tured in Senghor's introduction and Damas' poem may appear to be mo-tivated by the political events and conditions to which these texts allude (the burgeoning of African independence on the one hand, and the rise of Nazi power on the other), consideration of a broad selection of poems suggests that the self-modeling of French culture on a universal pattern well precedes the modern, colonial period, and should not be tied (too exclusively) to particular political circumstances. Rather, poetic representations of French identity appear to consistently oscillate between imposing two contrary sides of the same "reality": one establishing France's image as a kind of exemplary, ethnically unmarked synthesis and apogee of culture; the other evoking nostalgic, intimate images of more specific traditions.

The identification of France with culture *per se* is striking, for example, in one of Du Bellay's most baldly patriotic sonnets from the *Regrets*, where the poet, feeling exiled in Rome, performs a kind of cultural usurpation. He begins by putting his own country in the place of Rome – representing France as the "mother of arts, arms and laws," in short, of civilization – and then manages to paint himself among the (modern) Romans, as a lost sheep (in Christian terms) abandoned to the savagery of nature and wild wolves. What is more, Du Bellay's symbolic rearrangement of France's own historical relation to Rome grounds its coherence in a symbolic inversion of the myth of Rome's foundation (in which the city's founders Remus and Romulus, descendents of Aeneas, are portrayed as saved and suckled by a she-wolf):

> France, mere des arts, des armes & des loix,
> Tu m'as nourry long temps du laict de ta mamelle:
> Ores, comme un aigneau qui sa nourisse appelle,
> Je remplis de ton nom les antres & les bois.
> [. . .]
> Entre les loups cruels j'erre parmy la plaine,
> Je sens venir l'hyver, de qui la froide haleine
> D'une tremblante horreur fait herisser ma peau. [. . .][3]

> *France, mother of arts, of arms, and of laws,*
> *You long nourished me with the milk of your breast:*
> *Now, like a lamb who calls his nurse,*
> *I fill the caves and woods with your name.*
> *[. . .]*
> *Amongst cruel wolves I wander across the plain,*
> *I feel winter coming, whose cold breath*
> *Bristles my skin with a trembling fright. [. . .]*

At the same time, this undoing of Rome's foundational myth and appropriation of its civilization does not keep Du Bellay, elsewhere in the same collection, from disconnecting his own ancestral, intimately experienced, "native" French culture from the general idea of civilization, nor from representing Rome's cultural power as an alien threat. The sonnet 'Heureux qui, comme Ulysse . . .' specifically compares Roman and French culture, evoking the former through imposing images of domination and power, and associating the latter with the stuff of lyricism – personal feeling, subjectivity, and love. Furthermore, by inscribing these comparisons under the sign of a fragile analogy between his own separation from his homeland and that of ancient Greek heroes, the poet not only encapsulates the material of epic poetry into the confines of the sonnet, but also associates himself with a cultural power that precedes and (exceeds) that of Rome, at the same time as he situates both lyric poetry's and French culture's domain outside the framework of politics:

Heureux qui, comme Ulysse, a fait un beau voyage,
Ou comme cestuy là qui conquit la toison,
Et puis est retourné, plein d'usage & raison,
Vivre entre ses parents le reste de son aage!

Quand revoiray-je, hélas, de mon petit village
Fumer la cheminee, & en quelle saison
Revoiray-je le clos de ma pauvre maison,
Qui m'est une province, & beaucoup davantage?

Plus me plaist le sejour qu'ont basty mes ayeux,
Que des palais Romains le front audacieux:
Plus que le marbre dur me plaist l'ardoise fine,

Plus mon Loyre Gaulois que le Tybre Latin,
Plus mon petit Lyré que le mont Palatin,
Et plus que l'air marin la doulceur Angevine.[4]

Blessed is he who, like Ulysses, made a great voyage,
Or like that one who conquered the [Golden] Fleece,
Then returned, full of experience & reason,
To live amongst his kin the rest of his time.

When, alas, will I see my little village's
Chimney smoke again, and in what season
Will I see again my poor house's enclosure,
Which to me is a province, and much more?

I like better the abode that my ancestors built
Than the haughty fronts of Roman palaces:
Better than hard marble, I like fine slate,

Better my Gallic Loire than the Latin Tiber,
Better my little Lyré than Mount Palatine,
And better than sea air, that Angevine sweetness.

Putting forward the love of the poet's own home, in a particular (albeit traditional) regional French landscape, and presenting his attachment to these as a matter of sentiment and personal taste, rather than as the effect of his commitment to a state, this lyric poem, in its praise of appealing but unassuming French places ("mon petit village," "ma pauvre maison," "mon petit Lyré") is not "political" in the ordinary sense. Yet, by virtue, perhaps, of Du Bellay's ostensible choice of stylistic simplicity – in, for example, the repeated possessive adjectives and intimate tonalities of the homeland's description, and in the anaphoras establishing its superiority in the tercets – this sonnet has long been the most widely known and often recited poem of the French language. As such, it may well function as France's most powerful political poem of all. In any case, we already see in this Renaissance context that the primacy of French culture can be affirmed as much by its abdication of power, and its dissociation from nationalism and imperialism, as by the affirmation of these things.

Similar paradoxes come to light when we look back on the political implications of formal issues. We saw, for example, that the strict controls of Classical diction and prosody corresponded historically with the absolute monarchy of Louis XIV, in the second half of the seventeenth century. But this analogy was not rationalized by the particular power or glory of the "Sun King." Rather, in accordance with the Monarch's own thinking, Boileau's *Art poétique* insists that rules, hierarchy, clarity, and standardization are *universally* appropriate in matters of poetry (as of politics), because consonant with human reason. Similarly, though the nineteenth century's freeing of French verse is expressly linked by Hugo and Mallarmé to the French Revolution and its overturning of restrictions, free verse itself is not seen by these poets as something particularly French or suited to the French language. Rather, as we saw above with Senghor, and will explore more deeply further, French revolutions in poetry (as in politics) tend to be treated as exemplary, good for all nations and all times.

Conversely, in our considerations of forms and genres, we saw that when the sonnet was imported from Italy during the Renaissance, it was not considered to be of universal value until it was fully appropriated. On the one hand, a cultural rivalry with Italy is openly expressed (by Sébillet, Du Bellay and others) during the initial period where the sonnet is being "Gallicized" by the Pléiade poets. On the other hand (contrary to the case of England, where the Petrarchan sonnet continues to exist side by side with the Shakespearian and Spenserian English forms), once the sonnet becomes fully integrated into French culture it loses the specific trace of its formal Italian signature, and strives to grow out of its original generic connection with love poetry. Moreover, as the imported form helps, in the process of its assimilation, to elevate the status of the alexandrine, its integration exemplifies how central the idea of universal validation is to French poetry's identity, illustrating its privileging of flexible, global constructs as opposed to structures associated with locally or generically restricted traditions.

We also saw that when words and figures are deemed to be of high or low stylistic register, these lexical distinctions – though Hugo and others may use political allegories to dramatize various issues – have more to do with class structure than with anything exclusively French, reflecting a socio-political order that extends over Europe. Within that general frame, moreover, what stands for "Frenchness" (as Hugo's own practice shows) is neither any special orientation toward the high or low stylistic register, nor any preference for a language originally rooted in French earth. Rather, it is the consistent drive to categorize words and figures along class and other structural lines and the preoccupation with standardization itself. Thus, in the Classical era, expressions not assimilated into the normal language of "cultured" people in Parisian salons and at Court (provincialisms and foreign terms alike, regardless of the respectability of their lineage – Latin, Italian, or Normand) were considered improper "French," as were both excessively refined and vulgar words. By contrast, and in reaction to this identification of proper French with a stable norm, precious language and slang flaunt their exclusive association with particular types of people at extreme ends of the social scale. We should note, however, that both these aberrations of "normal" French, which find a place in poetry, are also centralized and controlled by the cultural life of Paris, whereas the various *patois* or dialects of the provinces (until recent times, when the monolithic French identity has begun to break apart, in response, perhaps, to the pressure of European integration) have rarely found their way into French poetry at all. They could instead fight to re-establish their own tradition, as happened, for example, in the nineteenth century, with the effort of the Provençal poet Frédéric Mistral (1830–1914) to revive the Occitan language and poetic heritage.

Finally, the stealth, or indirect, character of much of French poetry's politics becomes apparent when we consider the relative weakness of lyric poetry's place within French culture during the historical period when the nation's preoccupation with political power was most overt, that is from the mid-seventeenth century, when the monarchy reached its apogee, through the period of the French Revolution and the First Empire. The beginning of this period was to be sure a great age for dramatic verse, but not for poetry in general. With the prominent exceptions of Boileau and La Fontaine, who are associated with highly specialized genres, all of the early canonical French poets we have discussed (medieval, Renaissance, and Baroque, including the "Classical" Malherbe) precede this period. And the eighteenth century as a whole is generally acknowledged to be the age of prose, often dismissive of every kind of poetry despite reams of academic verse produced by writers as talented as Voltaire. Similarly, the nineteenth century's heights of Romantic lyricism are not reached in poetry proper – as they are in the "poetic" prose of Rousseau (1712–1778) and François-René de Chateaubriand (1768–1848) – until well after the 1815 demise of Napoleon.

In the modern period, where there has been, in France as elsewhere, a general tendency to equate revolutionary politics with "avant-garde" poetics that shun national like other kinds of limits, Paris especially has been represented as an uncircumscribed center of modern life and international culture; hence the German writer Walter Benjamin's description of it as the "capital of the nineteenth century."[5] Fostered by the longstanding internal tradition of centralization, this cosmopolitan view of Paris as both a positive and a negative allegorical point of convergence, in which not only all varieties of regional French but also European and exotic, ancient and modern cultures are superimposed, is especially emphasized beginning with Baudelaire. It prevails not only in *Le Spleen de Paris*, but also in the many ambivalent depictions of Parisian life in *Les Fleurs du mal*, as in these two stanzas from 'Le Cygne' ('The Swan'):

> Paris change! mais rien dans ma mélancolie
> N'a bougé! palais neufs, échafaudages, blocs,
> Vieux faubourgs, tout pour moi devient allégorie,
> Et mes chers souvenirs sont plus lourds que des rocs.
>
> [. . .]
>
> Je pense à la négresse, amaigrie et phtisique,
> Piétinant dans la boue, et cherchant, l'œil hagard,
> Les cocotiers absents de la superbe Afrique
> Derrière la muraille immense du brouillard [. . .][6]

> *Paris changes! but nothing in my melancholy*
> *Has budged! new palaces, scaffolding, blocks,*
> *Old outskirts, all is becoming allegorical for me,*
> *And my dear memories are heavier than rocks.*
>
> *[. . .]*
>
> *I think of the negress, emaciated and consumptive,*
> *Treading in the mud, and searching haggard-eyed*
> *For the absent coconut palms of superb Africa*
> *Behind the immense wall of fog [. . .]*

This image of Paris as a pivotal network of "correspondances" also prevails in early twentieth-century lyric poetry, as we saw with Apollinaire's 'Zone,' where the Eiffel tower (built for the 1889 Exposition Universelle), a welcoming symbol of international modern culture, oversees the bridges of Paris as a metaphorical shepherdess. This striking metaphor may itself allude to another contemporary poem by the Catholic poet Charles Péguy

(1873–1914). His 1913 litany-like *Tapisserie de sainte Geneviève et de Jeanne d'Arc* (*Tapestry of Saint Geneviève and of Joan of Arc*) weaves together numerous images of the patron Saint of Paris and the soon-to-be-canonized French national heroine (who helped oust the English during the Hundred Years' War). The opening sonnets portray this synthetic figure as an "antique bergère" (antique shepherdess) who on Judgment Day will guide the entire world along with Paris back to God: "Le troupeau tout entier à la droite du père" (The entire flock to the right of the father).[7]

With a more geographic and modernist perspective, this view of Paris as the center of the universe is also conveyed by the poetry of Blaise Cendrars (1887–1961), who broke with his Swiss roots and joined the foreign legion of the French army (losing his right arm in World War I) to become an honorary Frenchman: that is, paradoxically, a citizen "du monde entier" (of the whole world). His 1913 *Prose du Transsibérien et de la petite Jeanne de France* (*Prose of the Transsiberian and of Little Jeanne of France*), originally published on a two-meter fold-out interspersed with "simultaneous colors" by Sonia Delaunay, suggestively links transculturalism with transgeneric, multimedia aesthetics. It recounts one of the poet's first railway adventures, accompanied by a good-hearted French prostitute named (with a characteristic reversal of the sacred and profane) "la petite Jehanne de France." She repeatedly intervenes in the poem with the following refrain: "Dis, Blaise, sommes-nous bien loin de Montmartre?" (Say, Blaise, are we very far from Montmartre?) Naming also many far-flung places the poet has visited over his lifetime, the 400 free-verse lines of this semi-lyric, semi-epic "Prose" (lines which Cendrars himself referred to as "formules") are explicitly tuned to the world's train rhythms, which the poet knows "by heart":

> En ce temps-là j'étais en mon adolescence
> J'avais à peine seize ans et je ne me souvenais déjà plus de mon enfance
> J'étais à 16000 lieues du lieu de ma naissance
> [. . .]
> Maintenant, j'ai fait courir tous les trains derrière moi
> Bâle-Tombouctou
> J'ai aussi joué aux courses à Auteuil et à Longchamp
> Paris-New York
> Maintenant, j'ai fait courir tous les trains tout le long de ma vie
> Madrid-Stockholm
> Et j'ai perdu tous mes paris
> [. . .]
> Je reconnais tous les pays les yeux fermés à leur odeur
> Et je reconnais tous les trains au bruit qu'ils font
> Les trains d'Europe sont à quatre temps tandis que ceux d'Asie sont à
>   cinq ou sept temps [. . .]

During that time I was in my adolescence
I was barely sixteen and I could no longer remember my childhood
I was 16,000 leagues from the place of my birth
[. . .]
Now I've made all the trains run behind me
Basel-Timbuctoo
I've also played the races at Auteuil and Longchamp
Paris-New York
Now, I've made all the trains run the whole length of my life
Madrid-Stockholm
And I've lost all my bets / [P]arises
[. . .]
I recognize all countries with my eyes closed from their odor
And I recognize all trains by the noise they make
The trains of Europe are in four-beat time while those of Asia are in five
*   or seven-beat time [. . .]*

The poem ends with repeated apostrophes to Paris, invoked first as the grand
and noble hearth of correspondences:

Ô Paris
Grand foyer chaleureux avec les tisons entrecroisés de tes rues et tes
    vieilles maisons qui se penchent au-dessus et se réchauffent
Comme des aïeules
[. . .]

O Paris
Great welcoming hearth with the intersecting fire-brands of your streets
*   and your old houses that lean over them to get warm*
Like grandmothers
[. . .]

Then, as the poet's mood grows dark, there is a shift toward more disturbing,
painful images, equating Paris, in the end, with torture and even "capital"
punishment:

Ô Paris
Gare centrale débarcadère des volontés carrefour des inquiétudes
[. . .]
Je suis triste je suis triste
J'irai au *Lapin agile* me ressouvenir de ma jeunesse perdue
Et boire des petits verres
Puis je rentrerai seul

Paris
Ville de la Tour unique du Grand Gibet et de la Roue[8]

O Paris
Central station wharf of desires crossroad of anxieties
[. . .]

I am sad I am sad
I'll go to the **Lapin Agile** *to remember my lost youth*
And have a few drinks
Then I'll go home alone

Paris
City of the unique Tower of the Great Gibbet and the Wheel

A similar ambivalence, on the part of French poets, concerning the ideological implications of their culture's universalist stance, can be observed in contrasting modalities of Orientalism (the taste for everything Oriental and its exploration or exploitation in art), beginning with Hugo's *Les Orientales* (*Orientalia*) and the "Poèmes hindous" (*Hindu poems*) of Leconte de Lisle. While widespread twentieth-century imitations of such verse forms as the haiku generally convey a receptive attitude toward Eastern models, poets can engage in Orientalist poetics to very different effects. Some, such as Rimbaud and Artaud, look toward the Orient for a positive, abstract model of otherness, whose representation symbolizes, paradoxically, a spiritual journey within the self. By contrast, the diplomat Claudel, whether plotting the conquest of Asian hordes or mocking the Sanskrit alphabet in his Symbolist plays *Tête d'Or* (*Golden Head*) and *Le Repos du septième jour* (*The Seventh-day Repose*), performs a kind of poetic negation of the other that is consistent with imperialist discourse, and seems to use Oriental symbols or contexts to promote a Christian view of the world. At the same time his poetry, attempting to transcend a traditional Western distinction between sign and object, allows itself to be impregnated with the virtues of Oriental alternatives.[9] Thus his *Cent phrases pour éventails* (*One Hundred Phrases for Fans*), appropriating a Japanese mode of writing, can give haiku-like poems the rough appearance of ideograms, dislocating the normal order of alphabet-based language – sometimes down to the syllable, whose letters are separated: remue/r (mov/e) – to suggest the silent visual unity of the poem.[10]

Stèles (*Steles*), one of the most beautiful collections of turn-of-the-century French poetry, by the navy doctor Victor Segalen (1878–1919), develops a highly original poetic form that takes its cue from the inscribed ritual boundary markers celebrating various things throughout China. In 'Perdre le Midi quotidien' ('To Lose the Quotidian South/Midday'), we learn that the poet's objective is not to attach himself to any particular exterior place, but rather to "Éviter la stèle précise" (Avoid the precise stele), in order finally to

> Tout confondre, de l'orient d'amour à l'occident héroïque, du midi face au Prince au nord trop amical, – pour atteindre l'autre, le cinquième, centre et Milieu
>
> Qui est moi.[11]

Confuse all, from the orient of love to the heroic occident, from the Prince-facing
south to the too friendly north, – to reach the other, the fifth, center and
Middle
Which is me.

In 'Conseils au bon voyageur' ('Advice to the Good Traveler') we see, moreover, that Segalen's ideal conception of being-in-the-world mingles and confounds not only opposite places but also the contraries of movement and stasis, solitary adventure and communion, without "synthesizing" them:

Ville au bout de la route et route prolongeant la ville: ne choisis donc pas l'une ou l'autre, mais l'une et l'autre bien alternées.

[. . .]

Garde bien d'élire un asile [. . .]

Ainsi, sans arrêt ni faux pas, sans licol et sans étable, sans mérites ni peines, tu parviendras, non point, ami, au marais des joies immortelles,

Mais aux remous pleins d'ivresses du grand fleuve Diversité.[12]

City at the end of the road and road extending the city: don't choose therefore
the one or the other, but the one and the other well alternated.

[. . .]

Take care not to elect a refuge. [. . .]

Thus, without stopping or missing a step, without halter or stable, without
merit or hardships, you will make it, not at all, friend, to the marsh of immortal
joys,

But to the rapture-filled eddies of the great river Diversity.

The massive prose and versets of Saint-John Perse (1887–1975), though ostensibly less "personal" in their narrative, epic style and themes, also employ exoticism to unhinge poetry's domain from any particular space. Born in a French family long established in the Antilles, and then exiled in the United States under the Vichy government, Saint-John Perse, like Claudel, had a significant career as a diplomat. But he insisted on a separation between his political life and his art. His 1960 acceptance speech for the Nobel prize simultaneously emphasizes modern poetry's detachment from all narrowly defined worldly interests and its deep connection with all areas of human life, defining its universality in the widest possible terms: "it is with one embrace, as in one great stanza, that it holds in the present the whole past and future, the human with the superhuman, and all the space of the planet with universal space."[13]

Thus *Anabase* (*Anabasis*), though loosely patterned on Antique epic voyages (principally, Plutarch's and Arrian's accounts of Alexander the Great's ascent into Asia, and Virgil's *Aeneid*), presents itself as an autoreflexive, "critical" poem, creating, in Steven Winspur's words, "its own model Reader along with an ideal other-world of Reading for us to discover."[14] In the concluding lines, the identification of poetry with a universal creative process that transcends all historical events is evident in the reference to voyaging signs, and in the symbolic evocation of the earth's "breath," whose harvest is "feather." Though ancestral origins and the foundation of cities are richly invoked, it is not these that the heroic traveler – or dreamer – seeks, but rather the symbolic course of the journey itself:

> Ô généalogiste sur la place! combien d'histoires de familles et de filiations? [. . .]
>
> mais par-dessus les actions des hommes sur la terre, beaucoup de signes en voyage, beaucoup de graines en voyage, et sous l'azyme du beau temps, dans un grand souffle de la terre, toute la plume des moissons! . . .
>
> jusqu'à l'heure du soir où l'étoile femelle, chose pure et gagée dans les hauteurs du ciel . . .
>
> Terre arable du songe! Qui parle de bâtir? – J'ai vu la terre distribuée en de vastes espaces et ma pensée n'est point distraite du navigateur.[15]
>
> *O genealogist on the square! how many histories of families and filiations? [. . .]*
>
> *but above and beyond the actions of men on earth, many signs traveling, many seeds traveling, and under the azyme of fair weather, in a great breath of the earth, all the feather of harvests! . . .*
>
> *until the evening hour when the female star, a thing pure and engaged in the heights of heaven . . .*
>
> *Arable land of dream! Who speaks of building? – I saw the earth distributed into vast spaces and my thought is not distracted from the navigator.*

As *Anabase* well demonstrates, epic poems are not necessarily nationalistic, nor political in the narrow sense; nor is their distinction from lyric and dramatic poems – especially in the modern era – always clear-cut. Hugo's unfinished, life-long project of *La Légende des siècles* (*The Legend of the Centuries*), which embraces many lyric poems within it, traces the history of the world from the Fall to the dawn of the twentieth century, traveling through every myth from the Bible and Islam to Christian epics and the lives of great poets: this poem of poems is as good an example as any of French culture's characteristic attempts to embrace the universe as its own.

In the broad sense, epics are simply long poetic narratives that relate heroic exploits and stories of origins whose material is both ascribed to the past and relevant to a present collectivity (thus Greek mythology provides much of the material for Homer's *Odyssey* and *Iliad*, while Milton's *Paradise Lost* is based on the Judeo-Christian story of the Fall).

Discovered in a single manuscript at Oxford in 1832, *La Chanson de Roland* (*c*.1090), the oldest and most famous *chanson de geste*, or song of "exploits," corresponds to this broad definition, as well as to others more pointedly nationalistic, such as that proposed by Hegel in the nineteenth century: "[. . .] the collective world-outlook and objective presence of a national spirit, displayed as an actual event in the form of its self-manifestation, constitutes [. . .] the content and form of the true epic poem."[16] As such, *La Chanson de Roland* is at times considered to be the foundational epic of the French nation. This status is paradoxical, however, since the text – if not the story – was unknown until the same nineteenth century, and the question of its origins has been particularly problematic. Many scholars first stressed the poem's popular roots in song forms called "cantilènes"; then others vehemently rejected that view, insisting rather on the intervention of clerics in its composition, and on the genius of a singular poet. More recent specialists have leaned toward synthesizing these various theories. What all agree on, however, is the epic's powerful effect. As Gérard Moignet has pointed out: "*The Song of Roland* has the merit of evoking French patriotism in an incomparable way: *sweet France, Land of the Ancestors* are constantly present in the heroes' minds. The song is our first great national poem, and perhaps the only one."[17]

The epic recounts the defeat suffered by Charlemagne's rear-guard, led by "Roland the Valiant" (the King's nephew) and his companion "Olivier the Wise," and its subsequent avenging. An obscure 778 battle at Roncevaux is presented as having been set up by a treason, leading Charlemagne to retreat prematurely from a seven-year holy war aimed at driving the Moors out of Spain. Woven into the fundamental themes of feudal loyalty and the defense of faith against the "Infidels," we indeed find all the patriotic elements developed by future French poems. For example, as Charlemagne's army reenters French territory, the epic evokes the same sentimental attachment to the ancestral homeland later expressed in Du Bellay:

> Puis que il venent a la Tere Majur,
> Virent Guascuigne, la tere lur seignur;
> Dunc lur remembret des fius et des honurs,
> E des pulcele e des gentilz oixurs;
> Cel nen i ad ki de pitet ne plurt.[18]

> *When they arrive at the Land of their Ancestors,*
> *They see Gascony, the country of their Lord;*
> *Then they remember their fiefs and their domains,*
> *The young girls and noble wives:*
> *There is not one who doesn't cry with tenderness.*

Invocations of the honor and glory of France recur as refrains throughout the poem. For instance, at the onset of the battle, Aëlroth, the enemy King Marsile's nephew, threatens:

> "Enquoi perdrat France dulce sun los,
> Charles li magnes le destre braz del cors."

> *"Today, sweet France will lose its renown,*
> *And Charlemagne, his body's right arm."*

To which Roland (predictably) responds:

> "Oi n'en perdrat France dulce sun los.
> Ferez i, Francs, nostre est li premers colps!
> Nos avum dreit, mais cist glutun unt tort."[19]

> *"Today sweet France will not lose its renown,*
> *Strike, Francs, the first blow is for us.*
> *We have right on our side, and these cowards are wrong."*

An "extraordinary torment" of natural disasters hits many regions when the battle turns against Roland,[20] and the warrior, blessed by God but victim in part of his own heroism (urged by Olivier, he has long refused to sound his horn for help), mourns his companions' deaths as much for his "sweet country" as for himself.[21] Finally, Roland's moving last words to his sacred sword, Durendal, which conquered "[. . .] païs e teres tantes, / Que Carles tient, ki ad la barbe blanche" (so many countries and lands / that Charles of the white beard holds), evoke "France l'asolue" (holy France) as a monolithic, "universal" power: the lands mentioned include not only countries like Scotland, but also provinces such as Brittany and Anjou, which were not in fact taken in Charlemagne's time, but centuries later, by William the Conqueror.[22] This geographic redefinition works hand in hand with another anachronism: Charles, who was not crowned Holy Roman Emperor till Christmas Eve 800, is referred to at the time of the battle and from the poem's opening line as "Carles li reis, nostre emperere magnes" (Charles the king, our emperor, the Great).[23]

The "national" function of *La Chanson de Roland* is thus as much an anachronistic projection at the moment of its writing, at the end of the eleventh century, as in the moment of its discovery in the nineteenth. In its "original" form (whatever that might have been), the legendary narrative of Roland's heroic deeds may not have been any more politically centered or nationalistic than the eighth-century Old English epic *Beowulf*, based on a Norse legend. The synthetic theory of the *Chanson*'s genesis helps to explain both the intensity with which Charlemagne's holy power is glorified and the (erroneous) temporal and geographic expansion of his empire in the poem. One solution to the debate over popular vs. individual origins is the thesis that the poem was composed by a certain Turoldus (whose signature appears at the end of the manuscript) – a monk who was also William the Conqueror's half-brother. He would have reshaped the story he heard in a *cantilène* sung at the Battle of Hastings (1066) to more closely reflect his own experiences during William's conquest of England. Be this as it may, the quintessentially "French" status of the Roland legend is also paradoxical from the perspective of sheer literary glory, since the *Chanson*'s most important antecedent is a recently discovered Spanish text, while the story's greatest later developments are two Italian Renaissance epic romances: Boiardo's *Orlando Innamorato* (*Roland in Love*, 1494), and Ariosto's *Orlando Furioso* (*Mad Roland*, 1506).

The Italian appropriation of the Roland material may explain why, when the time came for the Pléiade poets to attempt the supreme French epic, they turned to other myths. In the *Deffence*, Du Bellay does, however, recommend following Ariosto's example, who borrowed from the French language "the names & story of his poem" and blended the epic with romance: "choose for me one of those beautiful old French romances such as a *Lancelot*, a *Tristan* [. . .]."[24] Du Bellay argues that French poets should take up these indigenous materials, as opposed to modeling their epics directly on Classical works (such as Virgil's *Aeneid*) which glorify the state – sensing, perhaps, a difference between poetry's moment of ideal partnership with political rulers at the onset of the Augustan age and the more equivocal relations joining French Renaissance poets to their kings, who were not always interested in verse: "Certainly if we had Maecenases & Augustuses, the Heavens & Nature are not so much the enemies of our time that we would not also have Virgils."[25]

As leader of the Pléiade, Ronsard was expected by his peers to write the epic which would crown the renaissance of French poetry. He managed to write four books of his *Franciade* once he was finally commissioned by Charles IX. But this epic remained unfinished, partly owing to its patron's death, and for antithetical poetic reasons. On the one hand, seeking to make his poem conform to the model of the *Aeneid* (contrary to Du Bellay's advice), Ronsard based it on a myth glorifying the foundation of the French nation, whose hero Francus was (like Aeneas) supposed to be of Trojan origin. Unfortunately, contrary to the Roland story, this myth had no roots in the French imagination and was fast losing its currency. On the other hand, Ronsard's own poetic imagination was considerably stayed by Charles IX's requirement that his work be historically accurate and incorporate a complete genealogy of the French Kings. Thus *La Franciade*'s failure can be attributed to the fact that it was at once too historical or political, and not enough. A similar conundrum would affect all further epics written in the Classical mold, such as Voltaire's *Henriade* (1728), a work celebrating the reign and combats of Henry IV, whose 1598 *édit de Nantes* put an end to the wars of religion in France.

The problem of the Classical French epic raises the issue of the connection between the poet and the state. French poets seldom experienced the privileged partnership with the sovereign that Virgil enjoyed in Rome. As far as the Middle Ages are concerned, it is important to remember that poets could have a stronger allegiance to other bodies, such as the church, as happens in the mid-thirteenth century, for example, with the political verse of Rutebeuf. The poet does not hesitate to berate a king as holy as Saint Louis (who eventually died in the Crusades) for not being zealous enough in motivating his Christian knights. Referring back nostalgically to the times of Roland, *La Complainte de Constantinople* (*Constantinople Lament*) wails, for example, that "Ogier [one of Roland's cousins] and Charlemagne are dead" and that "Loyalty is dead and perished."[26] And *La Complainte d'outremer* (*The Overseas Lament*) serves as literal recruitment for a crusade to the Holy Land, admonishing the King and his vassals to take up a larger cause than the national one:

> Ha! rois de France, rois de France,
> La loi, la foi et la creance
> Va presque toute chancelant.
> Que vous iroie plus celant?
> Secorez la, c'or est mestiers,
> Et vous et li quens de Poitiers
> Et li autre baron ensamble.
> N'atendez pas tant que vous emble,
> La mors l'ame, por Dieu, seignor![27]

> *Ah! King of France, King of France,*
> *Religion, faith, and devotion*
> *Are all on the verge of collapse.*
> *Why hide this from you any longer?*
> *Rescue them, now that you must,*
> *You and the Earl of Poitiers*
> *And all the other barons together.*
> *Don't wait till death steals away*
> *Your Soul, by God, lord!*

In fact, the strongest link between poetry written in French and the realization of state-based political objectives occurs neither in the form of "poetry" in the ordinary sense, nor in France. In the second half of the fifteenth century, the so-called *Grands Rhétoriqueurs* – a group of poet-historiographers originating in the Low Countries – served their princely patrons in a more direct political fashion than the Pléiade poets ever would, writing in both verse and prose to immortalize military exploits and others affairs of state – weddings, births, and deaths. The Flemish (Francophone) Jean Molinet (1435–1507), an "Indiciaire" (orator/historian) who began his career in the service of the Duke of Burgundy and ended it in the service of the German Empire, is exemplary of this tradition of politically employed writers – who were often enemies of the French state. Thus, in *La Journée de Therouenne* (*The Battle of Therouenne*), Molinet joyfully celebrates the defeat of the French by the Flemish:

> Chantés, notés, deschantés, gringotés,
> Petis enfans, qui sçavés contrepoint
> Et nous monstrés par vos chans fleurettés
> Comment Franchois ont estés escrottés,
> Rués par terre et gallés mal a point.
> Regratiés Dieu et n'oubliés point
> Que c'est œuvre saincte et miraculeuse,
> Pour reprimer leur vantise orguilleuse.[28]

> *Sing, play, harmonize, vocalize,*
> *Little children, who know counterpoint,*
> *And show us by your flowery songs*
> *How the French were trashed,*
> *Crushed to the ground and beaten to a pulp.*
> *Give thanks to God and do not forget*
> *That this was a Holy and miraculous work*
> *To stop their proud bragging.*

The mingled references to prowess in song and in battle suggest the complicity of poetry and military might, just as the various hammering rhyme effects suggest aggressivity and brute force through an overwhelming proliferation of verbal play:

> Chantés comment Franchois furent domptés,
> Batus, boutés, pilliés, esparpailliés,
> Desordonnés, desrompus, desmontés [. . .][29]

> *Sing how the French were tamed,*
> *Beaten, pushed out, trampled, scattered,*
> *Disbanded, disjointed, dismounted [. . .]*

This kind of poetic evocation of violence, which borders on the humorous and parodical because of its rhetorical excess and repetitiveness, will find immediate development in the early Renaissance novels of François Rabelais (*c*.1494–1553), and a distant echo in Jarry's late nineteenth-century plays and songs. Molinet's poem also mocks the royal emblem of France and its legendary hero, while appropriating the image of French warriors as lions (earlier used in *La Chanson de Roland*) – here representing, of course, the Roman-styled Flemish "Scipions":

> O fleur de lys, plaine de scorpions,
> Tu ne sçaras tantost quel sainct requerre.
> Rolland est mort; nos vaillans Scipïons
> Viennent en bruit, ils sont fiers que lions [. . .][30]
>
> *O fleur de lys, full of scorpions,*
> *Soon you will not know which Saint to beseech.*
> *Roland is dead; our valiant Scipions*
> *Are making a stir, they are as ferocious as lions [. . .]*

Although French *Rhétoriqueurs* such as Jean Marot and Guillaume Cretin were employed as poets and chroniclers by Kings Louis XII and Francis I, they did not hold as prestigious a position as the "Indiciaire" had in Burgundy. And Jean Marot's son, Clément, withdrew from the task of chronicling current events, abandoning prose and shifting his poetry to a more lyrical and personal vein. This is not to say that he refrained altogether from expressing political views poetically. On the contrary, his epigram on the execution of Samblançay, a finance minister of Francis I, who was widely considered to have been unfairly tried and sentenced for embezzlement, is one of the most successful political poems of French literature:

> Lors que Maillart Juge d'Enfer menoit
> A Montfaulcon Samblançay l'âme rendre,
> A vostre advis, lequel des deux tenoit
> Meilleur maintien? Pour le vous faire entendre,
> Maillart sembloit homme, qui mort va prendre:
> Et Samblançay fut si ferme vieillart,
> Que l'on cuydoit (pour vray) qu'il menast pendre
> A Montfaulcon le Lieutenant Maillart.[31]
>
> *When Maillart, the Judge from Hell, took*
> *Samblançay to Montfaulcon to give up the ghost,*
> *In your opinion, which of the two held*
> *Himself up the better? Well, to tell you how it went,*
> *Maillart seemed the one about to meet death:*
> *And Samblançay was such a firm old man,*
> *That one thought (in truth) it was he who was taking*
> *Lieutenant Maillart to hang at Montfaulcon.*

While this "snapshot" recording of a hanging at the Parisian gallows of Montfaulcon does not constitute an outright attack on the King (who still subsidized Marot's Muse), its neat repeated paradoxes and final punch do deliver sharp criticism. Realizing perfectly both the formal economy and the pointed wit characteristic of the satirical epigram, this commentary on a single political event shows well Marot's relative – if dangerous – poetic freedom and his personal detachment from representing the views of the French state. In the eighteenth century, Voltaire would write countless similarly styled epigrams.

The Pléiade poets who followed Marot simultaneously reclaimed and rejected the relative autonomy that his withdrawal from historiography and shift of perspective implied. They could not accept the earlier *Rhétoriqueurs'* subordination of their art to political expediency, but they wanted poetry to participate in and be sustained by the political sphere nonetheless. What the explosion of lyric poetry under their watch would show, however, is that direct political patronage is no more necessary to poetry's flowering than is poetry immediately required to sustain political power. This helps to explain both the failure of the group's epics and its successful exploitation of the poetic themes of failure and exile in works such as Du Bellay's *Regrets*.

Among the Pléiade poets, Ronsard was best able to negotiate the contradictions inherent in the group's ambivalent political stance. Aside from his failed epic, he managed to produce a massive œuvre of lyric poetry on every subject, along with effective satirical and political poetry in the *Discours des misères de ce temps* (*Discourse on the Miseries of These Times*). The first *Discours* involved him in political combat against the Protestant 1562 rebellion. But the last and most famous of these, the *Responce aux injures* (*Response to the Insults*) – while settling scores with the Protestant ministers who attacked him – takes advantage of a truce to defend his right to compose whatever kind of verse he chooses, on the basis that poets are fundamentally free spirits who give and take nothing but pleasure:

> En riant je compose en riant je veux lire,
> Et voila tout le fruit que je reçoy d'escrire:
> Ceux qui font autrement ils ne sçavent choisir
> Les vers qui ne sont nez sinon pour le plaisir:
> Et pource les grans Rois joignent à la Musique
> (Non au Conseil privé) le bel art Poëtique.[32]

> *Laughing I compose, laughing I wish to read,*
> *And that is the only fruit I gain from writing:*
> *Those who do otherwise don't know how to choose*
> *Verses that are born only for pleasure:*
> *And that is why great Kings conjoin to Music*
> *(Not to the private Counsel) the beautiful Poetic art.*

Ronsard's claiming of a lyrical, apolitical status for his very political *Discours* is curiously reversed by Hugo's hyperbolic claims for the political force of his own verse in the 'Réponse à un acte d'accusation,' a poem drawn from one of his most personal and least political collections, *Les Contemplations*. Apart from the fragmented, universal epic mentioned above, Hugo did, however, write a significant body of directly political poems, in the tradition of Ronsard's first *Discours* and of the early seventeenth-century epic *Les Tragiques* (*Tragic Fates*), by Agrippa d'Aubigné (1552–1630). These are mostly to be found within another collection written in exile, *Les Châtiments* (*Punishments*, 1853), which combines satirical invectives against Napoleon III (whom Hugo had helped to elect, but turned against following the 1851 coup d'état by the "prince-président"), and visionary patriotic flights celebrating the glory of France and the final reconciliation of society. In the poem 'Ultima verba' ('Last Words'), at the end of the last section, the solitary poet assumes the guise of a biblical prophet to excoriate "Napoléon le Petit" (Napoleon the Little):

> Je serai, sous le sac de cendre qui me couvre,
> La voix qui dit: malheur! la bouche qui dit: non!
> Tandis que tes valets te montreront ton Louvre,
> Moi, je te montrerai, César, ton cabanon.[33]
>
> *I will be, under the sackcloth and ashes that cover me,*
> *The voice that says: woe to you! the mouth that says: no!*
> *While your lackeys will show you around your Louvre,*
> *I will show you, Cæsar, your padded cell.*

D'Aubigné's 1616 *Les Tragiques* is a huge and resolutely un-Classical epic in seven books, expanding on the tradition of Ronsard's *Discours* (albeit from an opposite religious perspective) as well as on the work of another Pléiade poet, Étienne Jodelle (1532–1573), the author of the first tragedy in the French language. As Hugo would do, but even more savagely, d'Aubigné indicts French sovereigns, from a perspective that is both historical and eschatological. He vituperates the late Kings Charles IX and Henry III for their corruption and for their persecution of the Huguenots during the Wars of Religion, also exalting the martyrs of the 1572 "Saint-Barthélemy" massacre. The final books, "Vengeances" and "Jugement," prophesy the death of all perpetrators, including the murder of the turncoat Protestant Henry IV (which had occurred in 1610) and the eventual destruction of Paris, "this new Babel," along with the rest of the world on Judgment Day.

In one of the most moving and horrible depictions of "Misères" ('Miseries'), the first book, d'Aubigné uses touches of local color and realistic reportage to lead toward an allegorical "portrait" of war-torn France. He first relates a direct encounter with a wounded, dying man:

> Ce demi-vif la mort à son secours appelle
> De sa mourante voix, cet esprit demi-mort
> Disoit en son patois (langue de Périgort):
> "Si vous estes François, François, je vous adjure,
> Donnez secours de mort, c'est l'aide la plus seure [. . .][34]

> *This half-alive man calls death to his rescue*
> *With his dying voice, this half-dead soul*
> *Said in his patois (the language of Périgord):*
> *If you are French, as a Frenchman I beseech you,*
> *Rescue me with death; that's the surest aid [. . .]*

But it is not so much this man's own terrible condition, as the monstrous image he evokes of his wife – killed while trying to save her murdered child – that d'Aubigné offers as a symbolic representation of his country; a mother showering her starved, dying infant not with milk and tears, but with the blood spurting from her own dry flesh's wounds:

> [. . .] il ne sortoit plus d'eau
> De ses yeux consuméz; de ses playes mortelles
> Le sang mouilloit l'enfant; point de laict aux mammelles,
> Mais des peaux sans humeur: ce corps séché, retraict,
> De la France qui meurt fut un autre portraict.[35]

> *[. . .] no more water sprang*
> *From her consumed eyes; from her mortal wounds*
> *Blood wet the child; no milk in the breasts,*
> *But fluidless skins; this dried, withered body*
> *Was of France dying another portrait.*

The intimate fusion of d'Aubigné's visionary lyricism with political and religious intent is rare in French poetry. In the twentieth century, however, a similar conjunction has been noted in African and Caribbean poets. It is interesting, in this respect, to set d'Aubigné's allegorical vision of a tortured, withered France (where the poet's concrete concern for the very roots of his country emerges in details ranging from the mention of a native dialect, the Périgord *patois*, to the focus on the allegorical motherland's dried-up breasts) against the many positive images in Senghor's anthology equating "Négritude" and the African homeland with a kind of originary, nourishing human flesh. In his preface for this anthology, entitled "Orphée Noir" ("Black Orpheus"), the existentialist philosopher Jean Paul Sartre (1905–1980) insists on many poets' association of their emerging, "original" black voices with a symbolic return not only to their own physicality and to "raw" nature, but also to a native land. He also underscores the Negritude poets' conscious coupling of a "retractive reclaiming" of their identity with a contrary "generous expansion" toward the world, thus expressing the historical oppression and suffering of an entire race. This perhaps is what leads Sartre – who criticizes both the alleged political indifference of the Symbolists and the "gratuitous" revolutionary poetics of the Surrealists – to conclude: "For once at least, the most authentic revolutionary project and the purest poetry are springing from the same source."[36]

Yet Sartre does not take much account of the rhetorical differences in style and in tone distinguishing the poems he ideologically links, and as such falls short of illuminating just how they work politically, as well as how they work as poems. For example, the general perspective he stresses produces antithetical effects in Aimé Césaire's verse and prose Surrealist epic *Cahier d'un retour au pays natal* (*Notebook of a Return to the Native Land*) (originally composed in 1939) and Senghor's brief "chant" (song) 'Femme Noire' ('Black Woman'). The first poem, characterized by Breton as "nothing less than the greatest lyric monument of this time,"[37] opens up a new road within Surrealist poetics by virtue of a decision (which Sartre does note) to shake off paralyzing ideological contradictions. By contrast, Senghor's poem deliberately weaves African themes and imagery in the French poetic tradition, at the risk of appearing ideologically timid. The black woman (like Baudelaire's exotic lover in 'L'invitation au voyage') is equated with a "promised land" and a "lyrical source." "Savanna of pure horizons," she incarnates all the fruits of the earth and the earth itself, while her function is essentially to anoint male prowess: "calm oil on the flanks of the athlete, on the flanks of the princes of Mali." Thus, it is not surprising that Senghor's praise ends in the immortalization of her beauty's passing, and that her death is treated as a source of (poetic) regeneration, in lines reminiscent of Ronsard's 'Sur la mort de Marie':

> Femme nue, femme noire!
> Je chante ta beauté qui passe, forme que je fixe dans l'éternel
> Avant que le destin jaloux ne te réduise en cendres pour nourrir les
>   racines de la vie.[38]
>
> *Nude woman, black woman!*
> *I sing of your passing beauty, form that I am fixing in the eternal*
> *Before jealous fate reduces you to ashes to nourish the roots of life.*

More unsettling and complex both in its formal elements and literary references, Césaire's *Cahier d'un retour au pays natal* – which traces the poet's trajectory from Europe (where he was educated) back to his native Martinique, and finally to the reclaiming of his own African roots – has also struck most readers as more directly political and universal in scope. This may be partly because Césaire's return to himself and his African roots was originally framed within the context of a Marxist – that is, European – political allegory, which he ultimately renounced. Attempting to reconcile the age-old contraries of "dream" and "action," the poem seeks to cathartically carry the poet and readers alike through the moment of "negativity" which the black revolt against racial oppression represents, to a place where all differences, including that of color (and class), will finally be erased. Thus, Sartre explains that if Césaire's blacks can ultimately represent all workers, it is because they embody a kind of historical anachronism, remaining more immediately connected to agricultural production than to industry.

Be this as it may, the historical "light" brought forward by Césaire nevertheless distinguishes itself from that of the recent European tradition, associated formerly with religion and more recently with scientific and technological gains (partly sustained through colonial oppression). It is a new light and a call to arms of that "patient force" which lies latent in all humanity, inhabits all the elements, and is ultimately the soul and movement of the earth itself:

> ô lumière amicale
> ô fraîche source de la lumière
> ceux qui n'ont inventé ni la poudre ni la boussole
> ceux qui n'ont jamais su dompter la vapeur ni l'électricité
> ceux qui n'ont exploré ni les mers ni le ciel
> mais ceux sans qui la terre ne serait pas la terre
> gibbosité d'autant plus bienfaisante que la terre déserte
> davantage la terre
> silo où se préserve et mûrit ce que la terre a de plus terre
> ma négritude n'est pas une pierre, sa surdité ruée contre la
>   clameur du jour
> ma négritude n'est pas une taie d'eau morte sur l'œil mort
>   de la terre
> ma négritude n'est ni une tour ni une cathédrale
>
> elle plonge dans la chair rouge du sol
> elle plonge dans la chair ardente du ciel
> elle troue l'accablement opaque de sa droite patience.
>
> Eia pour le Kaïlcédrat royal!
> Eia pour ceux qui n'ont jamais rien inventé
> [. . .]
> véritablement les fils aînés du monde
> poreux à tous les souffles du monde
> aire fraternelle de tous les souffles du monde
> lit sans drain de toutes les eaux du monde
> étincelle du feu sacré du monde

chair de la chair du monde palpitant du mouvement même du
    monde![39]

o friendly light
o fresh source of light
those who invented neither gun powder nor the compass
those who never knew how to conquer steam or electricity
those who explored neither the seas nor sky
but those without whom the earth would not be the earth
gibbosity all the more beneficent as the earth deserts
more and more the earth
silo which preserves and matures that which the earth has
that is most earth
my negritude is not a stone, its deafness hurled against the
    clamor of the day
my negritude is not a speck of dead water on the dead eye
    of the earth
my negritude is neither a tower nor a cathedral

it plunges into the red flesh of the soil
it plunges into the burning flesh of the sky
it pierces opaque despondency with its righteous/erect patience

Eia for the royal Kaïlcedrat!
Eia for those who never invented anything
[. . .]

truly the eldest sons of the world
porous to all the breaths of the world
fraternal eyrie of all the breaths of the world
drainless bed of all of the waters of the world
spark of the sacred fire of the world
flesh of the flesh of the world palpitating with the very movement
    of the world!

Thus Césaire's poem handles equations between negritude and nature
very differently from Senghor's; where the latter gives a passive, "feminine"
figure to politically "engaged" lyric poetry, the former assumes a more revolutionary, symbolically "virile" stance, transforming anti-African prejudice
into incantation. For many black Francophone poets since Senghor and
Césaire, however, equations between black identity and nature, like equations between woman and nature, are problematic regardless of how they are
handled, because they imply an essentialist approach to the question of identity per se. In response to this problem and others, recent Caribbean poets
have opted to embrace instead of "Négritude" a wider, more heterogeneous
concept of cultural identity, under the term "Créolité."[40]
    Similar issues are raised by the expression of female identity in poetry.
Insofar as women are associated with nature by many poetic traditions,

women poets often face a choice of reworking such representations, or rejecting them along with the very notion of a feminine nature – as did the novelist Simone de Beauvoir (1908–1986) in her essay *Le Deuxième Sexe* (*The Second Sex*, 1949). By the same token, feminist poetry often rebels against political poems by men insofar as the poetic/political liberation they sing uses a gendered code to subordinate women through "love poetry" or glorify the filial, "fraternal" power of men. While Thérèse Plantier's previously cited 'Hommes po hommes à lunettes' is a satirical invective mocking political men in general, it is easy to see that it is also parodical, attacking the ideology inherent in most of the political poems we have seen thus far.

Many equally powerful feminist poems are, however, less direct in their political statements. This is the case, for example, with a biting lyric by the Egyptian poet Joyce Mansour (1928–1986), 'Noyée au fond d'un rêve ennuyeux.' Although Mansour's text does not constitute a direct response to either Senghor's or Césaire's poems, it exposes the sexist idealism they share, by aggressively overturning some key images:

> Noyée au fond d'un rêve ennuyeux
> J'effeuillais l'homme
> L'homme cet artichaut drapé d'huile noire
> Que je lèche et poignarde avec ma langue bien polie
> L'homme que je tue l'homme que je nie
> Cet inconnu qui est mon frère
> Et qui m'offre l'autre joue
> Quand je crève son œil d'agneau larmoyant
> Cet homme qui pour la communauté est mort assassiné
> Hier avant-hier et avant ça et encore
> Dans ses pauvres pantalons pendants de surhomme[41]

> *Drowned at the bottom of a boring dream*
> *I'd strip the leaves off man*
> *Man that artichoke draped in black oil*
> *That I lick and stab with my well-polished / very polite tongue*
> *Man whom I kill man whom I deny*
> *This stranger who is my brother*
> *Who offers me the other cheek*
> *When I pierce his teary lamb's eye*
> *This man who for the community was assassinated*
> *Yesterday before yesterday and before that and still before*
> *In his poor sagging superman trousers*

'Drowned at the bottom of a boring dream' introduces the poet in the same kind of subordinated place where Senghor leaves his naked black woman – nourishing "les racines de la vie," a place very like the ultimate water bed that Césaire associates with Negritude ("lit sans drain de toutes les eaux du monde"). In the next few lines, the petal-stripping of the metaphorical man-artichoke recalls and reverses the deflowering language of both Ronsard's Renaissance love poetry and the image of the woman-oiled man in 'Femme noire,' undermining also some of the plunging, phallic imagery of Césaire's verse. As the expression "cœur d'artichaut" refers, moreover, to a man too susceptible to falling in love, and the poet's (fingers' and tongue's) treatment of the artichoke is at once sweetly complacent and violent, her response to the lover appears at the same time docile, diminishing, and ultimately destructive. And her response to the man presented in the second half of the poem, who takes the form not of lover, but of an epic hero, her would-be political savior, is even more devastating. In a parallel movement to her undoing of the pathetic lover in the first lines, the unknown brother whom she "denies" and "kills" and who in a Christian-like manner refuses to fight her, is represented as a shrunken superman, a sacrificial lamb whose crying eye she again pierces out.

Contemporary feminism has not always known how to assimilate the most powerful woman poet of the French canon: Louise Labé (*c.*1524–1565), a Renaissance author from Lyons who, on the strength of a few sonnets and elegies, was placed by her contemporaries on the level of the legendary Greek poetess Sappho. Labé's love poetry can appear too accepting of male domination when considered in modern, anachronistic terms. However, if one takes into account their literary historical context, her love sonnets are not subtly but outrageously feminist, in the basic sense of redefining and claiming the woman's right to a lyric voice.

In a dedicatory prose preface to her œuvre, Labé encourages her sex generally to "elevate their minds beyond the distaff and spindle,"[42] and put their conceptions in writing so as to seize for themselves the same level of honor, glory, and pleasure traditionally reserved for men. In her own case it is primarily in the area of lyric poetry that she stakes her claims and demonstrates her own equality with men. She does this hyperbolically in several ways. First, her sonnets present a radical reversal of the gender roles constructed in Petrarchan and *fin'amor* love poetry models, which present the beloved "Dame" as a serene, dispassionate, divine being, and the poet a suffering, ardent, ever faithful, unrequited lover. Labé expresses such burning feelings of passion for an unfaithful lover – for example in these opening stanzas from sonnets II and XVIII – that her poems were read for centuries as evidence that she was an insatiable slut:

> O beaus yeus bruns, ô regars destournez,
> O chaus soupirs, ô larmes espandues,
> O noires nuits vainement atendues,
> O jours luisans vainement retournez [. . .][43]

O beautiful brown eyes, o averted looks,
O hot sighs, o spilt tears,
O black nights vainly awaited,
O shining days vainly returning [. . .]

Baise m'encor, rebaise moy et baise:
Donne m'en un de tes plus savoureus,
Donne m'en un de tes plus amoureus:
Je t'en rendray quatre plus chaus que braise.[44]

Kiss me again, rekiss me and kiss:
Give me one of your most savory [kisses],
Give me one of your most passionate:
I'll give you back four hotter than coals.

If the lack of syntactical connections creates confusion as to who is doing what to whom until the end of sonnet II[45] – thus mixing male and female roles –, the opening stanza of sonnet XVIII could not be more forceful in expressing female desire. Contemporary poets knew the concreteness of Labé's images to be a sign of the poet's supreme erudition (as opposed to conveying the quality of her love life), looking back to the sensual poetry of Sappho.

Above all, Labé's insistence on her own crying must be recognized not as a submissive acceptance of the woman's role but as a claiming of her right to write. As we saw from Christine de Pizan's 'Je chante par couverture,' it was not considered appropriate for medieval or Renaissance women to express their passionate sufferings in song. This overturns the conventional "femininity plot" of these periods on multiple levels. In her defense of crying in Sonnet XIV, moreover, Labé wholly identifies herself not so much with the act of loving, as with the recollection and musical expression of the lover's feelings – which defines lyric poetry in her time:

Tant que mes yeux pourront larmes espandre,
A l'heur passé avec toy regretter:
[. . .]
Tant que ma main pourra les cordes tendre
Du mignart Lut, pour tes graces chanter:
[. . .]
Je ne souhaite encore point mourir.
Mais quand mes yeus je sentiray tarir,
Ma voix cassée, et ma main impuissante,

Et mon esprit en ce mortel séjour
Ne pouvant plus montrer signe d'amante:
Prirey la Mort noircir mon plus cler jour.[46]

As long as my eyes will be able to spill tears,
To regret the hour passed with you:
[. . .]
As long as my hand will be able to pluck the strings
Of the sweet lute, to sing your graces:
[. . .]
I do not yet wish to die.
But when I will feel my eyes drying,
My voice broken, my hand without strength,

And my spirit in this mortal sojourn
No longer able to show a lover's sign:
Then I will ask Death to blacken my brightest day.

Labé's verse helps us to remember that just as political poetry, however direct it may seem, retains some distance from political action, lyric poetry is not consubstantial with love, but rather talks about or is the sign of it. Similar arguments could be made in defense of other important women poets whose "feminism" has often been dismissed, such as the Romantic Marceline Desbordes-Valmore, or the early twentieth-century poet Anna de Noailles (1876–1933).

Of Flemish origin, Desbordes-Valmore wrote political songs such as 'Dans la rue' ('In the Street'), in which "La Femme" mourns a massacre in Lyons following the silk-workers' uprising in the 1830s. This piece has been thought to be the model for Rimbaud's famous poem 'Le Mal,' condemning violence. Yet one of her most subversive texts, 'Le Ver luisant' ('The Glow-worm'), taking the form of a La Fontaine-styled fable, might not be considered to convey a political message insofar as its representation is allegorical, that is, indirect. The woman's voice is symbolized by an allusion to Philomela – the mythological victim of a rape, who was turned by the gods into a nightingale after her tongue was cut out. "Amante de ses pleurs et de la solitude" (Lover of her tears and of solitude), this songbird exhausts her heart in a "lamentable cri."[47] But the poem takes on a decidedly feminist air as soon as we recognize that the glow-worm's portrait is also an allegorical mockery, filled with allusions to the Romantic hero/poet/genius, as configured, for example, in the poems of Hugo and Alfred de Vigny (1797–1863). In the end, Desbordes-Valmore's melancholic songbird radically diminishes this male figure's stature much in the manner of Mansour: by eating him.

Because the signifying process of poetry implies some measure of indirection – as Michael Riffaterre has put it, "a poem says one thing and means another"[48] – it will always be complicated to judge what in poetry is political and what is not, let alone to isolate the content of what the political message is. In order to do this, one will have to reconnect one's reading with some other, more prosaic representations of the political reality in question, and to know something about the poem's cultural and historical context. Yet because it is in the nature of poetry to twist words and create ambiguities, the relations between poems and the political realities they refer to are often themselves ambiguous and twisted. Often, the most politically involved poets are the most aware of this conundrum, and represent the tensions between poetry and more direct forms of political action and speech dramatically within their own works. Such is the case, for example, with Gaston Miron, widely considered the preeminent poet of Québec, and one of the moving forces of its 1960s Independence movement.

Following in some respects the example of Saint-John Perse, Miron chose in various ways and at various times to separate his poetry from his public political life. At one point he refused to collect his poems in a book, for fear that this kind of monumentalization, regardless of his poems' message – which advocated both national and communist revolution – would interfere with or undermine his own political activism. And the distinction that Miron drew between poetry and politics remains articulated in the double structure of the most important work published in his lifetime: *L'Homme rapaillé* (*Reassembled Man*); *rapailler* is a not a French but a Québécois word, meaning to reassemble scattered fragments. When finally published in 1970, the book presented itself as a duality, dramatically underscoring the conflict between different modalities of poetry and prose, and between revolutionary poetry and revolutionary action. The first part assembles verse lyrics with very uneven degrees of political and poetic covertness: in 'L'homme agonique'('Agonizing/agonistic man'),[49] the poet claims to be writing as "le fou du roi de chacun" (everyone's king's fool), simultaneously under and against the old colonial act prohibiting political assembly: "je m'écris sous la loi de l'émeute" (I write myself under the [anti]-riot law); in 'Recours didactique,' the proud refrain: "je suis sur la place publique avec les miens," (I am on the public square with my people) openly proclaims his revolutionary action.[50] The second part is a collection of prose pieces, also entitled *Recours didactique* (*Didactic Recourse*), that again articulates with varying "directness" the main stages of his experience in attempting to engage poetry with politics in the peculiar situation of Québec. Though Miron may or may not have approved of the most recent, posthumous edition's decision to remove the work's prose pieces, considerations of the matter came long after the end of the 1960s movement, and thus well after the time when concern with the effects of his own direct political action could have been acute.

In an especially poetic prose piece entitled 'Aliénation délirante' ('Delirous Alienation'), which happens to be more obscure than the corresponding verses of 'Monologues de l'aliénation délirante' ('Monologues of delirious alienation'), Miron effectively conveys the political problem most central to his work as a poet: the difficulty of preserving his own Francophone expression in a sea of Anglophones, at the same time as he comes to grips with his own inevitable alienation (as a Québécois) from hexagonal French:

> *Il est ti flush lui . . . c'est un blood man . . . watch out à mon seat cover . . . c'est un testament de bon deal . . .*
>
> voici me voici l'unilingue sous-bilingue voilà comment tout commence à se mêler à s'embrouiller c'est l'écheveau inextricable[51]
>
> He is a little flush/spender he is . . . he's a blood man . . . watch out for my seat cover . . . it's a hell of a good deal . . .
>
> *here here I am the unilingual sub-bilingual here is how everything starts to get mixed to get tangled it's the inextricable skein*

Though the double jeopardy of French and English that the Québécois poet experiences is in certain ways unique, linguistic and cultural alienation is to some degree a problem that every poet from a colonized land faces, whether or not he or she "directly" expresses it. (The preeminent woman poet from Québec, Anne Hébert [1916–2000], for example, expresses it less directly than Miron does.) To take another distant example, let us consider Rabéarivelo's quotation, in a poem from his 1928 collection *Volumes*, of a Mallarmé line we have already encountered, from the 'Tombeau d'Edgar Poe':

> *Donner un sens plus pur aux mots de la tribu*
> et l'imprégner du sang de mes morts [. . .][52]
>
> To give a purer meaning to the words of the tribe
> *and impregnate it with the blood of my dead ones [. . .]*

In Mallarmé's poem, the line seems to represent the ideal poet's philosophical refinement of everyday language (though it is important to remember that the poet Mallarmé is celebrating is not himself French, or universal, but American, thus coming out of a colonized culture). The challenge that the African poet pulls off is not that (eternal) one, but nearly the opposite: "plus pur" now means that the words of the French tribe will be made to carry the blood and the dead of the very people they are colonizing.

When Miron returns to writing and publishing poetry, after a period where he acted out his alienation in a fashion reminiscent of Rimbaud's *Une saison en enfer* (followed by a period of silence), he describes this

first as an attempt to combat "the confusion engendered in [his] mind by
linguistic duality," and second as an effort to establish Québécois literature
as such: "Today, I know that all poetry cannot be other than national insofar
as it warrants literary existence. [. . .] My conviction is that here literature will exist collectively and no longer as an individual phenomenon, the
day that it takes its place among national literatures, the day it becomes
Québécois."[53] For Miron, then, in the mid-1960s, as for Rabéarivelo in
the late 1920s, the first challenge of the non-French poet of French expression is to appropriate the language as a native one, and the second,
to establish one's own individual voice as the expression of a unified, autonomous cultural community, whether or not this be ultimately defined
as a nation. Today, Québec remains of course a province of Canada, while
Césaire's native Martinique has become a department (as opposed to a territory) of France; Sénégal and Madagascar became independent republics
in 1960. But all of these places are rapidly establishing autonomous literary
traditions.

Particular political conditions can and do then generally shape the relations of poets to language and culture, but they are not the sole determining
factor in poets' perceptions and representations of the relations between
poetry and politics. We have seen a wide range of poetic responses to the
tensions arising between the natural and the cultural, the individual and
collective, the self and the other, and other conceptual contraries whose
interaction motivates strong relations between poetry and politics as much
as it pulls them apart. Though I have naturally anchored my discussion of
French poetry's political implications on a "national" perspective – treating
only in passing the politics of race and gender – it is important to remember
that the "monolithic" universalism of the French poetic tradition has, it
seems, "always already" half-negated this perspective, through a variety of
attempts to redefine and displace the cultural boundaries of France. By the
same token, readers of poetry in French will increasingly realize that owing
to an ever-greater emphasis on cultural diversity within France, the non-
universalist, non-French tradition is rapidly becoming as important inside
hexagonal France as in Francophone countries far away.[54]

We will conclude with Surrealism – the poetic movement which appears
to be the least concerned with national identity, the most concerned with
politics, and the central influence of twentieth-century poetry of French
expression inside and outside France. Surrealism offers as much complexity
and contradiction in its representations of poetry's relations with politics as
any of the other examples we have seen thus far. To begin with, the movement's ideology progressed within a decade from one extreme to the other
of the "engagement" scale. It moved from an essentially anarchical position

in the early 1920s – a position first proclaimed by Tzara and other Dadaists that set out to destroy all social hierarchies and political systems, refusing to serve any interests but those of the mind's free, unfettered expression – to most group members' willingness to serve (with varying degrees of commitment) the "borderless" interests of communism. Breton himself officially joined forces and broke with communism a number of times, and he did not hesitate to "excommunicate" poets from Surrealism on the basis of their non-adherence to the central lines of his own thought.

Within this general framework, the pressures of war and occupation forced Surrealists – who at first held much in common ideologically as well as stylistically – far apart, dividing even those who belonged to the same political parties. Because Dada shunned the very notion of group politics, it could gather under its wing poets who had acted or thought differently in response to World War I: some rejecting, others embracing the general violence. The same was not true of Surrealism in response to World War II. A number of poets evolving out of the movement wrote wartime works of poetry that were neither nationalistic or political in the narrow sense, marking only a "universal" form of resistance. This is the case, for example, with René Char's 1943–1944 poetic notebook *Feuillets d'Hypnos* (*Leaves of Hypnos*), which, though accompanying the poet's actual fighting for the French Resistance, presents itself as recording

> [. . .] la résistance d'un humanisme conscient de ses devoirs, discret sur ses vertus, désirant réserver *l'inaccessible* champ libre à la fantaisie de ses soleils, et décidé à payer le *prix* pour cela.[55]

> [. . .] *the resistance of a humanism conscious of its duties, discreet about its virtues, wanting to reserve the* inaccessible *free field for the fantasy of its suns, and determined to pay the* price *for this.*

However, hardcore Surrealists of the communist persuasion tended to divide themselves into two camps: those who thought it their political duty to accessibly treat war and resistance issues in their poetry, and those who did not. Leading the first group, Aragon reverted to alexandrines to express traditional, patriotic themes in lines such as these (with their joint references to French geography and the Roland story), published in a 1943 clandestine poem entitled *Le Musée Grévin* (*The Grévin Museum*, a Paris wax museum):

> Je vous salue ma France où l'oiseau de passage
> De Lille à Roncevaux de Brest au Mont-Cenis
> Pour la première fois a fait l'apprentissage
> De ce qu'il peut coûter d'abandonner un nid[56]

I salute you my France where the bird of passage
From Lille to Roncevaux from Brest to Mont-Cenis
For the first time has come to learn
What it can cost to abandon the nest

Following a slightly different track, the poem 'Liberté' by Éluard, from the 1942 collection *Poésie et vérité* (*Poetry and Truth*), reappears alongside resistance poems by Aragon and others in a 1943 pamphlet published in Rio de Janeiro, entitled *L'Honneur des poètes* (*The Honor of Poets*). This *hymne*-like poem presents equally accessible (and popular) lyrics, though it celebrates the more "universal" ideal of freedom:

> Sur mes cahiers d'écolier
> Sur mon pupitre et les arbres
> Sur le sable sur la neige
> J'écris ton nom
>
> Sur toutes les pages lues
> Sur toutes les pages blanches
> Pierre sang papier ou cendre
> J'écris ton nom[57]
>
> *On my school notebooks*
> *On my desk and the trees*
> *On the sand on the snow*
> *I write your name*
>
> *On all the pages read*
> *On all the blank pages*
> *Stone blood paper or cinder*
> *I write your name*

Benjamin Péret (1889–1959), Éluard's former friend, political comrade, and literary cohort, levels a terrible attack on this poem and others in a 1945 piece entitled 'Le Déshonneur des poètes' ('The Dishonor of Poets'), published in *Poésie et Révolution* (*Poetry and Revolution*) in Mexico (Péret left France toward the beginning of the war and was barred from immigrating to the United States, because of his ties with the Communist party). His criticism is especially interesting because it insists on poetry's indivisibility of "form" and "content" in one moment, only to pull them apart in the next; and because it emphasizes a divide in the Surrealists' revolutionary ideology that implicates their poetry, as opposed to their other forms of political action. It shows that what separates their perspectives is the open-ended question of what in poetry is effectively political or revolutionary, and what is not.

Péret dismisses most of the poems on the basis of sheer quality and then links an aesthetic complaint with an ideological problem:

> Not one of these "poems" surpasses the poetic level of pharmaceutical advertising, and it is not by chance that the great majority of their authors has believed it necessary to return to Classical rhyme and alexandrines. Form and content necessarily maintain a very strict relation to each other, and in these "verses" they react on each other in a mad dash to the worst reaction.[58]

The objectionable "content" that Péret stresses is an alloy of religious and nationalistic dogma. He sees this everywhere, coming even from former communists and atheists such as Aragon and Éluard; if not always explicitly, at least in the form of allusions, and in the technical aspects of the verses themselves. Aragon's particular offense in the selection of poems has been to evoke the "saints and prophets," and Lazarus' tomb; Éluard's, to formally "[. . .] return to the litany, no doubt in obedience to the famous slogan: 'The priests are with us'."[59]

For Péret, poetry "understood as the total liberation of the human mind" has no business representing political or any other ideological position, even under war and occupation: "[. . .] poetry does not have to intervene in this debate by other than its own means, by its own cultural significance, leaving poets free to participate as revolutionaries in routing the Nazi adversary by revolutionary means [. . .]." The fact that Péret feels it necessary to purge French resistance poetry of its Christian and nationalist roots, "miasmes of the past infesting this pamphlet," in order to defend the mind's total liberation, could not be more logical from his own political point of view. We should note, however, that in doing this Péret rejoins at least one branch of his own French universalist tradition, claiming in a paraphrase of Marx (on revolution) that "poetry has no homeland because it belongs to all times and all places."[60]

Whether or not we accept Péret's premise, it is fitting to move from it to a more direct examination of such "universal" ideas. How do poets writing in French tend to present such basic constructs as the self, the sign, and the world? How do they poetically signify the nature of their interrelations? Where do they say poetry comes from? To what dimension of being, or presence, does it ultimately belong? To explore these questions, we shall now turn to the no less fundamental and no less problematic matter of poetry's relationship to philosophy.

Chapter 5

Poetry and philosophy

Though French poets have often been explicitly engaged with specific philosophical traditions, the concerns of philosophy, in the basic sense of reflection on the nature of being and truth (the domain of metaphysics), of good and evil (ethics), and of beauty (aesthetics), have in fact been central to most Western poetry. What is the nature of being in the world? Of concrete and abstract reality's representation in signs (linguistic and otherwise)? Of the divine or human subject, or self, that creates and perceives? The link between these universal problems and poetry – where it comes from, what it is, what it does – has long been recognized, and is encouraged by the term's etymology, which through the Greek verb *poiein* (to make) is often made to suggest an analogy between the poet's craft and creation.

A deep-rooted connection between Western poetry and metaphysics also emerges when we consider that the divine presence or first principle has often been conceived of by the Christian tradition as an ideal, self-reflecting form of language. Indeed, in European literature and philosophy, the Greek Logos and Christian Word have tended to be fused since Antiquity. The term *logos*, meaning "word," "speech," "reason," variously used by Greek philosophers to refer to the "intellectual part of the soul" (in Plato), to the argument coming from "first principles" (in Aristotle), and to the divine order and regulating forces of creation (in Stoicism and Neoplatonism), was adapted in Christian theology to refer to the Word of God, in particular "to the instantiation of his agency in creation, and in the New Testament, to the person of Christ."[1]

A seminal example of the Greek *logos*' synthetic translation into the Christian Word is the opening of *The Gospel According to John*: "In the Beginning was the Word, and the Word was with God, and the Word was God."[2] This verse has often been echoed in French poetry, sometimes quite provocatively so, as in the 'Suite' to Hugo's 'Réponse à un acte d'accusation,' a poem which begins thus:

> Car le mot, qu'on le sache, est un être vivant.
> La main du songeur vibre et tremble en l'écrivant;

> *For the word, let it be known, is a living being,*
> *The hand of the dreamer vibrates and trembles while writing it;*

and ends as follows:

> Car le mot, c'est le Verbe, et le Verbe, c'est Dieu.[3]
>
> *For the word is the Word, and the Word is God.*

The equation established here elevates ordinary human language to the level of the divine Word and to God himself, from signification or representation to creation, which was clearly not the Gospel's intent.

Building on a longstanding "logocentric" conception of metaphysical being, many important figures throughout French literature, like Hugo, affirm in one way or another that poetry finds its model and source in divine speech – a language that "makes" instead of merely "saying." From the late nineteenth century forward, however, and often following the lead of German philosophy, French poets have tended to preserve this idea of language while negating its source, insisting rather, with various inflections, that poetry's function is to compensate for the absence of God and divine language, and to articulate truth in their place.

Universalizing, theoretical, and reflexive in its general thrust, it is not surprising that French poetry has revolved around and helped to disseminate a number of key philosophical perspectives throughout the history of Western culture. We already touched on the impact of the Platonic conception of love in French Renaissance poetry, and on Plato's and Aristotle's roles in establishing the origins of European literary genres. In this chapter, we will dwell further on these philosophers' influence as well as underscore French poetry's links with German philosophy in the last two centuries. It should be noted, however, that the privileged position which modern French poets have accorded to the latter can be explained in large measure by the increasing significance that the German philosophers themselves have accorded to poetry, in a tradition that begins with the declaration of poetry's supremacy among other arts in the *Critique of the Aesthetic Judgment* by Immanuel Kant (1724–1804) and culminates in the presentation by Martin Heidegger (1889–1976) of pure or self-reflexive poetry as the origin of man's conscious, historical existence itself. What is more, French poetry's engagement with the German philosophical tradition (as with the sixteenth and seventeenth centuries' poetic usage of the Classical philosophers and their Italian adaptations) does not present itself as the subservient expression of "foreign" doctrine, but rather as the gleaning and cultivation of "universal" concepts around which French poetic currents (more typically down-to-earth than metaphysical) gain strength, take shape, and organize themselves. Accordingly, we will ask less whether a poem advocates or illustrates a philosophical position – as Voltaire did, for example, against Leibnizian optimism, in his 1755 *Poème sur le désastre de Lisbonne (Poem on the Lisbon Disaster*) – than whether a given philosophical position might help us to understand what a poem sets out to do.

Such an autonomous conception of poetic culture does not, however, apply to the Middle Ages, an overwhelmingly religious era during which philosophy, at once transnational and enclosed within theology, often viewed poetry as a seductive lie, while poetry, like other arts, oscillated between the expression of religious doctrine and the development of a lay culture competing with or derived from the Christian model (as was the cult of love in the *fin'amor* tradition). Influenced by the scholastic (logic-based) philosophy of their time, many French medieval poets personify concepts such as Reason and Nature, reflecting on the distance between God and a human world submitted to sin and Fortune, and on the way to bridge that distance. They occasionally assume the stance of the preacher (as Rutebeuf does) and question the ethical worth of human activities, including their own art, but in general they do not pretend to be directly inspired by God. By contrast, a central paradox of the Renaissance is that it brought "pagan" poetry to an unprecedented degree of autonomy, but also used poetry (notably in the Reformation movement) to convey more direct forms of individual religious expression. In some cases the theological framing of knowledge and morals gave way to "pure" faith and the voice of God, for which poetry was now seen as a privileged channel.

This paradox can be seen, for example, in Clément Marot's 1541–1543 beautiful translations of the Old Testament Psalms (which Calvinists would eventually appropriate for their French hymn book). Though Marot's role in the growth of secular poetry was second to none, he also embraced a form of lyricism whose origin, destiny, and worth he actually believed to be divine. Personal inspiration thus fully merges with the sacred. His verse dedication describes the Psalms as having been originally "dictated" to King David by the Holy Spirit, and presents their similarly animated French translations as bequeathing themselves naturally to the "most Christian King," Francis I.

Similarly, Marguerite de Navarre (1492–1549), Francis' Protestant-leaning sister, extolling the spiritual writings of the thirteenth-century mystic Marguerite Porete in her long allegorical poem *Les Prisons* (*The Prisons*), celebrates the authenticity and power of their connection with Holy Scripture, the "[. . .] Esprit dans la parolle encloz / [. . .] Et ce beau mot qui descend de la cime / Du ciel treshault" ([. . .] Spirit enclosed in the word / [. . .] And that beautiful word that comes down from the pinnacle / Of highest heaven). Indeed, Marguerite de Navarre presents Porete's book (for whose heretical ideas the author was burned at the stake in 1310 by the French Inquisition) as being so much lit by the flame of charity that "[. . .] rien qu'amour n'estoit son argument, / Commancement et fin de son parler [. . .]" (nothing but love was the argument, / Beginning and end of its speech).[4]

In the late 1540s Marguerite de Navarre herself wrote a series of religious poems set to traditional song music, the *Chansons spirituelles* (*Spiritual Songs*). As the following stanzas show, she often manages to point the fashionable language of Petrarchism directly to Jesus Christ himself, thereby reconverting and spiritualizing the conventions of love poetry (which otherwise would become increasingly "pagan" in her time):

> Hélas, je languis d'Amours
> Pour Jésuchrist, mon espoux.
>
> [. . .]
>
> Dites à l'Amy de mon âme,
> Que de sa divine Flamme
> La vueille brusler tousjours,
>   Hélas.
>
> Et que rien ne veult prétendre,
> Que d'estre brulée en cendre
> Par ce feu qui est sy doux,
>   Hélas.[5]
>
> *Alas, I languish with Love*
> *For Jesus Christ, my spouse.*
>
> *[. . .]*
>
> *Tell the Lover of my soul,*
> *That with his divine Flame*
> *It may always burn,*
>   *Alas.*
>
> *And that it wants nothing*
> *But to be burned to ash*
> *By this flame which is so sweet,*
>   *Alas.*

We saw that the construction and images of Scève's *Delie* (1544) drew, on the contrary, Petrarch's own Christianized representation of love in a more pagan direction, celebrating the beauty of the beloved muse idolatrously and for its own sake; Délie is treated as a source and means of "divine" inspiration, but not as a spiritual conduit to and from the Christian God. In the years that follow, Pléiade poets who continue to voice Platonician theories of reality, beauty and poetic inspiration (theories first interpreted for the Italian Renaissance by the Florentine Marsilio Ficino, but originally elaborated in such Socratic dialogs as *The Republic*, *The Symposium*, *Ion*, and *Phaedrus*), tend to do this in a manner less obviously Christian and more abstract or intellectual than in earlier Petrarchan-styled poems. Thus, the best-known sonnet of Du Bellay's 1549 love collection *L'Olive* conveys on the whole a more synthetically "Classical" than Christian conception of the world, presenting worldly beauty as the mere reflection of what the poet's soul should truly desire and aspire to – the unchanging, immaterial realm of Platonic Ideas:

> Si nostre vie est moins qu'une journée
> En l'éternel, si l'an qui faict le tour
> Chasse noz jours sans espoir de retour,
> Si périssable est toute chose née,
>
> Que songes-tu, mon âme emprisonnée?
> Pourquoy te plaist l'obscur de nostre jour
> Si pour voler en un plus cler séjour,
> Tu as au dos l'aele bien empanée?
>
> La, est le bien que tout esprit desire,
> La, le repos ou tout le monde aspire,
> La, est l'amour, la, le plaisir encore.
>
> La, ô mon ame au plus hault ciel guidée!
> Tu y pouras recongnoistre l'Idée
> De la beauté, qu'en ce monde j'adore.[6]

> *If our life is less than a day*
> *In the eternal, if the year that makes the turn*
> *Chases our days without hope for return,*
> *If everything born is perishable,*
>
> *What are you dreaming of, my imprisoned soul?*
> *Why does the obscurity of our day please you*
> *If in order to fly to a clearer place*
> *You have your wings well fixed to your back?*
>
> *There, is the good that every spirit desires,*
> *There, the rest to which all the world aspires,*
> *There, is love, there, also pleasure.*
>
> *There, o my soul, guided to the highest heaven!*
> *You will be able to recognize the Idea*
> *Of the beauty, which I in this world adore.*

To be sure, this sonnet expresses the most influential philosophical dogma of its time: it reiterates (with Christian overtones) Plato's conception that the natural world in which we live is nothing but the shadow, or cavernous reflection, of metaphysical reality, the world of Ideas or unchanging Forms (a theory set forth in *The Republic*). It also implies, as a consequence, that the poet's beautiful representations express nothing but second-hand, illusory dreams of what reality ultimately is (thereby also seeming to embrace Plato's concept and critique of mimesis, which presents art as an illusory imitation of reality). However, through the searching questions of the quatrains and the insistant directives of the tercets, Du Bellay's sonnet voices these ideas in such a way as to stress not so much the truth and goodness of the ideal world, as just how difficult it is to keep one's attention focused on it. The last line makes it clear that what the poet adores at the moment is not an Idea imagined elsewhere, but a particular beauty of this present world.

French poetry also ambiguously draws on and blends various elements of Classical and Christian doctrine in its representations of the nature of the relationship between signs and referents, or words and things. The question of whether words have, in a given poetic context, a natural or arbitrary relation to the things and ideas they represent is something that we discussed briefly in Chapter Two, in connection with various kinds of descriptive poetry. In the wider context of language in general, and without regard for the special way words are used in poetry, Plato in fact offers two famously opposing views of this problem in the *Cratylus* (many have argued that his own position was uncertain). Cratylus, one of the characters in this dialog, asserts the fundamental unity of words and things, arguing that there is both a transcendent and natural motivation behind proper and common nouns; his interlocutor Hermogenes asserts, on the contrary, the disjunctiveness of language and the world, insisting that there is only a conventional, or arbitrary, relation between words and their (conceptual) signifieds or (actual) referents. In the age-old debate around this general issue, which has been of equal concern to poets, philosophers, and theologians, theorists of language have leaned toward Hermogenes' view and emphasized the conventionality of words.[7] Ferdinand de Saussure, for example, one of the founders of modern linguistics, actually defines the standard linguistic sign as arbitrary, and uses the term "symbol" for particular types of verbal or other signs which appear to have "un rudiment de lien naturel" (some element of a natural link) between the signifier and the signified.[8]

Poets have tended, however, to emphasize language's natural or divine motivation and deep-rooted connection with the world, whether they see this as a cause or an effect of their own poetic operations. This inclination makes sense, for it greatly elevates the power of the poet, granting him an important role in exposing philosophical or religious truth. The poet's chosen speech may be seen to simply draw out or enhance the inherent power of language, exposing long-lost meanings buried in etymologies, or otherwise revealing through word-play the hidden connections between words and things. Or, on the contrary, the poet's manipulations of language, whose effect normally establishes persuasive connections between words and their referents, may be seen to expose the absence of any truth beyond or outside language, suggesting that metaphysical reality itself is a poetic construct, or fiction. And, as might be expected, there are endless variations on each of these points of view.

Modern French Catholic poets, for example, tend to affirm that there is a divine model and origin for their poetry. Thus Claudel patterns the innovative *versets* of his early twentieth-century *Cinq grandes odes* and other works on the ancient rhythms of biblical poetry: in this conception rhythm itself is the element that is divinely inspired. But even among poets of this type, the positing of a divine origin can take unexpected turns, as happens in the work of Pierre Jean Jouve (1887–1976). More profoundly, perhaps, than the Surrealists, who perceived themselves as the ultimate explorers of the Freudian unconscious, Jouve manages to integrate very pointed aspects of Freud's psychoanalytic theory into his poetic world, even as he builds its themes and structure around Catholic imagery and doctrine. His flexible appropriation of psychoanalysis in fact repeats in some respects the French Renaissance poets' integration of Classical mythology and Platonism. Thus, in the following passage from 'Fairy' in *Diadème* (*Diadem*, 1949), the words that the poet uses are not at all represented as directly motivated or divinely inspired, but rather as irreparably corrupt and fallen from the Queen of Heaven. Inevitably removed by sin from the original purity and creative energy drawn from the Virgin Mary, this world's words are depicted as carrying their energies, along with the sacred seed of their ancestors, into the mouth of a Moloch-like Eros. This God is, of course, the mythological and psychoanalytic personification of sexual desire, a force which Freud, in *Beyond the Pleasure Principle*, describes as inextricably bound with Thanatos, the impulse toward destruction and death:

> LES MOTS N'ONT LEUR NAISSANCE et leur souffle d'enfants
> Ma reine que de toi: s'ils jettent par le sombre
> Dans la bouche d'Eros énorme et dévorant
> Une liqueur sacrée des aïeux très profonde;
>
> Puis un esprit cruel les confronte en poème
> Qui est un mot nouvellement pour l'univers
> Où tout l'aveugle ciel rayonne de la reine
> Par illusion vaste, éternel, et divers.[9]

> *Words only have their birth and their child's breath*
> *From you my queen: while they throw through the dark*
> *In the mouth of enormous and devouring Eros*
> *A sacred liqueur of their ancestors very deep;*
>
> *Then a cruel spirit confronts them in a poem*
> *Which is newly a word for the universe*
> *Where the whole blind sky radiates from the queen*
> *By illusion vast, eternal, and diverse.*

In the second stanza, the "cruel spirit" that "confronts" (or faces and orders) fallen words in the poem is not the loving mind of God, or one inspired by the divine spirit. Rather, it is the fallen, imperfect and harsh judgment of the poet. Accordingly, his creation brings a new kind of word, or being, into the world, one which parallels the Word's incarnation through the Virgin birth. But this creation is only a blind reflection, a simulacrum of heaven, much like the shadows of the cave in Plato's *Republic*. What the poet creates may appear to be as "vast, eternal, and diverse" as the universe itself, but this is only "through illusion." Jouve then shows how even poems adhering to "traditional" religious doctrine can subvert the parallels and connections they set forth between poetry and the word of God.

Thus, while it may be tempting to view early French poetry as globally linked to a divine language model and source, from which modern poetry is generally cut off, this pseudo-historical perspective would be far too simplistic and flatten crucial philosophical variations among different groups and periods. Seventeenth-century Classical poetry, for example, without abandoning a blend of Christian and Antique philosophical models, generally turns away from the typical Platonician Renaissance discourse fusing the poet's representations of spiritual and worldly passions with metaphysical idealism and divine inspiration. Classical poems predominantly pattern themselves instead on a more Aristotelian world view.

In his *Poetics*, Aristotle reverses, for example, Plato's conception of mimesis and of the tragic poet in particular, who had been condemned in *The Republic*, like the painter, as an "imitator" of reality, a creator of illusory representations, "two removes from the king and the truth."[10] In doing this, Aristotle redeems art in general. Most significant for our purposes, he attributes dignity and worth to mimesis, or art as imitation, by redefining it as the representation of human behavior and actions according to certain universal laws. Thus for Aristotle, a poetic text, while it is imitative of both a divine and natural order, is not inherently false, nor is it necessarily inferior to the creations of the natural world. Indeed, poetry represents, for him, one of the highest forms of truth insofar as it is modeled on patterns of order and measure, and presents characters that reflect not just particular individuals, but universal types. Aristotle also rejects the notion of divine inspiration, or poetic madness, set forth in Plato, and views the poet as working as much through his intellect as the philosopher does in creating his own verisimilar representations of truth. The *Poetics* in fact establishes many of the underlying rhetorical principles and philosophical grounds for French Classical poetry's deep concern with reason, order and measure – concerns that we saw expressed in Boileau's *Art poétique*. Finally, Aristotle dismisses "Cratylism," arguing the conventionality of linguistic signs. Following his lead, French poetry then concerns itself most, in the Classical era, with expressing truth as it is reflected in the laws of nature and of human behavior, grounding itself on a bedrock of conventions, and emphasizing the value of reason over that of the passions.

In the Romantic era, along with a privileging of the passions and an attack on mimesis – art is now supposed not to represent nature, but to be one with it – the belief in divine inspiration and divine language returns, as with a vengeance. But the nineteenth century's revival of Renaissance ideals of poetry's divinity remains unwittingly influenced by the relative rationalism and worldliness of Classical poetry. The notion of inspiration becomes, for example, at once typified and individualized in the Romantic Genius, a new kind of poet or poetic persona seen to be at once superior to and at odds with society. Alfred de Vigny's aloof, noble 'Moïse' (Moses) presents us with a compelling avatar of this Romantic hero, whose direct connection to God is at once assumed and protested:

> "L'Orage est dans ma voix, l'éclair est sur ma bouche;
> Aussi, loin de m'aimer, voilà qu'ils tremblent tous,
> Et, quand j'ouvre les bras, on tombe à mes genoux.
> Ô Seigneur! j'ai vécu puissant et solitaire,
> Laissez-moi m'endormir du sommeil de la terre."[11]

> *"The storm is in my voice, the lightning on my mouth;*
> *Thus, far from loving me, see how all people tremble,*
> *And, when I open my arms, each one falls to my knees.*
> *O Lord! I have lived powerful and solitary,*
> *Let me now sleep the sleep of the earth."*

And the notion of divine inspiration can take on an even more accursed and alienated, melancholic turn, as in Nerval's 'El Desdichado.' It is crucial to note, moreover, that in nineteenth- and twentieth-century poems divine inpiration often tends to be drawn straight from nature, without precise reference to religious or philosophical dogma. As for divine language, as we saw with Hugo, though poems may often echo Holy Scripture, such references often have little to do with the poet's belief in the truth of the letter of sacred texts, or in the divine roots of ancient Hebrew. Rather, the ordinary words of the French language, which Hugo helped to make free and available for the poet's use, begin to be perceived as "divine."

Though the perception of God in nature, the exaltation of genius, and the privileging of the passions over reason may be said to have indigenous roots in the works of Jean-Jacques Rousseau, many of the metaphysical and aesthetic concepts underlying nineteenth-century French poetry crystallized in the writings of Kant, F. W. J. Schelling, and the brothers A. W. and Friedrich Schlegel. Thanks in part to their strong ties with such important German poets as Goethe and Novalis, these philosophers' ideas permeated early nineteenth-century Parisian literary circles. Most notably, they were vulgarized by *De l'Allemagne* (*On Germany*), an 1813 treatise of enormous influence by the novelist and salon animator Germaine de Staël (1766–1817).

What is perhaps most important in Romantic doctrine for the history of French poetry is the idea, introduced by Schelling, that beauty is "the infinite represented in the finite," which A. W. Schlegel rephrases thus: "the beautiful is a *symbolic* representation of the infinite."[12] Throughout the nineteenth century, this conception leads to an ever-stronger belief in the absolute value of aesthetic beauty, and also to the elevation of art over other modes of human expression and communication, insofar as it offers a sensorial apprehension of the Ideal.[13] Drawing on Kant's theory of the sublime, Goethe also develops several more pointed ideas which would long be at play in theoretical discussions of French literature, such as a hierarchical distinction between allegory and symbol.

We have already used these terms in their widest literary senses, employing "symbol" to refer either to something that represents something else, or to the concretization of an abstract idea; and "allegory" to refer to complex, detailed figurative representations (such as those in Charles d'Orléans' 'Le temps a laissié son manteau,' the *Fables* of La Fontaine, and Baudelaire's 'L'Invitation au voyage'). The German Romantics' distinction between allegory and symbol involves a more specfic definition of these terms, which illuminates the connection between particular poetic devices and general philosophical ideas. They redefine and favor the symbol as a natural and motivated, sense-oriented type of sign, which arrests our attention on its own modality even as it also evokes something beyond itself; the allegory they view, on the contrary, as an arbitrary, conventional, pre-set modality of representation, in which the sign conveys as immediately and transparently as possible an immaterial concept.[14]

We find striking examples of the French Romantics' penchant for symbols thus defined in Nerval's *Chimères* and Hugo's *Contemplations*. In the latter's 'Ce que dit la bouche d'ombre' ('What the Shadowy Mouth Says'), a spectral voice coming from a seaside gorge speaks to the poet of a nature whose elements obscurely address and signify God:

> Tout parle; l'air qui passe et l'alcyon qui vogue,
> Le brin d'herbe, la fleur, le germe, l'élément.
> T'imaginais-tu donc l'univers autrement?
> Crois-tu que Dieu, par qui la forme sort du nombre,
> Aurait fait à jamais sonner la forêt sombre,
> L'orage, le torrent roulant de noirs limons,
> Le rocher dans les flots, la bête dans les monts,
> La mouche, le buisson, la ronce où croît la mûre,
> Et qu'il n'aurait rien mis dans l'éternel murmure?[15]

> *Everything speaks; the breeze that passes and the kingfisher that sails by,*
> *The blade of grass, the flower, the germ, the element.*
> *Did you then imagine the universe otherwise?*
> *Do you think that God, by whom form comes from number,*
> *Would have made the dark forest forever resonate,*
> *The storm, the torrent rolling with black silts,*
> *The rock in the waves, the beast on the mount,*
> *The fly, the thicket, the blackberry-growing bush,*
> *And that he would have put nothing in the eternal murmur?*

The poem goes on to reveal an entire – and dark – cosmogony while celebrating nature's power to suggest it. Renaissance poetry can sound very much like this kind of symbolism, as in these lines from Ronsard's 'Hymne de l'Automne' ('Autumn's Hymn'), where the poet represents himself as directly inspired (in this case, by Apollo) to interpret nature's divine secrets:

> Il me haussa le cœur, haussa la fantaisie,
> M'inspirant dedans l'ame un don de Poësie,
> Que Dieu n'a concedé qu'à l'esprit agité
> Des poignans aiguillons de sa Divinité.
>   Quand l'homme en est touché il devient un Prophete,
> Il prédit toute chose avant qu'elle soit faite,
> Il cognoist la nature et les secrets des Cieux,
> Et d'un esprit bouillant s'élève entre les Dieux.[16]

> *He lifted my heart, lifted my imagination,*
> *Inspiring in my soul a gift for Poetry,*
> *Which God only grants to the spirit moved*
> *By the sharp spurs of his Divinity.*
>   *When a man is thus touched he becomes a Prophet,*
> *He predicts everything before it takes place,*
> *He knows nature and the secrets of the Heavens,*
> *And with an ardent spirit rises up amongst the Gods.*

In the lines that follow this passage, the emphasis is on "listening" to nature: the poet interprets the symbols of the natural world to reveal its hidden order. Further in the poem, however, Ronsard switches from his initial (and mythical) inspiration to his actual mythological education:

>   [. . .] et de là je vins estre
> Disciple de Dorat, qui long temps fut mon maistre,
> M'apprist la Poësie, et me monstra comment
> On doit feindre et cacher les fables proprement,
> Et à bien desguiser la verité des choses
> D'un fabuleux manteau dont elles sont encloses [. . .][17]

>   *[. . .] and from there on I became*
> *The disciple of Dorat, who was long my teacher,*
> *Who taught me Poetry, and showed me how*
> *One should properly feign and hide in fables,*
> *And to well disguise the truth of things*
> *With a fabulous cloak in which they are enclosed [. . .]*

Here, "Poësie" means something that is learned, the art of starting from a known if difficult truth and constructing a cover of "fables" (meaning mostly pagan mythology) to adorn, protect, and hint at it. Paradoxically, it is at the very moment when a "Nymph" (or earthly spirit) sends him off to live alone in nature that the poet learns (in college) how to discern and present truths through the enticing veil of mythology. Ronsard had learned from his teacher, the Neo-Latin poet Jean Dorat (*c.*1508–1588), that poetry is at heart a "théologie allégorique" (allegorical theology): it communicates the truth about God and nature in a deliberately disguised form (this idea was used to defend poetry against the accusation of being a lie). This deliberateness (finding an outward sign for a truth that is already conceived) would be the mark of what the Romantics called "allegory." But for Renaissance poets there is no contradiction: they are both sensitive to the symbolic power of natural and supernatural signs, and eager to wrap precise meanings in elaborate myths.

Earlier poets (down to the *Grands Rhétoriqueurs* of the late fifteenth century), while pretending to reveal the divine order of the world, do not necessarily claim to be themselves – individually – connected to a divine source. Medieval allegories, such as the thirteenth-century *Roman de la Rose* (*Romance of the Rose*), typically are very long didactic narratives in verse, using personifications to develop a basic metaphor (such as the garden of love, or the pilgrimage of human life), often explicitly translating the meaning of the symbols they propose. Religious allegories show the entire natural world itself to be a representation of the truth set forth in Scripture. This outlook is also evident in shorter religious poems, as in these opening lines from the "argument" of a *Chant Royal* by Jean Parmentier (1494–1529) honoring the Immaculate Conception of the Virgin Mary:

> Par le haut ciel et sa creatïon,
> tout pur, tout beau, sans que alteratïon
> par mixte effect peust degaster sa forme,
> j'entens Marie en sa conceptïon,
> très pure et necte, où n'a eu mixtïon
> de vil péché, qui tous humains difforme.
> C'est le beau ciel plain des orbes et spheres,
> par quoy j'entens toutes vertus prosperes [. . .][18]

> *By the high heaven and its creation*
> *all pure, all beautiful, without alteration*
> *by any mixed effect being able to ruin its form,*
> *I mean Mary in her conception,*
> *pure and clean, where there was no mixture*
> *of vile sin, which deforms all humans.*
> *This is the fair heaven full of orbs and spheres*
> *by which I mean all prosperous virtues [. . .]*

Here the emphasis falls from the start on the divine, immaterial reality that the natural world is said to represent; at the same time the connection is willingly explained by the poet who uses it to construct his allegory. This figurative approach is very different from that of the indirect symbolic representation examined earlier in Baudelaire's prose 'Invitation au Voyage.' There, it is the poet's sensorial contact with his lover that seems to give rise to an expanding figurative 'tableau' – a detailed, metonymic image of her that also appears, paradoxically, to be allegorical. 'L'Invitation au voyage' in fact presents an especially ambiguous mixture of the German Romantics' notions of the allegorical and symbolic, for it emphasizes the natural source of the poet's mysterious images at the same time that it exposes or explains their motivation, and even suggests, by virtue of the prose's reworking of a previous verse version, that the poem's symbolic order has been "conventionally" pre-encoded or fixed by another text.

Thus, though they may not always be framed in philosophical terms, questions of whether and how universal truths may be expressed by a living, creative voice that articulates powerful connections between words, concepts, feelings, and the material things of this world, are continually raised with vastly different perspectives throughout the history of French poetry. Yet, more often than not, these questions are not unequivocally answered. As with the indirectness of poetic political messages, this philosophical ambiguity cannot be unilaterally explained. It has as much to do with the formal, rhythmic nature of poetry, its inherent favoring of rhetorical indirection and its strong appeal to the passions and the senses, as it does with the basic fact that truth itself is not immediately accessible, and remains in this world impossible to behold.

A famous sonnet by Baudelaire, entitled 'Correspondances' ('Correspondences'), well illustrates the equivocal nature of poetry's philosophical statement. The sonnet, which is generally considered to be an *art poétique* – a poetic statement of Baudelaire's own poetic theory – alludes through its title to a theological system developed by the Swedish mystic, natural scientist and biblical scholar Emmanuel Swedenborg (1688–1772), which had enormous impact throughout Europe in the Romantic period. Swedenborg's theory of correspondences sets forth an elaborate network of relations between the visible and invisible worlds, establishing analogies amongst and within the physical, abstract, and spiritual planes. Though the intricacies of this system of "universal analogy" are rarely developed by nineteenth-century French writers, its synthetic explanatory force for them seems clear. Thus, Baudelaire does not hesitate to quote his own interpretation of the theory in 'Correspondances' when attempting to defend and explain to his compatriots the innovative music-dramas of Richard Wagner.[19]

As has also been the case with Wagner's operas, it happens that Baudelaire's 'Correspondances' is often seen to represent the transition between Romantic and modern aesthetics – to the extent that the sonnet functions like an echo chamber for many different kinds of earlier and later texts:[20]

> La Nature est un temple où de vivants piliers
> Laissent parfois sortir de confuses paroles;
> L'homme y passe à travers des forêts de symboles
> Qui l'observent avec des regards familiers.
>
> Comme de longs échos qui de loin se confondent
> Dans une ténébreuse et profonde unité,
> Vaste comme la nuit et comme la clarté,
> Les parfums, les couleurs et les sons se répondent.
>
> Il est des parfums frais comme des chairs d'enfants,
> Doux comme les hautbois, verts comme les prairies,
> – Et d'autres, corrompus, riches et triomphants,
>
> Ayant l'expansion des choses infinies,
> Comme l'ambre, le musc, le benjoin, et l'encens,
> Qui chantent les transports de l'esprit et des sens.[21]

> *Nature is a temple where living pillars*
> *Sometimes let confused words escape;*
> *Man passes there through forests of symbols*
> *Which observe him with familiar looks.*
>
> *Like long echoes becoming confused from afar*
> *In a mysterious and profound unity,*
> *Vast like the night and like clarity,*
> *Perfumes, colors, and sounds correspond / answer each other.*
>
> *There are some perfumes fresh like children's flesh,*
> *Sweet like oboes, green like prairies,*
> *– And others, corrupt, rich, and triumphant,*
>
> *Having the expansion of infinite things,*
> *Like amber, musk, benjamin, and incense,*
> *Which sing the transports of the spirit and senses.*

The sonnet begins by positing a resemblance and connection between the natural, divine, and human worlds (establishing what some have referred to as the "vertical" dimension of Swedenborg's theory), since nature is metaphorically affirmed to be a temple, a holy place, made up of animated, human-like speaking pillars. The evocation of "paroles" or spoken words – which in this context are implicitly divine as well as hyperbolically natural and human – consolidates the connection between these realms, though God, the supposed origin of divine speech, is not named.[22] Indeed, there is no clear will or agency of any kind attributed to the oxymoronic "vivant piliers" making up the "forêt de symboles." Rather, language just emerges sometimes in jumbled words ("confuses paroles") in a world where traditional distinctions between man and nature or subjects and objects are either no longer in play, or dramatically reversed. Thus, "L'homme," normally the speaker, the one considered to be the sole interpretor and manipulator of natural and divine signs, becomes the one who simply passes through (or by) the talking, symbolic trees, who observe him knowingly.

A dramatic syntactic reversal in the second stanza works similarly to overturn our normal sense of the distinction between the human, natural, and supernatural realms, by disordering spatial and temporal sequence. While line 2 refers to a profound unity, giving the poem a mysterious divine center (in accordance with Swedenborg's theological representations of God as the ultimate point of reconciliation of differences, at the beginning and end of all things), the poem's grammar actually emphasizes disorder and difference as much as unity and order. "Echoes," unlike Platonic ideas, are supposed to be secondary effects of natural things. Yet here, they come first, and are shown to be blending into a unity, instead of emerging from it. The disjunction and syntactic inversions of lines 5 and 8, which constitute the stanza's framing simile, add significantly to the sonnet's obscurity. At the same time, in line 7, the contraries of darkness and light in the central similes following the "profonde et ténébreuse unité" (which we might expect to find inextricably fused), are simply set side by side: "vaste comme la nuit et comme la clarté." This establishes a realm of universal analogy, in which the various "vertical" levels of creation are simultaneously unified and distinct, ordered and disordered, and can play interchangeable roles.

As is typically required by the sonnet structure, the tercets elaborate on the same general idea, but attack it from a different angle. Here, the Swedenborgian notion of the interconnectedness and interchangeability of all things will be explored in its "horizontal" dimension, from the perspective of the single worldly plane introduced in line 8, where "Les parfums, les couleurs, et les sons se répondent." This last line of the second quatrain seems to affirm the truth of synesthesia,* a psychological principle asserting the authenticity of exchanges between different modes of sensorial experience. Yet, we find the same ambiguous, paradoxical construction of unity (and of the divine underpinnings of nature and language) in the tercets as we do in the quatrains. For example, the first line seems to emphasize a natural link between words and things, by exposing particular analogies between fresh perfumes and certain fresh and "natural," sense-perceived things – specified things whose precise analogical interrelations appear to be reflected in language. Thus, the adjective "doux," which in French extends from taste to every other sensation (smell, touch, sound, and sight), conveying softness as much as sweetness, here works as a logical lever, connecting fresh perfumes both to the tenderness of children's flesh and the soothing sound of the oboe. Then the verbal pivot of this musical instrument's name, the "hautbois" (originally meaning "high wood") connects all these sensations to the visual greenness of the "prairies." Without necessarily accepting that this first string of analogies depends wholly on the multiple meanings of the words "doux" and "hautbois," we may then agree with Jonathan Culler that the poem links the psychological theory of synesthesia with "verbal art," showing that natural correspondences coincide with "verbal echoes."[23] Thus, there are elements of arbitrariness at play in our inherent or innate "sense" of the natural order and interconnectedness of things. But conversely, in the corrupt, excessive perfumes that triumph in the poem's last lines, there are also, inevitably, core elements of "naturalness." Though the original, organic elements may be both rotten and artificially refined in the perfume-making process (as with the case of musk, an animal gland secretion), they cannot be eradicated from these strong scents' sensorial decadence and spiritual power.

Thus, all of the sonnet's perfumes, the first, fresh ones like the last, decadent ones – which signify no particular analogical relations, but rather the "expansion of infinite things" by either natural or verbal association – remain tied to the natural world like all other things, including "man" and language. Baudelaire sees the order of exchanges between things as "universal," embracing all reality – even though we may read certain correspondences to be more naturally motivated, and others more verbally determined, and even though order itself, in his poems, may appear sometimes analogical (reflecting an order of nature), and sometimes arbitrary (consisting of a mere association in a series). Indeed, as Paul de Man has stressed, the repeated term "comme" (like), on which all the sonnet's analogies rely, subtly changes meaning in the poem's next to last line, taking on the sense of "such as" to introduce the list of powerful scents. This important semantic shift replaces the logic of analogy with that of enumeration.[24] But enumeration can be, even more than analogy, an adequate mode of suggesting the infinite. Finally, though the last "image" of singing perfumes may appear to be the most arbitrary, it actually carries the principle of synesthesia set forth in line 8 to a neat conclusion. And it does this through a stylistic privileging and elevation of olfactory transformations that recurs throughout Baudelaire's poetry. It thus introduces nicely the last line of Baudelaire's *art poétique*, which affirms, through the synesthetic figure, poetry's powerful capacity to move or transport "l'esprit et les sens" (the etymology of "metaphor" is in fact "to carry over," or "to transfer"). Readers can freely interpret these "transports" to be verbal, or natural/physical, or spiritual, or all three, just as the last coupling of the terms "esprit" and "sens" can suggest simultaneously a unity-in-duality of the mind, or the spirit (or both), and of the physical senses, or the words' verbal senses (or both).

It is common to see two "opposing" currents of modern poetry coming out of Baudelaire. Both of these overturn conventions associated with Christian and Classical idealism, but in different ways. The first, which continues to present itself as inspired and visionary, is perhaps best represented by the revolutionary poetics of Rimbaud, whose work still seeks to reveal a superior, "unknown" truth through poetry. Poets of Rimbaud's ilk, far from relying, like their predecessors, on traditional means of divine inspiration, reverent imitation of sacred models, and universal principles of measure to reveal truth, tend to follow an inverse trajectory. They turn their attention inward, toward the exploration of the self's own mind and senses, cultivating both moral evil and aesthetic ugliness, as Lautréamont does, and as Baudelaire had done in *Les Fleurs du mal*, describing rotting corpses or his own depressed state of "spleen," and exposing private vices. And they view the poet, as Rimbaud portrays him in his "Lettre du Voyant" ("Letter from the Seer"), and in *Une saison en enfer*, as a criminal and monstrous figure engaged in a metaphysical revolt, stealing, like Prometheus, the "fire" of knowledge and creation from the Gods. These poets, who are in some respects direct heirs to the Romantics, also tend to treat their models iconoclastically; they purposefully adopt an order of disorder, an anarchichal poetic method which Rimbaud describes as "un long, immense et raisonné *dérèglement* de *tous les sens*" (a long, immense and reasoned *disordering of all senses*).[25] This current reaches its fullest expansion in Dada and the Surrealist movement.

A second current overturns traditional conceptions in a less confrontational way. It lays aside, rather than inverts (or perverts), the mythic, moral and visionary dimension of the poet's persona and presents itself instead as depersonalizing the poetic process. It focuses the reader's attention on the poetic riches inherent in language, rather than developing the Romantic obsession with subjectivity or expanding previous notions of the inspired lyrical voice. This current, which has been widely associated with the influence of Mallarmé, posits "nothingness" in the place of God and presents poetry as a deliberate, painstaking work performed on language by the conscious human mind. Poets of the Mallarméan type underscore the primacy of chance and of chaos, both in the natural universe and in the world of language (Mallarmé even recommends the ceding of poetic initiative to words),[26] but contrary to Rimbaud-styled poets, they seek to constrain this principle, rather than to give it free rein.

Developing in certain respects the formal poetic values of the mid-nineteenth-century neo-Classical, Parnassian school, this current – which tends to attribute to poetry no other philosophical "end" than the poem's own perfect beauty, the attainment of an autonomous aesthetic ideal – indeed reaches new heights in the hermetic, chiseled perfection of Mallarmé's sonnets. But Mallarmé adds a tragic dimension to this perspective. We need only recall 'Le vierge, le vivace et le bel aujourd'hui,' where the "present" allegorical swan/poet/sign's own dream of the ideal, or desire to realize its own perfect song and flight, is explicitly linked to a lucid, paralyzing self-consciousness. The swan's refusal either to ignore or to be carried away by illusory transports of the mind and senses (of the very same kind that Baudelaire celebrates) is what keeps him trapped in a ghostly present and grounded in metaphysical despair. Paradoxically, this philosophical double-bind creates in Mallarmé one of the richest new sources of beauty for modern poetry, just as the dying swan's agonizingly sterile conditions generate multiple intricate layers of pristine imagery and crystalline sound.

The 'Sonnet en yx' ('Sonnet in yx') perhaps the best known of Mallarmé's sonnets, holds up a similar conundrum, underscoring the "void" that grounds modern poetry, but it does this from an angle that appears less subjective. Indeed, this poem, which Mallarmé himself described as a "sonnet nul et se réfléchissant de toutes les façons" (a nullified/non-existent sonnet and one reflecting itself in all ways) does not focus, even symbolically, on any lyrical voice or poetic presence at all. Rather, it evokes the dispersed, reflexive, allegorical effects of the absence at the poem's own empty center:

> Ses purs ongles très haut dédiant leur onyx,
> L'Angoisse ce minuit, soutient, lampadophore,
> Maint rêve vespéral brûlé par le Phénix
> Que ne recueille pas de cinéraire amphore
>
> Sur les crédences, au salon vide: nul ptyx,
> Aboli bibelot d'inanité sonore,
> (Car le Maître est allé puiser des pleurs au Styx
> Avec ce seul objet dont le Néant s'honore.)
>
> Mais proche la croisée au nord vacante, un or
> Agonise selon peut-être le décor
> Des licornes ruant du feu contre une nixe,
>
> Elle, défunte nue en le miroir, encor
> Que, dans l'oubli fermé par le cadre, se fixe
> De scintillations sitôt le septuor.[27]

> *Her pure nails very high dedicating their onyx,*
> *Anguish this midnight, suspends, torch-bearer,*
> *So many vesperal dreams burnt by the Phoenix*
> *Which no cinerary amphora gathers*
>
> *On the credence-tables, in the empty salon: no ptyx,*
> *Abolished trinket of sonorous inanity,*
> *(For the Master has gone to draw tears from the Styx*
> *Taking this sole object that Nothingness honors itself with.)*
>
> *But near the vacant window to the north, a gold*
> *Agonizes according perhaps to the décor*
> *Of unicorns kicking up fire against a nix,*
>
> *She, defunct, nude/cloud in the mirror, even*
> *As, in the oblivion closed by the frame, forthwith is*
> *Being fixed in scintillations the Septet.*

Mallarmé himself provided the clearest commentary on what this sonnet "represents" in describing how the details of an "etching full of Emptiness and Dream" could render its emotional and visual effects:

> [. . .] a nocturnal open window, the two shutters fastened; a room with no one inside, despite the stable mood that the fastened shutters convey, and in a night made of absence and interrogation, without furniture, except for the plausible sketch of some vague console-tables, the frame, bellicose and agonizing, of a mirror hanging on the far wall, with its reflection, stellar and incomprehensible, of the Big Dipper, which links solely to the sky this dwelling abandoned by the world.[28]

The circular and reflexive quality of this sonnet's auto-negating, self-cancelling representation, and the centrality within it of the unknown word "ptyx,"[29] first used here to name the non-existent object featured in the second stanza (the "aboli bibelot d'inanité sonore"), have generated much theoretical debate. Some critics have invested the word "ptyx" with symbolical meanings, others have emphasized rather its non-referential status, its value as a pure verbal artifact serving only to complete the difficult rhyme pattern in "-yx." And relying with equal justification on the poem's original title – 'Sonnet allégorique de lui-même' ('Sonnet Allegorical of Itself') – to support their views, readers have interpreted the sonnet to represent things as different as a ritual evocation of philosophical Nothingness, a parodical spoof, or a mechanical "exercise in verbal exercise."[30]

Readers' perceptions of Mallarmé's texts typically reverse themselves in this way, and this divided response is appropriate insofar as his poetics is profoundly paradoxical. Indeed, we shall see that Mallarmé's emphasis on the purity and autonomy of poetic form, which we have highlighted in relation to his sonnets, is diametrically reversed in less traditionally constructed texts that appear to annex the features of other art forms. Considered from this new perspective, Mallarmé is a "revolutionary" poet to the degree that he became, along with Rimbaud and Lautréamont, one of the most crucial influences for twentieth-century avant-garde poets. Mallarmé's insistence on the autonomy of poetry inaugurates, nonetheless, an important rebirth of Classicism in modern times, particularly through the influence of his most prominent disciple and commentator, Paul Valéry. It is Valéry more than any other poet who preserves a tradition of formalism in early twentieth-century French verse. At the same time, Valéry's theory of poetry as an "art of language," "where sound and sense take on equal importance" and give "the illusion of their profound intimacy,"[31] has been crucial for the development of French criticism during the later half of the twentieth century, beginning with the Structuralist reflection on language and figures.

While Valéry wrote masses of private and public theoretical reflections on poetry and other arts, one of the pillars of his own poetic theory is the firm distinction that he draws between poetry and philosophy. Of overly conceptual or intellectual poets (which he himself has been perceived to be), he wrote disparagingly: "Poètes-philosophes (Vigny, etc.). C'est confondre un peintre de marine avec un capitaine de vaisseau . . ." (Poet-philosophers [Vigny, etc.] This confuses a sea-scape painter with a ship captain . . .)[32] What is more, at the very moment when he describes poetry as an intellectual exercise, Valéry refuses to grant it any kind of metaphysical or absolute truth value. He presents the poem instead as a verbal apparatus whose meaning the reader can freely interpret according to his own lights, while being emotionally affected by the text.[33] And though he admits that the first line comes to the poet as a gift from "the Gods" (or chance),[34] he sees great poetry on the whole not as the byproduct of enthusiasm, be it divinely inspired or decadently induced, but as the work of constructing one's own original voice through a conscious "misappropriation" of literary influences − a process that Valéry famously described as follows: "There is nothing more original, nothing that is more one-self than to nourish oneself with others. But they must be digested. The lion is made of assimilated sheep."[35]

This view of poetry can be grasped from 'Le Rameur' ('The Rower'), an allegorical representation of the poet's journey, which assimilates and transforms the water imagery of a number of nineteenth-century poems. Among these are Baudelaire's 'Voyage,' which presents poetry as a daring exploration of everything, including death, for the discovery of the "new;" several of Mallarmé's sea poems, which convey paradoxical pictures of the poet's quest, suggesting failure and success, movement and immobility; and especially Rimbaud's 'Le Bateau ivre' ('The Drunken Boat'), which unleashes the poet/boat, completely unguided, on the "poem of the sea." Included in *Charmes*, a collection published in 1922 (five years after his great poem *La Jeune Parque* (*The Young Fate*) put an end to twenty-five years of poetic silence), Valéry's 'Rameur' presents the poet as a patient laborer, who, far from being simply carried away by the beauty of the world (and others' poetic renderings of it), works against the natural current of inspiration:

> Penché contre un grand fleuve, infiniment mes rames
> M'arrachent à regret aux riants environs;
> Âme aux pesantes mains, pleines des avirons,
> Il faut que le ciel cède au glas des lentes lames.
>
> Le cœur dur, l'œil distrait des beautés que je bats,
> Laissant autour de moi mûrir des cercles d'onde,
> Je veux à larges coups rompre l'illustre monde
> De feuilles et de feu que je chante tout bas.[36]

Bent against a great river, infinitely my oars
Tear me reluctantly from the pleasant surroundings;
Soul with heavy hands, filled with their oars,
The sky must cede to the passing-bell of slow waves/blades.

Heavy-hearted, my eye distracted by the beauties that I beat,
Letting circles of water around me grow,
I want with wide strokes to rupture the illustrious world
Of leaves and of fire that I sing very low.

Further stanzas develop the poet's progress toward the end of his journey –
an end which is only death – and underscore his resistance to being swayed
by the illusory "charms" of this world. Valéry's use of the word "charmes,"
here and in the collection's title, plays on the term's original (musical and
magical) sense of incantation. His conscious opposition to succumbing to
these "charms" and to following the river's current anticipates, in a sense,
the lucid revolt that Camus and other existentialists in the 1940s would call
for in front of the meaninglessness of death:

Jamais, charmes du jour, jamais vos grâces n'ont
Tant souffert d'un rebelle essayant sa défense:
Mais, comme les soleils m'ont tiré de l'enfance,
Je remonte à la source où cesse même un nom.

Never, charms of the day, never have your graces
Suffered so from a rebel trying to defend himself:
But, just as the suns have taken me from childhood,
I must return to the source where even a name ceases.

The poem closes with the rower proudly embracing material darkness and
rejecting the ideal world:

Sous les ponts annelés, l'eau profonde me porte,
Voûtes pleines de vent, de murmure et de nuit,
Ils courent sur un front qu'ils écrasent d'ennui,
Mais dont l'os orgueilleux est plus dur que leur porte.

Leur nuit passe longtemps. L'âme baisse sous eux
Ses sensibles soleils et ses promptes paupières,
Quand, par le mouvement qui me revêt de pierres,
Je m'enfonce au mépris de tant d'azur oiseux.

Under the ringed bridges, the deep water carries me,
Vaults full of wind, of murmur, and of night,
They run across a brow that they crush with ennui,
But whose proud bone is harder than their door.

Their night is long in passing. The soul lowers under them
Its sensitive suns and its prompt eyelids,
When, by a movement that again covers me with stones,
I plunge forward with disdain for so much idle blue.

Yet Valéry's poems do not typically end on this somber note. In other texts, which often take death as their point of departure, conscious observation of the human condition and lucid emotional resistance to the world's charms give way finally to a kind of liberation, a tentative celebration of nature and the human spirit. This open, energized and energizing aspect of Valéry's conception of poetic creation is apparent in the flapping book and flying page imagery with which he closes his most famous poem, 'Le Cimetière marin' ('The Seaside Cemetery'):

> Le vent se lève! . . . il faut tenter de vivre!
> L'air immense ouvre et referme mon livre,
> La vague en poudre ose jaillir des rocs!
> Envolez-vous, pages tout éblouies!
> Rompez, vagues! Rompez d'eaux réjouies
> Ce toit tranquille où picoraient des focs![37]

> *The wind is rising! . . . one must try to live!*
> *The immense air opens and recloses my book,*
> *The pulverized wave dares to jut out from the rocks!*
> *Fly away, pages all dazzled!*
> *Break, waves! Break with rejoicing waters*
> *This tranquil roof where jib-sails were pecking!*

Other classically oriented twentieth-century poets, such as Catherine Pozzi (1882–1934), Valéry's lover (who remained largely unpublished and unrecognized in her lifetime), still hark back, as we saw Jouve does in Christian terms, to a more traditional conception of poetic inspiration – one that links it with a transcendent conception of love. Much in the vein of Louise Labé's Renaissance sonnets (to which her poem 'Nyx,' ['Nyx,' goddess of the night] pays homage), Pozzi celebrates love and her own devotion to it in a 1929 poem entitled 'Ave' ('Hail'), presenting them as the only sacred absolutes of her poetry. She does this even as she admits to the possibility of her own spiritual mortality and acknowledges that she may never know the source and identity (or even the "reality") of love:

> Très haut amour, s'il se peut que je meure
> Sans avoir su d'où je vous possédais,
> En quel soleil était votre demeure
> En quel passé votre temps, en quelle heure
> Je vous aimais [. . .][38]

> *Most high love, if it may be that I die*
> *Without having known from where I possessed you,*
> *In which sun your dwelling was,*
> *In which past your time was, in which hour*
> *I loved you [. . .]*

Notwithstanding being aware of her own impending death and loss of self-consciousness – which she expresses in a further stanza: "Quand je serai pour moi-même perdue / Et divisée à l'abîme infini" (When I will become lost to myself / And divided into the infinite abyss) – the poet expresses confidence that some avatar of her "name" and "image" will be remade by the nameless, faceless force of love. The love she salutes thus is and begets a kind of identity-in-difference that binds all things; it is the absent "center" of an infinite spectral vision (or "mirage"), both generating and following from her temporally severed devotion:

> Par l'univers en mille corps brisée,
> De mille instants non rassemblés encor,
> De cendre aux cieux jusqu'au néant vannée,
> Vous referez pour une étrange année
> Un seul trésor
>
> Vous referez mon nom et mon image
> De mille corps emportés par le jour,
> Vive unité sans nom et sans visage,
> Cœur de l'esprit, ô centre du mirage
> Très haut amour.

> *By the universe in a thousand bodies broken,*
> *From a thousand instants not yet gathered,*
> *From the ash of heaven winnowed unto nothingness,*
> *You will remake for a strange year*
> *One sole treasure*
>
> *You will remake my name and my image*
> *From a thousand bodies carried off by the day,*
> *Living unity wthout name and without face,*
> *Heart of the spirit, o center of the mirage*
> *Most high love.*

We find a different yet equally powerful sacralization of the poet's vision of love in a famous poem by Robert Desnos (1900–1945), who was considered by Breton to be one of the most authentic Surrealists because of his ability to immediately and faithfully transcribe the uncensored activity of his unconscious through hypnotic dream states. The 1926 prose poem entitled 'J'ai tant rêvé de toi' ('I've dreamed of you so much'), repeatedly links from its opening lines the intensity of the poet's love with that of his dreaming, suggesting that both of these states have a greater hold on him than material reality:

> J'ai tant rêvé de toi que tu perds ta réalité.
> Est-il encore temps d'atteindre ce corps vivant et de baiser sur cette bouche la naissance de la voix qui m'est chère?

J'ai tant rêvé de toi que mes bras habitués, en étreignant ton ombre, à se croiser sur ma poitrine ne se plieraient pas au contour de ton corps, peut-être.

Et que, devant l'apparence réelle de ce qui me hante et me gouverne depuis des jours et des années, je deviendrais une ombre sans doute.

I've dreamed of you so much that you are losing your reality.

Is there still time to reach that living body and to kiss on that mouth the birth of the voice which is dear to me?

I've dreamed of you so much that my arms accustomed, in embracing your shadow, to crossing themselves on my chest might not adapt to the contour of your body, perhaps.

And that, faced with the real appearance of that which has haunted and governed me for days and years, I would become a shadow no doubt.

The beloved woman becomes a ghostly being through the poet's imagination, and he dreams of her to the point of no longer waking up and losing sense of his own corporeality; in the final lines he anticipates becoming a "phantom among phantoms."[39]

Another well-known Surrealist love poem, from Éluard's 1929 collection *L'amour la poésie* (*Love/poetry*), shows, finally, how artificial (if pedagogically convenient) it can be to emphasize the opposing philosophical perspectives dividing poets into different movements:

La terre est bleue comme une orange
Jamais une erreur les mots ne mentent pas
Ils ne vous donnent plus à chanter
Au tour des baisers de s'entendre
Les fous et les amours
Elle sa bouche d'alliance
Tous les secrets tous les sourires
Et quels vêtements d'indulgence
À la croire toute nue.

Les guêpes fleurissent vert
L'aube se passe autour du cou
Un collier de fenêtres
Des ailes couvrent les feuilles
Tu as toutes les joies solaires
Tout le soleil sur la terre
Sur les chemins de ta beauté.[40]

The earth is blue like an orange
Never an error words do not lie
They don't make you sing any more
It's time for kisses to understand each other
Fools and loves
She her ringed mouth

All the secrets all the smiles
And what garments of indulgence
To believe her all naked.

The wasps flower green
Dawn slips around her neck
A string of windows
Wings cover the leaves
You have all the solar joys
All the sun on the earth
On the paths of your beauty

The first line of this poem presents a typical Surrealist image, a coupling of incompatible terms (of the kind we saw Breton recommend) that illuminates an unexpected truth about the world and thought. At the same time, the second line, as though denying the apparent mistake of the first, seems either to assert the general infallibility of truth in language, or to adopt the logic of formalism in poetry, affirming (as the neo-Classical, "anti-Surrealist" Valéry does) that it has no relation to any truth outside itself. But however one wishes to interpret the philosophical message that seems crypted in this poem, it presents itself – thanks to the central figure of the earth – as "universal," also suggesting like Baudelaire's 'Correspondances,' the simultaneous naturalness and arbitrariness of poetic signs. There are, for example, both "symbolic" and "allegorical" values in the rhetorical ornaments of stanzas one and two: the earth's (or the beloved's) "garments of indulgence" and the dawn's "string of windows." The poem celebrates, as many of the poems we have been examining do, a kind of cosmic communion and an all-embracing form of love.

This is not to say that particular philosophical "ideas" play no role in shaping poetic currents. On the contrary, beyond Surrealism, as in the Romantic period, the central ideological pull of French poetry comes again from concepts articulated in German philosophy, this time by Martin Heidegger. Heidegger is an important figure for French culture at large. His primary work *Being and Time* (1927) was key to the development of Sartre's *Being and Nothingness* (1944), the philosophical treatise grounding French existentialism. However, Heidegger's high conception of poetry could not be more different from Sartre's. With exceptions, such as his enthusiastic endorsement of the Negritude movement in *L'Orphée noir*, the French philosopher generally dismisses modern poetry as decadent, bourgeois self-indulgence.

In a number of writings devoted to the German Romantic poet Hölderlin, Heidegger, by contrast, attributes to a certain kind of "thinking" poetry – that is, a poetry reflecting on the fundamental nature of its own creations – the highest of all philosophical functions: the revelation of being, or presence itself. Acknowledging the absence of God and the finality of death and consciousness, his hierarchical view of poetic creation places the self-conscious, earth-bound, always ruptured unity between poetic language and the world at the foundation of truth. This perspective appeals strongly to many French poets in the second half of the twentieth century, beginning with René Char, who corresponded extensively with Heidegger. Without attempting to map the vast and problematic relations between recent French poetry and Heidegger's complex thought, let us cite the final "leitmotif" from a famous 1936 lecture that the philosopher gave on Hölderlin (translated and widely read in France the following year), and consider some of its reverberations in late twentieth-century French poetry. This phrase is in fact borrowed from Hölderlin's own verse: "Riche en mérites, c'est poétiquement pourtant / Que l'homme habite sur cette terre" (Rich in merit, it is nonetheless poetically / That man dwells on this earth).[41]

We shall begin with a 1958 essay, *L'Acte et le lieu de la poésie* (*The Act and Place of Poetry*), by Yves Bonnefoy (1923–), which puts together a "negative theology" very close to that of Heidegger, suggesting that presence, or being, can only be seized in this world through the articulation of its absence, or withdrawal. "Language," declares Bonnefoy "is not the Word."[42] Because modern poets cannot "escape the nothingness that eats away at things," they must, following Baudelaire, celebrate the "cruel lacunas of being in existence,"[43] and recognize the void that grounds human language, and thus poetry. Mallarmé's *Crise de vers* draws our attention to this central nothingness, pointing to the plurality of languages, and to such fundamental differences as that between ordinary (literal) and figurative expression, and writing and speech. For Bonnefoy, the connection between consciousness and the world can only be revealed through the breach inscribed and reflected in the self-conscious poetic language that connects them. His poetry thus hyperbolically embraces mortality and the most basic intimations of both contact and disconnection between matter and consciousness, as in the starkly celebratory poems of his 1953 collection, *Du mouvement et de l'immobilité de Douve* (*Of the Movement and Immobility of Douve*).

As in much of the previous poetry we have been examining, what we find in *Douve* is predominantly lyricism (the musical expression of subjective experience) gathered in a string of autoreferential love poems. The extreme originality and earthiness of Bonnefoy's beloved muse, however, is apparent from the outset in her name. Far from conjuring up a heavenly, transcendent being, in the tradition of Petrarch's Laura or even Scève's Délie, "Douve" evokes a hollowed, dug-out tract of earth, the water-filled moat surrounding castle fortifications, and other symbolic ditches. Thus, the opening lines of 'Vrai nom' ('True Name') (in accordance with the notion of the ontological "inhabitation" of the earth) show the poet, in anticipation of Douve's death, preparing to name the world after a series of negated manifestations of her former, beloved presence:

> Je nommerai désert ce château que tu fus,
> Nuit cette voix, absence ton visage,
> Et quand tu tomberas dans la terre stérile
> Je nommerai néant l'éclair qui t'a porté.
>
> Mourir est un pays que tu aimais. Je viens
> Mais éternellement par tes sombres chemins.[44]
> [. . .]
>
> *I will name desert that castle that you were,*
> *Night that voice, absence your face,*
> *And when you fall into the sterile earth*
> *I will name nothingness the lightning flash that bore you.*
>
> *Dying is a country that you loved. I am coming*
> *But eternally by your dark paths.*
> *[. . .]*

Note the masculine participle "porté": the poet addresses the "true name" instead of Douve herself, as though to further emphasize the distance between her and his own speech, however faithful.

Then a further poem, 'Vrai corps' ('True Body'), elaborates that it is only after Douve's burial – in the moment arising from the cold finality of her body's closure, and surviving the burning "frost" of the lovers' ultimate, most broken (and sealed) intimacy – that the poet will be able to speak of his beloved's "true body" and, paradoxically, from a position within her being:

> Close la bouche et lavé le visage,
> Purifié le corps, enseveli
> Ce destin éclairant dans la terre du verbe,
> Et le mariage le plus bas s'est accompli.
>
> Tue cette voix qui criait à ma face
> Que nous étions hagards et séparés,
> Murés ces yeux: et je tiens Douve morte
> Dans l'âpreté de soi avec moi refermée.
>
> Et si grand soit le froid qui monte de ton être,
> Si brûlant soit le gel de notre intimité,
> Douve, je parle en toi; et je t'enserre
> Dans l'acte de connaître et de nommer.[45]
>
> *Closed the mouth and washed the face,*
> *Purified the body, buried*
> *This lucent destiny in the earth of the word,*
> *And the lowest marriage is accomplished.*
>
> *Silenced that voice that cried to my face*
> *That we where haggard and separated,*

Walled up those eyes: and I hold Douve dead
In the harshness of herself with myself shut again.

And however great the cold that arises from your being,
However burning the frost of our intimacy,
Douve, I speak in you; and I enclose you
In the act of knowing and of naming.

Without sharing the same style, or aesthetic, or all the same ideas, a number of contemporary French and Francophone poets have a "Heideggerian" orientation similar to Bonnefoy's. We find, for example, a continual emphasis on the poem's establishment of our being in this world in the work of the Breton poet Eugène Guillevic (1907–1997), as in these brief maxims from his 1989 *Art poétique*:

Écrire le poème
C'est d'ici se donner un ailleurs
Plus ici qu'auparavant.

To write the poem
Is to give oneself from here an elsewhere
More here than before.

Le poème
Nous met au monde.[46]

The poem
Brings us into the world.

The poems of Philippe Jaccottet (1925–), a Swiss-born poet who has long resided in Provence and translated many German writers into French (including Hölderlin and Rilke), do not always strike the reader as predominantly reflexive and theoretical. Yet they record how the poet comes upon revelations of being in the natural world, as happens in this first section of 'Au petit jour' ('At Dawn'), a triptych from his collection *L'Ignorant* ('The Ignorant One,' 1958). Here, the very foundations of life are quietly explained and softly illuminated, as hidden beauty – the leaf-covered "abode of the violet" – is "established," constituting the "countryless" poet's "last refuge":

La nuit n'est pas ce que l'on croit, revers du feu,
chute du jour et négation de la lumière,
mais subterfuge fait pour nous ouvrir les yeux
sur ce qui reste irrévélé tant qu'on l'éclaire.

Les zélés serviteurs du visible éloignés,
sous le feuillage des ténèbres est établie
la demeure de la violette, le dernier
refuge de celui qui vieillit sans patrie . . .[47]

The night is not what one thinks, the reverse of fire,
fall of the day and negation of the light,
but a subterfuge made to open our eyes
to that which remains unrevealed as long as it is being lit.

Once distanced the zealous servants of the visible,
under the leaves of the darkness is established
the abode of the violet, the last
refuge of he who ages without a country . . .

In the last parts of the triptych, however, the poet cannot help asking how to say "cette chose qui est trop pure pour la voix" (this thing that is too pure for the voice). His lyricism remains fragile and conscious of what separates it from the world it celebrates.

Within the broad flow of Heideggerian influence, "opposing currents" seem again to have formed, tempting critics to divide contemporary French and Francophone poets into speculative, "textualist," "logolâtrique" (that is, word-idolizing) poets, and lyrical ones. Elaborating on these distinctions can be helpful when we are trying to understand the directions that French poetry has been taking of late.[48] Yet, the explanatory value of currents is limited from the start. One problem in this case is that speculative, word-reflexive, and lyrical elements tend to co-mingle. Another is that such currents tend to carry far more in their wake than poetry presenting itself as directly engaged with them; they often build on the works of poets who do not consider themselves to be involved with philosophical questions at all.

To be sure, some poetic works appear to be more conceptual, or language-driven, or object-oriented, or lyrical than others. And most poets have a marked philosophical orientation even though we may not think of them – or they might prefer not to be thought of – in that light. Francis Ponge has been central to many philosophical discussions of French poetry, though he often said that he was not involved in expressing philosophical ideas. Describing himself as a materialist, he claimed only the attempt to inscribe things in all their concreteness within the separate but multi-dimensional world of words. At first glance, his poems may also strike the reader as "purely objective," refusing speculativeness, logolatrism, or lyricism, or all three. In fact, as the philosopher Jacques Derrida has shown, there is no fundamental difference in the treatment of the sign, the subject, and the object in Ponge's writing; all of these elements are inextricably "bound" in an exemplary way[49] (as they must be everywhere from Derrida's own point of view). Critics like Michel Collot have also underscored how Ponge's own comments reveal an inherent, paradoxical subjectivity in his approach to objects and to words. The poet "admits that he is incapable of 'knowing [him]self, otherwise than through applying himself to things'"; and that "others will only be able to know [him] through the accent of [his] representation of the world." But he also maintains that words are themselves "mysterious objects," "immobile reserves of sentimental flights" coming to the aid of "man who no longer knows how to dance [. . .]."[50]

'Le Soleil placé en abîme' ('The Sun Repeated in a Mirror/Placed in the Abyss') – a poem often cited because of the philosophical symbolism of its object – formally develops both the concrete and the abstract (or signified, immaterial) nature of the thing/word that captures the poet's attention as he inscribes it into the text. As one reaches its conclusion, the poem fulfills several different objectives at the same time. Thanks to the following passage's remarkable typographical arrangement – showcasing the title, which sounds like that of an allegorical tableau – we notice that the poem is at the same time "purely" verbal and reflexive, and yet also performative and iconic, having to be "seen" by its reader. Underscoring the conventions of writing and printing, this humorous text actually performs and physically incorporates the "mirroring" act it refers to (*mise en abîme* is the literary term for a representation reflecting itself in the text): the sun named in the title and at the top of the text is made to "rise" within and above it.

LE SOLEIL SE LEVANT SUR LA LITTÉRATURE

QUE LE SOLEIL À L'HORIZON DU TEXTE SE MONTRE ENFIN COMME ON LE VOIT ICI POUR LA PREMIÈRE FOIS EN LITTÉRATURE SOUS LES ESPÈCES DE SON NOM INCORPORÉ DANS LA PREMIÈRE LIGNE DE FAÇON QU'IL SEMBLE S'ÉLEVER PEU À PEU QUOIQUE À L'INTÉRIEUR TOUJOURS DE LA JUSTIFICATION POUR PARAÎTRE BRILLER BIENTÔT EN HAUT ET À GAUCHE DE LA PAGE DONT IL FAIT L'OBJET, VOILÀ QUI EST NORMAL ÉTANT DONNÉ LE MODE D'ÉCRITURE ADOPTÉ DANS NOS RÉGIONS COMME AUSSI DU POINT DE VUE OÙ PUISQU'IL M'EN CROIT SE SUBROGEANT CONTINUELLEMENT À MOI-MÊME SE TROUVE ACTUELLEMENT SITUÉ LE LECTEUR.[51]

THE SUN RISING ON LITERATURE

THAT THE SUN ON THE HORIZON OF THE TEXT SHOULD SHOW ITSELF AT LAST AS ONE SEES IT HERE FOR THE FIRST TIME IN LITERATURE IN THE FORM OF ITS NAME INCORPORATED IN THE FIRST LINE SUCH THAT IT SEEMS TO RISE LITTLE BY LITTLE THOUGH STILL WITHIN THE JUSTIFICATION SO AS SOON TO APPEAR TO SHINE AT THE TOP AND TO THE LEFT OF THE PAGE WHOSE OBJECT IT IS, (THIS) IS NORMAL GIVEN THE MODE OF WRITING ADOPTED IN OUR REGIONS AND ALSO FROM THE POINT OF VIEW WHERE SINCE HE TAKES MY WORD FOR IT CONTINUALLY SUBSTITUTING HIMSELF FOR ME THE READER IS CURRENTLY LOCATED.

At the close of the poem, we find a passionate and parodical invocation of the sun's afternoon and evening presence, personified as a monstrous lover; also, an erotic image of the poet's completed act of entering and consecrating her (textual) being. This takes the form of a symbolic signature:

> Ô Soleil, monstrueuse amie, putain rousse! Tenant ta tête horripilante dans mon bras gauche, c'est allongé contre toi, tout au long de la longue cuisse de cet après-midi, que dans les convulsions du crépuscule, parmi les draps sens dessus dessous de la réciprocité trouvant enfin dès longtemps ouvertes les portes humides de ton centre, j'y enfoncerai mon porte-plume et t'inonderai de mon encre opaline par le côté droit.
>
> *Le soleil était entré dans le miroir. La vérité ne s'y vit plus. Aussitôt éblouie et bientôt cuite, coagulée comme un œuf.*[52]

> *O Sun, monstrous lover, red-haired whore! Holding your hair-raising/horrific head in my left arm, it is lying against you, all along the long thigh of this afternoon, that in the convulsions of sunset, among the tangled sheets of reciprocity finding at last the long open humid doors of your center, I'll thrust/plunge my pen in there and flood you with my opaline ink through the right side.*
>
> The sun had entered the mirror. Truth no longer saw itself / was no longer seen there. Dazzled forthwith and soon cooked, coagulated like an egg.

In the last italicized lines, the mirror into which the poet, the sun, and its symbolic "truth" ultimately disappear, corresponds quite concretely to the rhetorical figure of the *mise en abîme*. We might conclude that this image signals, for Ponge, the opacity as well as the ultimate figurativity of all things.

In a very different way, Michel Deguy (1930–) also disrupts traditional philosophical distinctions between subjects, objects, and signs, vehemently refusing the notion that there is an inside and an outside to poetic language. A translator and commentator of Heidegger, Deguy instead underscores both in poetry and theoretical prose (genres which often come together and overlap in his work) the rhetorical configuration of being. Thus "L'être-comme" ("Being-as"), a chapter from his 1987 *La Poésie n'est pas seule* (*Poetry is Not Alone*), glosses Éluard's 'La terre est bleue comme une orange' and other texts, exploring correspondences between the structure of presence, the (mimetic) image's re-presentation of material reality, and the linguistic pivot that holds rhetorical comparisons together.[53] This same knot of ideas is also central to many of his poems; in his collection of *Gisants* (a title evoking the recumbent statues on tombstones), it is, for example, immediately apparent in the title of the theoretical prose poem 'Compas-raison' ('Compass-reason/Comparison'). But Deguy's reflection on the nature of "being-as" is equally crucial to 'L'Iconoclaste' ('The Iconoclast'), a longer, more lyrical poem recently added to the collection, which an 'Avant-propos' refers to as a summary *art poétique*. I will cite this poem in a very fragmentary way and present its verses as a kind of coda to our discussion of French poetry's relations with philosophy. (The initial mention of "Guillaume" alludes to a *canso* by the *Troubadour* Guillaume IX, 'Farai un vers de dreyt nien' ['I'll make verse out of pure nothing']):

> Plutôt que de rien comme Guillaume
> Je puis écrire un poème avec tout-et-rien
> En tout rien tout bonheur
> Est-ce cela que l'on attend?
>
> Tu seras réduit en temps
> Sablier ton corps passe en âme
> Ton âme distendue
> Poussière maintenant heure par heure
> Tout devient temps. Le temps se perd
> La mort étend sa pulvérisation
> Que restera-t-il entre les seins de la parenthèse?
> Tes dernières paroles
> [. . .]
> Que ton visage n'exprime rien
> Je souhaite que s'y annule la différence
> Entre un dedans et un dehors
> [. . .]
> Trans-en-danse
> Le *trans* est la fiction
>
> Comme si là-bas était au-delà
> D'au-delà nul ne revient
> [. . .]
> Je cherche par où l'être-comme n'est pas l'être-à-l'image.
> Cherchant comme quoi il est et à quoi ressembler, l'homme-nous
> [. . .]
> Le principe est celui de l'hospitalité
> [. . .]
> L'imagination est l'hôte de l'inconnaissable
> Ayant plongé au fond de l'inconnu
> Elle en revient en poèmes chez les humains
> Leur dit avec les images
> C'est inimaginable mais c'est comme ça.[54]

> *Rather than from nothing like Guillaume*
> *I can write a poem with all-and-nothing*
> *In every nothing all happiness*
> *Is that what is expected? / we are waiting for?*
>
> *You will be reduced in time*
> *Hourglass your body passes into soul*

Your soul distended
Dust now hour by hour
Everything becomes time. Time loses itself
Death spreads its pulverisation
What will remain between the breasts of the parenthesis?
Your last words

[. . .]
Let your face express nothing
I wish to be anulled there the difference
Between an outside and an inside

[. . .]
Trans-in-dance
The trans *is the fiction*

As though over there was beyond
From beyond no one returns
[. . .]
I am seeking the way by which being-as is not being-in-the-image-of.
Seeking what we-man is like and what [he] should resemble
[. . .]
The principle is that of hospitality
[. . .]
The imagination is the guest/host of the unknowable
Having plunged to the bottom of the unknown
It comes back in poems where humans live
Says to them with images
It's unimaginable but it's like that.

We need not bring to light the full sense of these lines to see how they gather and echo many of the themes and problems we have discussed. The opening stanza sets forth, for example, the philosophical stakes of the text: whether or not we expect it, what will emerge from the poem is at once "all-and-nothing" – an unlimited, divided yet indivisible entity – which also constitutes the poem's materials. This position once established, the second stanza shifts to a more lyrical, subjective perspective, representing the poem's addressee and principle object, as so many of the above-cited poems have, as a woman withdrawing in and through time. What best resists time's pulverizing process is at the same time mortal and verbal: this woman's last words – that which emanates directly from her body, and yet remains disjunct from it. The operation on the word "transcendance" ("trans-en-danse") captures contemporary French poetry's characteristic break with that notion, redefining it as something which is not (really) of the order of the ideal (or the metaphysically true in itself), but rather, hyperbolically corporeal (like the activity of dance) and made up by man. The italicized repetition of the prefix "*trans*" recalls, moreover, the ambiguous status of the "transports de l'esprit et des sens" on which Baudelaire's 'Correspondances' closed. In the lines that begin with the affirmation "Je cherche," Deguy formulates the central concern of his poetics: the difference between "being-as" as *mode* of being and as *image* of being, the latter pertaining to the longstanding notion of representation posited in mimetic theories of poetry and art. It is the "principle of hospitality," and thus implicitly a new relational notion of the way in which poetry inhabits the world, that seems to provide a decisive if irremediably circular end to his quest. On this earth ("chez les humains"), concludes Deguy, the imagination is "l'hôte," that is, according to the French term's double meaning, at once the "indweller" and the "visitor" of the unknowable. Thanks to the imagination's return to us in the form of poems, we hear and see what unimaginable being is like.

This relational conception, which presents itself as universal, or, at least, as geographically and ethnically unmarked, curiously dovetails with another, more politically oriented discourse on the nature of poetry – a "poetics of relation" opposing all universalizing conceptions of identity, proposed by the Martinican poet, novelist and essayist Édouard Glissant (1928–). Following such ex-centric French poets as Segalen and Saint-John Perse, Glissant's verse and prose epic, *Les Indes* (*The Indies*, 1955),[55] does not present the poetic act as the foundation of an earthly presence, let alone the conquest and settling of a native land. Rather, it becomes the recounting of an incessant crossing impulse, symbolized by an eternal sea-voyage toward an always "other" imaginary place. A more recent collection, *Les Grands Chaos* (*The Great Chaoses*, 1993), travels back to Paris to describe a group of homeless people on Place Furstemberg, whom Glissant presents as emblems of the world's chaos – from which new languages and new poetry are emerging:

> Ceux qu'Histoire a débattus et jetés là. Mais aussi la parole déroulée de leur errance. Ils détournent la raison suffisante de ces langages dont ils usent, et c'est par des contraires de l'ode ou de l'harmonie: des désodes. [. . .] Leurs dialogues sont d'allégorie. Folles préciosités, science non sue, idiomes baroques de ces Grands Chaos. Venus de partout, ils décentrent le connu. Errants et offensés, ils enseignent. Quelles voix débattent là, qui annoncent toutes les langues qu'il se pourra?[56]
>
> *Those whom History has beaten / struggled with and thrown there. But the unfolded speech of their wandering as well. They misappropriate the sufficient reason of those languages that they use, and do so by the opposites of odes or harmony: dis-odes. [. . .] Their dialogues are allegorical. Mad preciosities, unknown science, baroque idioms of those Great Chaoses. Coming from everywhere, they decenter what is known. Wandering and offended, they teach. What voices are struggling/debating there, announcing all the languages that can be?*

Citing in his essays the theoretical models of Gilles Deleuze and Félix Guattari – thinkers who have argued against unified or single-root conceptions of being – Glissant rejects the very notion that poetry comes from or expresses any one thing at all. Comparing and connecting it to the continuous mixing of identities which affects all nations and all people, he views poetry as the site of encounters (sometimes violent and oppressive, sometimes liberating) between disparate modes of being: not as an anchor, but as an unmooring.

As fresh and challenging as this conception is, we have observed many similar transformations and interweavings throughout the whole of French poetry, which despite our emphasis on "French" aspects we have hesitated to define otherwise than as a network of poems composed in the language known as French. As for saying what "poetry" itself is, while we remember that it can be defined as an aesthetically marked form of language that draws attention to "itself," we have also seen that this reflexiveness in fact opens it up to a world of other things. Let us then briefly reflect, by way of conclusion, on yet another field of relations from which poetic language draws much of its power: poetry's kinship with other forms of art.

Epilogue: Poetry and other arts

The consideration of poetry's relationships with such domains as politics and philosophy helps, paradoxically, to reveal its own intrinsic nature, shedding light also on its status within the wider world of French culture. When we examine how poems wield, shun, and reflect power within the context of given socio-political realities, or when we explore, conversely, how they construct their own origins and aims from a more "universal" perspective, we come to know broadly what poetry says and does. Similarly, we can come to understand much about how poetry moves us by considering its relations with other art forms.

We have already encountered scattered aspects and examples of such relations. I shall now return to some of these references and draw on them as threads to bring our study to a close: the focus will be primarily French poetry's kinship with music and visual arts. The phrase *Ut pictura poesis* (as in a painting so in a poem) from the *De Arte poetica* (*On the Art of Poetry*) of the Latin poet Horace (65–8 BC) may well be the most celebrated statement on the nature of poetry: so, we'll give some interpretations of its meaning the last word. It is fitting, however, to start by evoking French lyric poetry's historical relationship to music, since, as we saw, it literally began with the courtly love songs of the medieval *Troubadours* and *Trouvères*, such as this "chanson" (song) by Thibaut de Champagne (1201–1253), which weaves the themes of music, nature, love, and death:

> Li rosignox chante tant
> Que mors chiet de l'aubre jus;
> Si bele mort ne vit nus,
> Tant douce ne si plaisant.
> Autressi muir en chantant à plainz criz,
> Ne je ne puis de ma dame estre oïz,
> N'ele de moi pitiez avoir ne daigne.[1]

> *The nightingale sings so much*
> *That it falls dead under the tree;*
> *No one ever saw such a beautiful death,*
> *So sweet and pleasurable.*

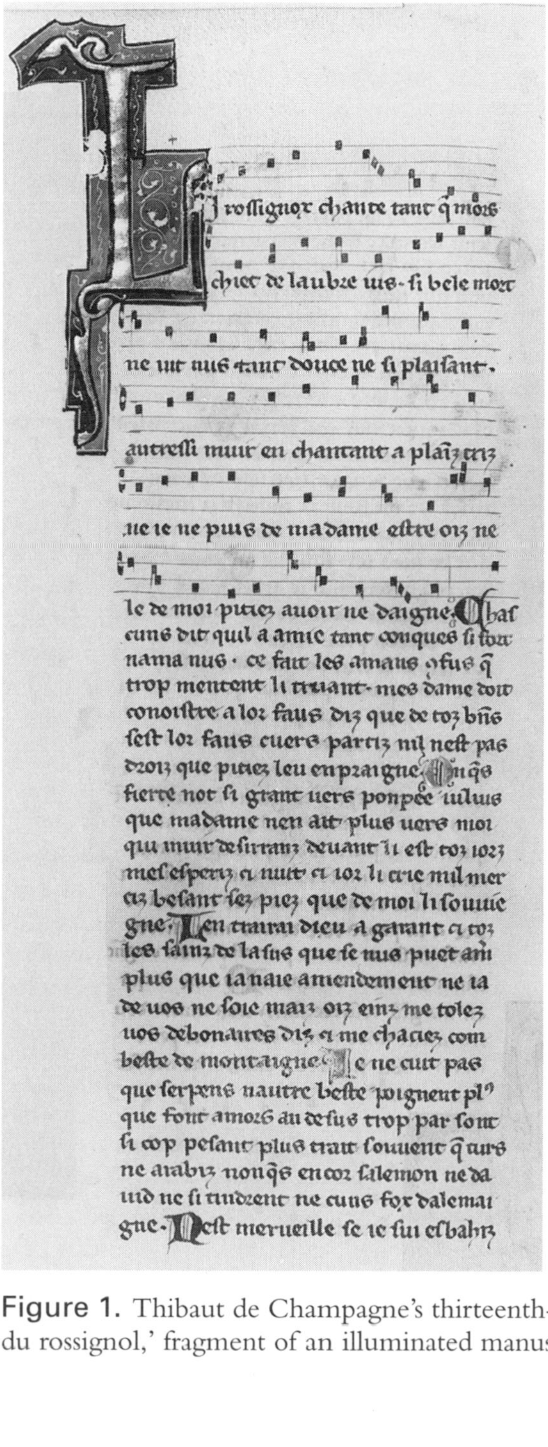

Figure 1. Thibaut de Champagne's thirteenth–century 'La Mort du rossignol,' fragment of an illuminated manuscript.

Similarly I die singing at the top of my voice,
I cannot make my lady hear me,
Nor does she deign take pity on me.

Evidence that French poetry retains some of its original, powerful connection with music in modern times can be found even in adamant statements affirming its independence. In 1924, Valéry defined, for example, the Symbolist movement in the following terms: "What was baptised: *Symbolism* can be summarized simply as the intention, common to many families of poets (otherwise enemies among themselves), to 'take back their own from Music.' "[2] In fact, this apparent contradiction – whereby poetry's autonomous fruition grows out of an ever-recurring rivalry with music – should be seen as central to the development of both arts in France from the start.

It is no accident that the first forms of unsung lyric poetry were developed in the fourteenth century by medieval France's greatest composer, Guillaume de Machaut, who, we remarked, divided his own œuvre of rondeaux and ballades into musically notated and un-notated pieces. The role that Machaut's musical expertise played in fixing and refining the intrinsic verbal music of short French verse forms might not seem obvious today. But we recall that verse itself is generally defined by rhythm and measure – properties which are also fundamental to music – and that the emerging distinctive features of French poetry's rhythms grow out of particular accentual and phonic traits inherent in the French language – sound features that Machaut as a poet-musician was bound to be sensitive to.

We saw, for example, that the progressive weakening and terminality of French accent in the Middle Ages relate to the numerical regularity of French verse as well as its heavy dependence on rhyme. Similarly, old French stanzaic structures, which originally accomodate a loose correspondence between homophonic vocalic sonorities and a relatively simple melodic structure (as with the assonantic *laisses* of the *Chanson de Roland*) develop through the fourteenth and fifteenth centuries into increasingly controlled and complex rhyme patterns having less and less to do with any particular tonal or melodic determination. The final imposition, in the Renaissance, of the rule requiring alternation of masculine and feminine rhymes completes, in a sense, the separation of poetic structures from musical ones. The rule had, at first, a musical foundation: organizing the distribution of terminal *e muets* (still heard in the sixteenth century), it facilitated the setting of poems to "syllabic" music (with one-to-one correspondence of notes and syllables), so that decasyllables, for example, would in fact alternate with hendecasyllables (counting the final e) in an expected, systematic way. However, as "melismatic" composition developed (in which a group of notes can be sung to a single syllable), the rule's musical motivation became obsolete.[3] By the same token, from the perspective of verse alone, which itself was growing more and more detached from serving the needs of music, the addition of a gender-balancing feature compensated (sometimes only visually) for the disappearance of any implied or actual musical support. From this point forward, most of the rules and conventions of the Classical age aim to clarify and enhance the internal proportions, sense, and rhythmicity of the alexandrine, the favored meter of a strictly standardized poetic language designed mainly to be read (or recited in the theater), lending itself only incidentally to song.

It can thus be said that the road to the ultimate stabilization of French verse began with Machaut's dual compositions, a practice whose theory was developed by his disciple Eustache Deschamps. In his 1392 *Art de dictier*, Deschamps draws an important distinction between "natural" and "artificial" music. The latter is defined as the art of making melodies "par figure de notes, par clefs, et par lignes" (by the figure of notes, key-signatures, and lines), be this with musical instruments or the human voice, and Deschamps insists that it can be learned by "le plus rude homme du monde" (the roughest man in the world). "Musique naturelle," by contrast, is defined as purely oral and verbal, as the art of making "la musique de bouche en proférant paroules metrifiees" (the music of the mouth proffering metered words) without recourse to musical notes, and it is deemed at once more basic to man's noble nature than melody making and more reflective of cultural refinement.[4] Deschamps has, of course, no objection to the marriage of natural (verbal) music and melody in song, which remains a predominant means of short poems' delivery through the Renaissance, but he sees verse as realizing in itself a higher, more pure form of music. Deschamps (like Machaut before him) considered music to be an art primarily concerned with number, balance, and proportion. Just as in Antiquity music was associated with mathematics rather than with grammar and rhetoric – as with Pythagoras' harmony of the spheres – in the Middle Ages it was perceived as the most exact expression of the principle of order. In adopting St. Augustine's conception that "Music is the science of good measurement" and in treating unsung verse as a kind of music analogous and allied to melody, Deschamps' poetic theory does not differ significantly from that of other major European poets of the Middle Ages, including Dante.[5]

Accordingly, the musical quality of early French poetry had little or nothing to do with mimesis, or imitative, onomatopoeic representations of the kind that would become important in modern times. Indeed, as James I. Wimsatt has shown, French medieval verse forms typically forgo even with developing specific points of conjunction between sound and sense.

Thus, Machaut the composer fixes, regulates and complicates the intrinsic rhythmic and harmonic features of his verse in notated and un-notated *ballades* alike, with little regard for establishing precise internal correspondences between purely verbal, or verbal plus melodic, sound "effects," and the *meaning* of particular words.[6] (Though, as might be expected, the semantic value of words is even less determinant in the unfolding of his complex melodic structures than in the composition of his un-notated pieces.) The meaning of the rhymed words, which are often "predictable," is not necessarily crucial to the harmonious feeling produced by their acoustic effect; in such cases, the sense is "ancillary," or subservient, allowing by its non-interference a kind of echoing of the sound:[7]

> Amours, ma dame et Fortune et mi oeil,
> Et la tresgrant biauté dont elle est plaine
> Ont mis mon cuer, ma pensee et mon veuil
> Et mon desir en son tresdoulz demaine;
>   Mais Fortune seulement
> Me fait languir trop dolereusement [. . .][8]

> *Love, my lady, and Fortune, and my eyes,*
> *And the very great beauty with which she is filled*
> *Have placed my heart, my thought, and my will,*
> *And my desire in her most sweet power;*
>   *However Fortune*
> *Makes me languish in great pain [. . .]*

Indeed, we saw that the rhyming elements of French words often consist of semantically neutral elements such as suffixes and grammatical endings. In connection with this fact, Wimsatt makes a further interesting distinction between the relative weight of meaning in the rhetorical sound figures of Middle English and French verse, pointing especially to the former's early favoring of alliterative effects which do underscore particular words' meanings to a far greater degree than rhyme. Through an English poet as important as Geoffrey Chaucer (1343–1400), the critic demonstrates the historical impact of medieval French verse forms on English prosody; the former introduces an initial, foreign element of regularity discouraging the latter's own natural accords of sound and sense. Though Chaucer's prosody, in poems such as 'To Rosemounde,' is inherently more accentual and semantically overdetermined by word-based stresses than is Machaut's, by virtue of its English language expression, it could not have evolved from native English lyrics, which rely on alliterative and assonantic effects. Rather, it is imitative of the un-notated ballads of Machaut.[9] In this light, Charles d'Orléans' double stature as a significant representative of both Middle English and Middle

French poetry in the fifteenth century, far from seeming a random political accident, appears logical and well prepared.

In the seventeenth century, as French poetry tends increasingly to deny its original affiliation with song, lyricism, we saw, gives way to other dramatic, satirical, and didactic forms – forms whose rules and conventions are set by powerful authorities (such as Boileau) and institutions (such as the Académie Française) at the heart of an increasingly autocratic and centralized French culture. Thus, it is not surprising that when lyricism regains strength in the Romantic period, and as music and poetry become more and more closely reallied in the nineteenth century, this happens, in turn, under the influence of other cultures, and operates against Classical rules and conventions, once touted as reasonable and natural, now looked on as arbitrary and artificial.

In his *Lettre sur la musique française* (*Letter on French Music*, 1753) and his *Essai sur l'origine des langues* (*Essay on the Origin of Languages*, posthumously published in 1781) the writer and composer Rousseau, who is often credited for having introduced lyricism into French prose, encouraged his contemporaries to embrace Italian vocal music's simple according of sound and sense, and reject the modern system of harmony developed by his rival composer Jean-Philippe Rameau (1683–1764). Rousseau saw Rameau's complex harmonic structures as a means of masking a fundamental void of expressivity and subjective feeling in French melodies (which he felt was determined by the monotone quality of the French language – its relative weakness of accent and melodiousness).[10] In the following decades, many of Rousseau's admirers would voice similar complaints regarding the traditional metrical devices of poetry, treating these as hollow trappings devised to disguise a lack of natural meaning and sincere feeling in French verse. This points to a reversal in the nineteenth-century conception of both music and literature. Partly under the influence of such important Romantic composers as Beethoven, Liszt, and Chopin, French poets no longer think of music in mathematical terms, but rather increasingly as a mimetic expression of the individual human passions and also of nature's own sublime creative force. Naturally, this changed conception of music also transforms through time their sense of what poetry's own intrinsic "musicality" should be.

Thus, Baudelaire's 1861 essay defending the music of Wagner especially welcomes the German composer's development of meaningful links between the words and music of his music-dramas: operas where the traditional fixed structures of arias and recitatives give way to newly mixed and contoured lines of "unending melody" which include mimetic elements – short recurring musical themes called *leitmotifs*. What is more, Wagner's ambiguous treatment of harmony and melody, and his substitution of onomatopoeic and alliterative effects for rhyme in his operas' librettos, may well have directly influenced the formal development of Baudelaire's own prose poems. In one of these, we saw how Baudelaire sought in purely verbal terms to do away with the constraints of number and measure, so as to produce the "miracle of a poetic prose, musical without [fixed] rhythm and without rhyme," and therefore adequate to express directly the movement of his own soul. Alongside its mockery of poetic conventions, the "music" of Laforgue's ground-breaking free verse tends similarly to be alliterative, onomatopoeic, and ironically calibrated on subjective feeling.[11]

In the Symbolist period generally, when the rules and conventions of Classical French verse are being most forcefully overthrown, just as in the seventeenth century when they are being most forcefully implemented, music functions more as a model and metaphor for poetry than as an implied or actual complement. When Boileau refers to "cadence" and "harmony" in his *Art poétique*, he is talking about the inherent rhythmic balance and euphoniousness of the alexandrine; whereas when Verlaine calls for "music above all" in his 'Art poétique' two centuries later, what he encourages first of all is a rupture with this even verse's weighty, well-poised sound (though he, of course, also undermines several other key aspects of Classical rhetoric, which he disdainfully labels "Littérature"). For Verlaine, in a light and breezy melodic way, as for Mallarmé, in a heavier, more elaborate and complex harmonic sense, modern French poetry, by following the course of a newly extended notion of music, can free, regenerate, and expand itself.

Thus, in *La Musique et les Lettres* (*Music and Letters*), a lecture delivered at Oxford and Cambridge in 1894, Mallarmé defines the two arts as wholly self-sufficient and yet inextricably related – as the "alternative sides" of one same phenomenon, which in the Hegelian philosophical tradition he calls "the Idea." Contemporary humanity, he states, can encounter the "Mystery" of being either by experiencing it through the senses in concert halls, or apprehending it silently in books on an individual basis. He sees this mystery as consisting of nothing but the aesthetic outpouring and mirroring of the innermost human self in its double condition of body and mind, or spirit. Though Mallarmé's language in the whole of his theoretical writings is remarkably poetic, lofty and obscure,[12] the types of music and literature that he deems capable of performing this revelation are mobile and diverse, ranging from such low genres as the song of a country woman to the high liturgy of the Catholic Mass. Thus, *Crise de vers* begins by expanding the notion of verse to include all "Littérature," or stylistically marked writing, and invokes different musical instruments as metaphors to represent the modalities and meters used by poets in France, be they orthodox or newly discovered and individualistic. And yet Mallarmé was as anxious to preserve Classical French verse and to assert its autonomy and supremacy as he was bold with experimentation and determined to bind poetry to the world by allying it with other arts.[13] The tentative theatricality of such classically measured texts as *L'Après-midi d'un faune*, which Debussy, in 1892, chose to transpose rather than to set to music, and the unfinished Mystery play *Les Noces d'Hérodiade* (*The Wedding of Hérodiade*) show this contradiction to some degree. But it is even more apparent in *Un coup de dés jamais n'abolira le hasard*, the text that Mallarmé himself, against all conventions, suggested that we recite with changing dynamics and intonations, along the lines of a musical score.[14]

Variously dispersed across the high, low, and middle spaces of eleven double pages, this text appears at first glance to be a random explosion of words. But in time and through repeated reflective readings (whether silently or out loud), the fragments reveal a dense, intricate, interconnected body of verse, whose sense is often paradoxical because of the plural possibilities offered by flexible syntactic conjunctions. In fact, the syntactic interrelations and thematic and compositional importance of the verse fragments prove to be meticulously correlated to different types and sizes of print, which guide the reader's eye. Too long and graphically complex to cite here, the poem tells of a cosmic disaster where symbolic figures, ranging from Mallarmé, the Master himself, to Hamlet and a mythical siren, ephemerally appear and disappear from the scene of a hypothetical shipwreck. Ultimately, as one of the main organizing themes of the poem intermittently states, "R I E N / [...] N'AURA EU LIEU / [...] QUE LE LIEU" (NOTHING / [...] WILL HAVE TAKEN PLACE / [...] BUT THE PLACE). And yet, as in the final line of the "Sonnet en yx," the last and lasting image of the text is that, irrepressibly hopeful, of a constellation – here stars representing an on-going metaphorical dice-roll, rather than the fixture of seven well-ordered rhymes. Whether or not we regard it as fateful, this heavenly mirroring of the writing on the page anticipates much of what we have seen in modern French poetry, including Ponge's reflexive, ideographic conclusion to 'Le Soleil placé en abîme.'

It is possible to see various iconic figures in the typographical arrangement of *Un coup de dés* (a listing ship, a whirlpool, a constellation). However, its aesthetic value, while materially concrete and emotionally expressive is, for the most part, representationally abstract. Mallarmé's 'Préface' describes it as a "mise en scène spirituelle exacte," a precise, dynamic visual representation of the poem's reading process before he presents it as a musical score. Because the visual dimension of the poem cannot be separated from its inscription and is therefore not as "open" to the reader's interpretation as the musical one (which, depending on one's viewpoint, the graphism might be seen either to determine or reflect), it has long been treated as the text's most fundamental and revolutionary aspect. But however critics might wish to weigh or interpret the musical and visual dimensions of this text, both have

EXCEPTÉ

à l'altitude

PEUT-ÊTRE

aussi loin qu'un endroit

fusionne avec au delà

hors l'intérêt

quant à lui signalé

en général

selon telle obliquité par telle déclivité

de feux

vers

ce doit être

le Septentrion aussi Nord

UNE CONSTELLATION

froide d'oubli et de désuétude

pas tant

qu'elle n'énumère

sur quelque surface vacante et supérieure

le heurt successif

sidéralement

d'un compte total en formation

veillant

doutant

roulant

brillant et méditant

avant de s'arrêter

à quelque point dernier qui le sacre

Toute Pensée émet un Coup de Dés

Figure 2. Last double–page of Stéphane Mallarmé's 1897 *Un coup de dés jamais n'abolira le hasard.*

played a major role in formally redefining modern poetry as well as in expanding its cultural role. The poem is generally recognized to have had a seminal impact on the whole of twentieth-century French poetry, but also to have been critical for artists and composers such as Marcel Duchamp, Pierre Boulez, and John Cage. In this sense, *Un coup de dés* contributes to the rise of France's cultural power at the turn of the century, an ascendency manifest not only in the separate fields of poetry, music, and the visual arts, but also in many types of multimedia works in Paris, where far-flung European artists, ranging from the Spanish painter Picasso to the Russian ballet impresario Diaghilev, gathered to work out aesthetic principles that still predominate in Western art.

In certain ways, the revolutionary enthusiasm of this modernist period, with its multiple manifestoes, mirrors the ebullient, collective cultural activity of the French Renaissance. However, the fact that the Renaissance was imported from Italy (the relatively weaker political force) led French poets of that time not so much to embrace the idea of an international movement (which humanism was in some respects) as to become involved in an intense rivalry with Italian culture. We saw this in some detail in our consideration of the sonnet form and in the thematics of Du Bellay's *Regrets*. This Franco-Italian rivalry often intersected with and played itself out as a rivalry between poetry and the visual arts, in a "paragone" (or comparison) of the sister arts' relative worth that raged through the sixteenth century.

Evidence of this growing competition can already be noted in the work of the *Rhétoriqueur* Lemaire de Belges. His "prosimètre" *La Plainte du désiré* (*Lament for the Desired One*, 1503), mourning the death of an illustrious young patron, the Count of Ligny, stages an allegorical competition between "Peinture" and "Rhétorique." Presented as the two principal handmaidens of "Nature," the two arts attempt in long, brilliant verse speeches to console her (and the public). Painting flaunts her wealth of resources,

> J'ay pinceaulx mille, et brosses, et ostilz,
> Or et asur tout plain mes cocquillettes;
> J'ay des ouvriers tant nobles et gentilz,
> Engins soubdains, agus, frecz et subtilz;
> J'ay des couleurs blanches et vermeillettes;
> D'inventions j'ay plaines corbeillettes [. . .][15]

> *I have a thousand brushes, fine and thick, and tools,*
> *Gold and azure aplenty in my little shells;*
> *I have such noble and gentle craftsmen,*
> *Quick minds, acute, fresh, and subtle;*
> *I have colors white and vermilion;*
> *I have basketfuls of inventions [. . .]*

and lines up a predominantly Italian array of "children" led by Leonardo da Vinci, with his "graces supernes" and remarkable mimetic skills. Yet, though she moves her listeners to tears, she fails to either represent Nature's pain or to console her. Rhetoric on the other hand, after enlisting the soothing aid of Music, is more successful insofar as she endeavors to retrace Ligny's historical destiny. Thus, Lemaire shows the consolation of Nature to depend on a more traditional, utilitarian form of rhetoric, whose focus would remain the recounting and illustration of the feats of great men.[16]

Despite this theoretical resistance, Lemaire's own writing, whether in the above *Plainte*, in the verse of the *Concorde des deux langages* (*Concord of the Two Languages*, *c.*1511) comparing the merits of French and Italian, or in his historical prose, is especially remembered for its vivid imagery and powerful mimetic descriptions. And as French poetry separated itself from history, its rivalry with Italian painting only intensified. Ronsard, who is also famous for his rich imagery, often used painting as a metaphor for his poetry, wrote poems based on ekphrasis* (the literary representation of either real or imagined works of art), and payed homage in verse to many artists of his day, as in his *Élégie à Janet* (*Elegy to Janet*), celebrating the preeminent court painter Jean Clouet.[17] And Du Bellay shows how entangled the inter-arts rivalry was with the Franco-Italian one when, writing his *Regrets* from his Roman "exile," he humbly closes one of his sonnets by comparing Ronsard to the great Michelangelo (thereby figuratively expatriating his paramount French rival in his place), and comparing himself in turn with Clouet, perhaps the world's "second-best," but still the most important portrait painter in France.[18] Ronsard for his part complained that the subsidies he needed for *La Franciade* were being squandered by his patrons, Kings Henry II and Charles IX, on expensive buildings designed and decorated by Italian architects and painters (among others).[19]

But what was the theoretical basis for this conflict between visual art and poetry? What was the aesthetical wealth that each was attempting to appropriate for itself? Whereas Horace's *Ut pictura poesis* simply states in context that well-made poems, like good paintings, can tolerate more light and scrutiny than bad ones, within the Renaissance "paragone" debates (and since) it has generally been seen to assert the essential equality and sameness of the two arts. At the same time, other statements from Antiquity underscoring differences in their modalities of representation were interpreted to affirm the supremacy of either poetry or painting. Most famously, Leonardo da Vinci, whose *Trattato de Pittura* (*Treatise on Painting*) aimed to elevate painting from the status of a mechanical to a philosophical art, countered the ancient Greek poet Simonides of Ceos' aphorism that "painting is mute poetry; poetry a speaking painting," with the statement that "the painter may call poetry blind painting" instead.[20] This points to the contrary nature of verbal and visual signs, which formed the conceptual core of the paragon debates. Da Vinci naturally privileges the sense of sight, and argues that visual (or material) images offer representations that are at once more natural, intellectually accessible, and emotionally powerful than those evoked with words. Ronsard and other poets tend naturally to argue for the artistic primacy of language, emphasizing the advantages (rather than the disadvantages) of its relative disjunction from nature or material reality – which allows literature to stand the test of time better than visual art – its semantic precision, and its diachronic (or temporal) unfolding through the mediation of a subject or living voice.

We will not linger here on the relations between poetry and visual arts during the periods of French lyric poetry's relative dormancy, though two points are worth emphasizing. The first is that lines and color, the basic modalities of visual representation, figure heavily in this period's philosophical discussions of the origins of language and poetry (including Rousseau's *Essai*) just as fundamental aspects of music do. The second, correlated point is that philosophical discussions of this kind in eighteenth-century France contributed significantly to the birth of Romanticism in England and in Germany. Morevoer, such important theoretical issues for Romantic poetry as the distinction between allegory and symbol, and the privileging (by Hugo and others) of Grotesque styles, often emerge from eighteenth-century debates on visual art objects. Thus, when Baudelaire assumes the role of a major nineteenth-century art critic, promoting as his own the very different aesthetics of the major Romantic painter Delacroix and the (minor) "painter of modern life" Constantin Guys, he is following in the tradition of such important philosophers as the *Encyclopédie* editor, Denis Diderot.

I will not dwell either on a discussion of the relationship between Symbolism and visual art, except to say that the Baudelairian theory of correspondences that it develops, and which we have repeatedly discussed, is by definition as involved with positing a relationship between verbal and visual art as it is with establishing one between music and poetry. We need only to recall Rimbaud's 'Voyelles' or to think of his theory of "Voyance." As for Mallarmé, he summarizes his own Symbolist poetics of suggestion in the following terms: "*Peindre, non la chose, mais l'effet qu'elle produit*" [Paint, not the object, but the effect that it produces],[21] a statement which both maintains the pictorial reference and displaces it decisively.

In the first decades of the twentieth century, Apollinaire filled the role of the preeminent French poet/art critic. The principal champion of Cubist painting in France, he coined, we saw, the term "surrealism" in his program notes for the revolutionary Diaghilev ballet *Parade*, and was also central to developing the verbal-visual graphic experimentation begun by Mallarmé.

Figure 3. 'La Colombe poignardée et le jet d'eau,' from Guillaume Apollinaire's 1918 *Calligrammes*.

Though his 1918 *Calligrammes* (*Calligrams*) were preceded in Italy by Marinetti's *Zang Tumb Tumb, parole in libertà,* (*Zang Tumb Tumb, words in Freedom*) and in France by Cendrars' innovative blending of verse with Delaunay's painting in *Prose du Transsibérien*, this collection is unquestionably one of the major inaugurating works of modern concrete poetry. 'LA COLOMBE POIGNARDÉE ET LE JET D'EAU' ('The Stabbed Dove and the Fountain'), perhaps the most moving and certainly the most famous of these visual poems, laments the scattering of the poet's friends in World War I. The poem is an iconic memorial, while remaining intensely lyrical: under a dove made of women's names, the fountain spouting from the eye (whose pupil is the exclamation "O") reanimates the age-old *ubi sunt . . .?* (where are . . .?) topos.[22]

Surrealism was started by poets, but painters such as Max Ernst or Giorgio de Chirico and photographers such as Man Ray soon played a crucial role in providing their own, non-verbal versions of the surrealist "image." Indeed, though music always remains relevant to lyric poetry, poetry's alliance (as opposed to rivalry) with visual art predominated in twentieth-century France – although Jacques Prévert, for one, is more known for lyrics to songs such as 'Les feuilles mortes' ('Dead Leaves') than for his whimsical collages.[23] Outside the domain of popular song, and notwithstanding the remarkable lyrics of singer-songwriters from Aristide Bruant to Georges Brassens, poet-musicians, like poet-music critics, are a rare breed, whereas poet-art critics and poet-artists are common. Claudel, Reverdy, and Bonnefoy, for example, count among the most respected French writers on painting, as does Jacques Dupin (1927–), another major contemporary poet. As for the tradition of the poet-graphic artist, though such radical practitioners as Isidore Isou, the 1940s "Lettriste," or the 1960s "Spatialiste" Pierre Garnier are still not considered "mainstream," the use of graphic effects and textual space has become crucial to most French poets: hence Deguy's verbal-visual operation on "trans-en-danse" in 'L'Iconoclaste,' and Ponge's typographical arrangement of 'Le Soleil placé en abîme.' 'La Nue' and many other poems by André du Bouchet (1924–2001), another important poet, recall the use of textual space in Mallarmé's *Un coup de dés*.[24] Artaud's first works were cryptic poems and his last were hallucinatory drawings. But the deep yet complex connection between poetry and visual art in the contemporary French tradition is perhaps best represented by the work of the poet-painter Henri Michaux, whose creations show as much the divergence as the convergence or analogy of verbal and visual expression.[25]

Michaux, as we saw, wrote in an ever-changing, chameleon-like poetic style – noted, paradoxically, for its utter individuality. Though first and foremost a poet, he recognized and embraced (notably in experiences with mescaline) such inherent advantages of visual art as its free instantaneous wholeness. But the image's all-at-onceness also calls forth from him its in-terpretive, diachronic complement: a reading. Thus his response to another painter's work, the *Lecture de huit lithographies de Zao Wou-Ki* (*Reading of Eight Lithographs by Zao Wou-Ki*), begins:

> Books are boring to read. No free circulation. We're invited to follow. The way is traced, unique.
>
> A painting is completely different: Immediate, total. To the left, also to the right, in depth, at will.
>
> No path, a thousand paths, and the pauses are not marked. As soon as one likes, the painting all over again, whole. In an instant, everything is there.
>
> Everything, but nothing is known yet. It is here that one must truly begin to READ.[26]

As might be expected, the "readings" that accompany Zao Wou-ki's lithographs are poems. Since poems, like pictures, are not ultimately meant for academic reading, let me here then end by allowing your own response to one of Michaux's most powerful drawings, *LA FACE À LA BOUCHE PERDUE* (*THE FACE WITH THE LOST MOUTH*). In the collection *Peintures et dessins*, the text that serves this image as a caption is printed in red on the page to the left – an arrangement which combines the effects of word and image even as it respects their autonomy. I have chosen this last offering because it captures French poetry's wanderings in our own time; also because it illustrates why, in truth, no introduction can communicate what poetry itself is; we have to listen up or look directly, then look and listen within.

> Nous n'avons plus nos mots. Ils ont reculé en nous-mêmes. En vérité, elle vit, elle erre parmi nous *LA FACE À LA BOUCHE PERDUE* . . .[27]
>
> *We no longer have our words. They have moved back in ourselves. In truth, it lives, it roams amongst us* THE FACE WITH THE LOST MOUTH . . .

Figure 4. 'LA FACE À LA BOUCHE PERDUE,' from Henri Michaux' 1946 *Peintures et dessins.*

Notes

Prologue

1. J. Du Bellay, *La Deffence et illustration de la langue françoyse*, ed. H. Chamard (Paris: STFM, 1970), pp. 27–28.
2. *Ibid.*, p. 40.
3. *Ibid.*, pp. 22–25.
4. *Ibid.*, pp. 38–41.
5. The asterisks signal the first occurrence of literary terms defined in the glossary.
6. *Ibid.*, pp. 100 and 41.
7. *Ibid.*, pp. 103–104 and 184–185.
8. *Ibid.*, p. 178.
9. S. Mallarmé, *Œuvres complètes*, ed. H. Mondor (Paris: Gallimard, 1945), p. 360.
10. *Ibid.*, pp. 360–361.
11. *Ibid.*, pp. 362–368.
12. *Ibid.*, p. 361.
13. A. Breton, *Manifestoes of Surrealism*, trans. R. Seaver and H. R. Lane (Ann Arbor: The University of Michigan Press, 1969), p. 26.
14. *Ibid.*, p. 27.
15. *Ibid.*, p. 25.
16. There are, of course, many fine English translations of much of the poetry presented in this book. My own literal translations strive merely to support (rather than to compete with) readers' efforts to understand the French, and to allow them to see ambiguities inherent in the original, by sometimes offering alternative translations for a single word or phrase.

Chapter One

1. Chrétien de Troyes, *Yvain ou le chevalier au lion*, ed. K. D. Utti, in *Œuvres complètes*, ed. D. Poirion *et al.* (Paris: Gallimard, 1994), p. 339, lines 1–6.
2. These words are cited in J.-M. Gouvard, *La Versification* (Paris: Presses Universitaires de France, 1999), pp. 9–10.

3. P. Fussell, *Poetic Meter and Poetic Form*, revised edition (New York: Random House, 1979), pp. 19–23.

4. C. Scott, *The Poetics of French Verse* (Oxford: Oxford University Press, 1998), pp. 15, 30.

5. F. de Malherbe, *Œuvres*, ed. A. Adam (Paris: Gallimard, 1971), p. 152, lines 1–6.

6. Scott, *The Poetics of French Verse*, pp. 19–21. See also Scott, "Mallarmé's Mercurial E," in *Forum for Modern Language Studies*, 34 (1998), pp. 43–55, and his comparative analysis of Mallarmé's and Bonnefoy's prosody, "The Mirage of Critical Distance: the Mallarmé of Yves Bonnefoy," in *Meetings with Mallarmé in Contemporary French Culture*, ed. M. Temple (Exeter: University of Exeter Press, 1998), pp. 200–201.

7. *La Chanson de Roland*, example cited in J. Mazaleyrat's *Eléments de métrique française* (Paris: Armand Colin, 1974), pp. 43–44.

8. *La Chanson de Roland*, ed. F. Moignet (Paris: Bordas, 1989), pp. 26, 28, lines 16, 25.

9. J. Marot, *Le Voyage de Gênes*, ed. G. Trisolini (Geneva: Droz, 1974), p. 86, line 68.

10. F. Villon, *Le Testament*, in *Poésies complètes*, ed. C. Thiry (Paris: Le Livre de Poche, 1991), p. 161, line 874.

11. Villon, *ibid.*, p. 211, line 1489.

12. Malherbe, *Œuvres*, p. 158, lines 1–4.

13. E. Deschamps, example cited by C. Thiry in M. Jarrety (ed.), *La Poésie française du Moyen Âge jusqu'à nos jours* (Paris: Presses Universitaires de France, 1997), p. 494.

14. G. Apollinaire, 'La Loreley,' in *Alcools*, in *Œuvres poétiques*, eds. M. Adéma and M. Décaudin (Paris: Gallimard, 1965), p. 115, line 12.

15. J. Racine, *Œuvres complètes I*, ed. G. Forestier (Paris: Gallimard, 1999), p. 205, lines 224–226.

16. *Ibid.*, p. 870, lines 1445–1446.

17. V. Hugo, *Théâtre complet I*, ed. J.-J. Thierry and J. Mélèze (Paris: Gallimard, 1963), p. 1155, lines 1–2.

18. A. Rimbaud, *Poésies*, in *Œuvres complètes*, ed. A. Adam (Paris: Gallimard, 1972), p. 32, lines 12–14.

19. A. de Lamartine, *Méditations poétiques*, in *Œuvres poétiques complètes*, ed. M.-F. Guyard (Paris: Gallimard, 1963), p. 39, lines 31–32.

20. C. Baudelaire, example cited in Mazaleyrat, *Eléments de métrique française*, p. 126.

21. N. Boileau, *Satires, epîtres, art poétique*, ed. J.-P. Collinet (Paris: Gallimard, 1985), pp. 229–230, lines 103–112.

22. R. Goscinny and A. Uderzo, *Astérix et Cléopâtre* (Paris: Dargaud, 1965), p. 7.

23. *Tel Quel* was a journal-based group founded by the novelist Philippe Sollers devoted to developing theoretical reflection on literature.
24. D. Roche, *La Poésie est inadmissible* (Paris: Seuil, 1995), p. 521, lines 1–3.
25. P. Corneille, *Œuvres complètes III*, ed. G. Couton (Paris: Gallimard, 1987), p. 1253, line 268.
26. V. Hugo, 'Quelques mots à un autre,' in *Les Contemplations*, in *Œuvres poétiques II*, ed. P. Albouy (Paris: Gallimard, 1967), p. 529.
27. C. Baudelaire, *Les Fleurs du mal*, in *Œuvres complètes I*, ed. C. Pichois (Paris: Gallimard, 1975), p. 53, lines 1–14.
28. P. Verlaine, *Jadis et Naguère*, in *Œuvres poétiques complètes*, eds. Y.-G. Le Dantec and J. Borel (Paris: Gallimard, 1962), p. 326, lines 1–4.
29. M. Desbordes-Valmore, example cited in Gouvard, *La Versification*, p. 146.
30. Baudelaire, *Œuvres complètes I*, pp. 275–276 (my translation).
31. Verlaine, *Fêtes galantes*, in *Œuvres poétiques complètes*, p. 108.
32. Rimbaud, *Poésies*, in *Œuvres complètes*, p. 53, lines 1–6.
33. G. Perec, *La Disparition* (Paris: Gallimard, 1989), p. 125, lines 1–2.
34. Rimbaud, *Illuminations* in *Œuvres complètes*, p. 140.
35. *Ibid.*, p. 123
36. *Ibid.*, p. 142, lines 1–4.
37. M. Krysinska, cited in *Poèmes de femmes des origines à nos jours*, ed. R. Deforges (Paris: Le Cherche Midi, 1993), pp. 80–81, lines 19–25.
38. Mallarmé, *Œuvres complètes*, ed. H. Mondor (Paris: Gallimard 1945), pp. 362–363.
39. Apollinaire, *Œuvres poétiques*, p. 39, lines 1–6, 11–12.
40. J. Laforgue, *Derniers vers*, in *Œuvres complètes II*, eds. M. de Courten, J.-L. Debauve, P.-O. Walzer and D. Arkell (Lausanne: L'Âge d'Homme, 1995), p. 297, lines 1–10.
41. G. Cretin, "[Epistre] Dudict Cretin audict de Bigue," in *Œuvres poétiques*, ed. K. Chesney (Geneva: Slatkine, 1977), p. 257, lines 37–39.
42. J. Goudezki in *Les Poètes du Chat Noir*, ed. A. Velter (Paris: Gallimard, 1996), p. 444, lines 12–13.
43. A. Allais in *L'Esprit fumiste et les rires fin de siècle*, eds. D. Grojnowski and B. Sarrazin (Paris: José Corti, 1990), p. 84, lines 7–8.
44. P. de Ronsard, *Le Second Livre des amours, II*, in *Œuvres complètes I*, eds. J. Céard, D. Ménager, and M. Simonin (Paris: Gallimard, 1993), pp. 254–255.
45. J. Roubaud, *Quelque chose noir* (Paris: Gallimard, 1986), pp. 85–86.

Chapter Two

1. T. Sébillet, *Art poétique françois*, in *Traités de poétique et de rhétorique de la Renaissance*, ed. F. Goyet (Paris: Le Livre de Poche, 1990), pp. 127–128.

2. J. Du Bellay, *La Deffence et illustration de la langue françoyse*, ed. H. Chamard (Paris: STFM, 1970) p. 113.

3. A. Chénier, 'Ode IV,' in *Œuvres complètes II*, ed. G. Walter (Paris: Gallimard, 1966), p. 181, lines 1–6.

4. P. Claudel, *Cinq grandes odes* (Paris: Gallimard, 1975), pp. 21–22.

5. Christine de Pizan, *Œuvres poétiques I*, ed. M. Roy (Paris: Firmin Didot, 1886), pp. 101–102.

6. Charles d'Orléans, *The French Chansons of Charles d'Orléans*, ed. S. Spense (New York and London: Garland Publishing, 1986), p. 76, lines 1–4.

7. Charles d'Orléans, *En la forêt de longue attente et autres poèmes*, ed. G. Gros (Paris: Gallimard, 2001), p. 210.

8. H. Morier, *Dictionnaire de poétique et de rhétorique* (Paris: Presses Universitaires de France, 1961), p. 48.

9. F. Villon, *Poésies complètes*, ed. C. Thiry (Paris: Le Livre de Poche, 1991), p. 311, lines 1–10.

10. C. Marot, *L'Adolescence clémentine*, ed. F. Lestringant (Paris: Gallimard, 1987), p. 216, lines 1–4.

11. G. Defaux analyses this in "Rhétorique, silence et liberté dans l'œuvre de Marot," in *Bibliothèque d'Humanisme et Renaissance*, XLVI (Geneva: Droz, 1984), pp. 299–322.

12. M. Scève, *Blasons*, in *Œuvres complètes*, ed. P. Quignard (Paris: Mercure de France, 1974), p. 363.

13. F. Ponge, *La Rage de l'expression*, in *Œuvres complètes I*, ed. B. Beugnot *et al.* (Paris: Gallimard, 1999), p. 366.

14. J. Du Bellay, *Divers jeux rustiques*, in *Œuvres poétiques V*, ed. H. Chamard (Paris: STFM, 1983), p. 16, lines 1–3, 7–8, 13–18.

15. R. Char, *Fureur et mystère*, in *Œuvres complètes* (Paris: Gallimard, 1983), p. 130.

16. J. de La Fontaine, *Œuvres complètes I*, ed. J.-P. Collinet (Paris: Gallimard, 1991), p. 33, lines 11–14.

17. *Ibid.*, pp. 44–45, lines 1–2, 7–15, 28–29.

18. A. de Musset, *Contes d'Espagne et d'Italie*, ed. M. A. Rees (London: Athlone Press, 1973), p. 111, lines 1–4. See also lines 97–100.

19. A. de Lamartine, *Méditations poétiques*, in *Œuvres poétiques complètes*, ed. M.-F. Guyard (Paris: Gallimard, 1963), p. 38, lines 9–12.

20. V. Hugo, *Les Rayons et les ombres*, in *Œuvres poétiques I*, ed. P. Albouy (Paris: Gallimard, 1964), p. 1093, lines 1–6.

21. Both the Spenserian (abab bcbc cdcd ee) and the Shakespearean (abab cdcd efef gg) sonnets are divided into three quatrains and a closing couplet.

22. T. de Banville, *Petit traité de poésie française* (Paris: Fasquelle Éditeurs, 1935), p. 200.

23. T. Gautier, *Émaux et camées*, ed. C. Gothot-Mersch (Paris: Gallimard, 1981), pp. 148, 150, lines 1–4, 52–56.

24. T. Sébillet, *Art poétique françois*, in *Traités de poétique*, pp. 107–108.

25. Francis Goyet makes this point in "Le Sonnet français, vrai et faux héritier de la grande rhétorique," in *Le Sonnet à la Renaissance des origines au XVIIe siècle*, ed. Y. Bellenger (Paris: Aux Amateurs de Livres, 1988), pp. 31–41.

26. F. Petrarca, *Canzoniere*, ed. G. Contini (Turin: Einaudi, 1982), p. 3. This sonnet was also translated by Marot (*Œuvres poétiques II*, ed. G. Defaux [Paris: Bordas, 1993], pp. 494–495).

27. M. Scève, *Delie object de plus haulte vertu*, in *Œuvres complètes*, ed. P. Quignard (Paris: Mercure de France, 1974), p. 13.

28. Plato's discourse on love is rediscovered and Christianized for Renaissance poets in Marsilio Ficino's fifteenth-century translation and commentary on *The Banquet*.

29. Pernette du Guillet (*c.*1520–1545) was herself a poet, who alluded to Scève in her posthumously published *Rymes*.

30. M.-M. Fontaine offers this analysis in "Le Système des *Antiquités* de Du Bellay," in *Le Sonnet à la Renaissance*, p. 68.

31. F. Jost, "Le Sonnet: sens d'une structure," in *Le Sonnet à la Renaissance*, p. 59.

32. See H. Morier's *Dictionnaire de Poétique et de Rhétorique*, pp. 381–397, and A. Gendre's *Évolution du sonnet français* (Paris: Presses Universitaires de France, 1996).

33. G. de Nerval, *Les Chimères*, in *Œuvres complètes III*, eds. J. Guillaume and C. Pichois (Paris: Gallimard, 1993), p. 645.

34. R. B. Gordon, "The Lyric Persona: Nerval's *El Desdichado*," in Christopher Prendergast's *Nineteenth-Century Poetry: Introductions to Close Reading* (Cambridge: Cambridge University Press, 1990), p. 99.

35. Paul Valéry, *Variété*, in *Œuvres I*, ed. J. Hytier (Paris: Gallimard, 1957), p. 444.

36. See A. Jarry's "Nécrologie" of Mallarmé in the 1899 *Almanach du Père Ubu*, in *Tout Ubu* (Paris: Le Livre de Poche, 1985), pp. 384–385.

37. J.-J. Rabéarivelo, 'À G. Henri de Burgada,' in *Volumes* (Antananarivo: Imprimerie de l'Imérina, 1928), p. 35. I would like to thank Richard Serrano for bringing this poem to my attention.

38. S. Mallarmé, *Poésies*, in *Œuvres complètes I*, ed. B. Marchal (Paris: Gallimard, 1998), pp. 36–37.

39. J. Roubaud, *Poésie: (récit)* (Paris: Seuil, 2000), p. 430.

40. R. Queneau, *Cent mille milliards de poèmes* (Paris: Gallimard, 1961).

41. Queneau, "Littérature potentielle," in *Bâtons, chiffres et lettres* (Paris: Gallimard, 1965), p. 335.

42. M. Grangaud, *Poèmes fondus* (Paris: P.O.L., 1997), p. 99, lines 4–6.

43. *Ibid.*, pp. 7–8. The poet also states that "In a poem, as in a living organism, each element communicates with all the others, regardless

of their respective positions"; and that "A melted, or implicit, poem is constituted by a circulation of meaning between incontiguous words of the explicit poem" (my translation).

Chapter Three

1. V. Hugo, *Les Contemplations*, in *Œuvres poétiques II*, ed. P. Albouy (Paris: Gallimard, 1967), pp. 496, 498.
2. Example cited in P. Fontanier, *Les Figures du discours* (Paris: Flammarion, 1977), p. 107.
3. P. Fontanier, *ibid.*, p. 64 (translation mine).
4. C. Baudelaire, *Le Spleen de Paris*, in *Œuvres complètes I*, ed. C. Pichois (Paris: Gallimard, 1975), pp. 301–303.
5. For an extensive analysis of the relationship between these poems, touching on some of these points and others, see B. Johnson's *Défigurations du langage poétique* (Paris: Flammarion, 1979), pp. 103–160.
6. Baudelaire, 'L'Invitation au voyage,' in *Le Spleen de Paris*, p. 303.
7. B. Johnson, *Défigurations du langage poétique*, p. 159.
8. C. Rifelj, *Word and Figure in Nineteenth-Century French Poetry* (Columbus: Ohio State University Press, 1987), pp. 68–99.
9. R. Jakobson, *Questions de poétique* (Paris: Seuil, 1973), p. 234 (translation mine).
10. R. Jakobson, "Linguistics and Poetics," in *Style in Language*, ed. T. A. Sebeok (Cambridge, Mass.: MIT Press, 1960), p. 358.
11. N. Boileau, *Art poétique*, in *Satires, Epîtres, Art poétique*, ed. J.-P. Collinet (Paris: Gallimard, 1985), p. 231, lines 147–160.
12. F. de Malherbe, *Commentaire sur Desportes*, ed. A. Sideleau (Montréal, Les Éditions Chantecler, 1950), p. 163.
13. *Ibid.*, p. 110.
14. *Ibid.*, p. 198.
15. *Ibid.*, p. 38.
16. *Ibid.*, p. 146.
17. *Ibid.*, p. 118.
18. *Ibid.*, p. 116.
19. *Ibid.*, p. 118.
20. *Ibid.*, p. 162.
21. *Ibid.*, p. 100.
22. M. Régnier, *Satyre IV*, in *Œuvres complètes*, ed. G. Raibaud (Paris: Nizet, 1982), p. 44, lines 111–114.
23. Boileau, 'Préface de 1701,' in *Satires, epîtres, art poétique*, pp. 49–50.
24. T. de Viau, *Œuvres complètes III*, ed. G. Saba (Paris: Nizet / Rome: Edizioni dell'Ateneo and Bizzarri, 1979), pp. 191 and 205, lines 8–10 and 328–330.

25. Saint-Amant, *Œuvres complètes II*, ed. Ch. Livet (Paris: Jannet, 1855), p. 214. See also R. G. Maber, *Malherbe, Théophile de Viau, and Saint-Amant: A Selection* (Durham: University of Durham, 1983), p. 63.

26. V. Voiture, 'Rondeau,' in *Anthologie de la poésie française du XVIIe siècle*, ed. J.-P. Chauveau (Paris: Gallimard, 1987), p. 257.

27. J. Lermina and H. Levêque, *Dictionnaire thématique argot* (Paris: Bibliothèque Charcornac, 1897) pp. 1–111.

28. *Ibid.*

29. J. Richepin, *Gueux des champs*, in *La Chanson des gueux* (Paris: Fasquelle, 1912), p. 85, lines 1–4, 12–14.

30. P. Verlaine, *Jadis et naguère*, in *Œuvres poétiques complètes*, eds. Y.-G. Le Dantec, J. Borel (Paris: Gallimard, 1962), p. 327, lines 17–20.

31. *Ibid.*, lines 21–28.

32. S. Mallarmé, 'Le Tombeau d'Edgar Poe,' in *Poésies*, in *Œuvres complètes I*, ed. B. Marchal (Paris: Gallimard, 1998), p. 38, line 6.

33. A. Rimbaud, *Une saison en enfer* ('Alchimie du verbe,' 'Délires' II), in *Œuvres complètes*, ed. A. Adam (Paris: Gallimard, 1972), pp. 106–109.

34. Lautréamont, *Les Chants de Maldoror*, 'Chant sixième, strophe 6,' in Lautréamont and G. Nouveau, *Œuvres complètes*, ed. P.-O. Walzer (Paris: Gallimard, 1970), p. 235.

35. A. Jarry, *Tout Ubu*, ed. M. Saillet (Paris: Librairie Générale Française, 1962), p. 19.

36. *Ibid.*, pp. 33, 41.

37. T. Tzara, *De nos oiseaux*, in *Œuvres complètes I*, ed. H. Béhar (Paris: Flammarion, 1975), p. 231, lines 1–16.

38. Lautréamont, *Poésies II*, in *Œuvres complètes*, p. 285.

39. A. Breton, *Manifestoes of Surrealism*, trans. R. Seaver and H. R. Lane (Ann Arbor: The University of Michigan Press, 1969), p. 26.

40. P. Reverdy, cited in A. Breton, *ibid.*, p. 20.

41. A. Breton, *ibid.*, p. 37.

42. A. Breton, 'Dernière levée,' in *Le Revolver à cheveux blancs*, in *Œuvres complètes II*, ed. M. Bonnet (Paris: Gallimard, 1992), p. 97, lines 13–15.

43. 'L'Union libre,' in *ibid.*, pp. 85–86, lines 1–6.

44. E. Jabès, 'Les Rames et la voile,' in *Le Seuil le sable. Poésies complètes 1943–1988* (Paris: Gallimard, 1990), p. 309.

45. H. Michaux, 'Glu et gli,' in *Qui je fus*, IX, 'Poèmes,' in *Œuvres complètes I*, eds. R. Berlour and Y. Tran (Paris: Gallimard, 1998), pp. 110–111, lines 1–32.

46. T. Plantier cited by the editor in *The Defiant Muse: French Feminist Poems from the Middle Ages to the Present*, ed. D. C. Stanton (New York: The Feminist Press, 1986), p. 203.

47. T. Plantier, 'Hommes po hommes à lunettes,' cited in *The Defiant Muse*, pp. 182–183, lines 1–7. I am also quoting Mary Ann Caws' English translation.

Chapter Four

1. L. S. Senghor, ed., *Anthologie de la nouvelle poésie nègre et malgache de langue française* (Paris: Presses Universitaires de France, 1997), p. 1 (my translation).
2. L.-G. Damas, *Pigments*, cited in Senghor, ed., *Anthologie de la nouvelle poésie nègre et malgache*, pp. 17 18.
3. J. Du Bellay, *Les Regrets*, Sonnet IX, in *Œuvres poétiques II*, ed. H. Chamard (Paris: STFM, 1970), p. 59, lines 1–4 and 9–11.
4. *Ibid.*, Sonnet XXXI, pp. 76–77.
5. See the essay under this title in W. Benjamin's collected *Reflections*, ed. P. Demetz, trans. E. Jephcott (New York: Shocken Books, 1986), pp. 146–162.
6. C. Baudelaire, *Les Fleurs du mal*, in *Œuvres complètes I*, ed. C. Pichois (Paris: Gallimard, 1975), pp. 86–87, lines 29–32 and 40–44
7. C. Péguy, *Œuvres poétiques complètes* (Paris: Gallimard, 1940), pp. 621–623.
8. B. Cendrars, *Poésies complètes* (Paris: Denoël, 2001), pp. 19–34.
9. Madhuri Mukherjee develops these points in "Symbolism and Orientalism in Rimbaud, Claudel, and Artaud" (New Brunswick, N. J.: Rutgers University Ph.D., 2000). For a general analysis of Orientalist discourse, see E. Said, *Orientalism* (New York: Vintage Books, 1979).
10. P. Claudel, *Cent phrases pour éventails* (Paris: Gallimard, 1942).
11. V. Segalen, *Stèles* (Paris: Gallimard, 1973), pp. 115–116.
12. *Ibid.*, p. 103.
13. Saint-John Perse, *Œuvres complètes* (Paris: Gallimard, 1972), p. 445 (my translation).
14. S. Winspur, *Saint-John Perse and the Imaginary Reader* (Geneva: Droz, 1988), p. 30.
15. Saint-John Perse, *Anabase* in *Œuvres complètes*, pp. 113–114.
16. G. W. F. Hegel, *The Philosophy of Fine Art*, IV, trans. F. P. B. Osmaton (New York: Hacker Art Books, 1975), p. 111.
17. G. Moignet, *La Chanson de Roland*, ed. G. Moignet (Paris: Bordas, 1989), p. 14 (my translation).
18. *Ibid.*, p. 80, lines 819–822.
19. *Ibid.*, p. 104, lines 1194–1195 and 1210–1212.
20. *Ibid.*, p. 118, line 1423.

21. *Ibid.*, p. 146, line 1861.
22. *Ibid.*, p. 174, lines 2333–2334.
23. *Ibid.*, p. 126, line 1.
24. J. Du Bellay, *La Deffence et illustration de la langue françoyse*, ed. H. Chamard (Paris: STFM, 1970), pp. 128–129.
25. *Ibid.*, pp. 132–133.
26. Rutebeuf, *Œuvres complètes I*, eds. E. Faral and J. Bastin (Paris: A. and J. Picard, 1959), p. 428, lines 127 and 129.
27. *Ibid.*, p. 445, lines 39–47.
28. J. Molinet, *Faictz et Dictz*, ed. N. Dupire (Paris: SATF, 1936), p. 128, lines 25–32. I would like to thank François Cornilliat for bringing this poem to my attention.
29. *Ibid.*, p. 129, lines 49–51.
30. *Ibid.*, p. 131, lines 113–116.
31. C. Marot, *Œuvres poétiques II*, ed. G. Defaux (Paris: Bordas, 1993), pp. 223–224.
32. P. de Ronsard, *Responce aux injures*, in *Œuvres complètes II*, eds. J. Céard, D. Ménager, and M. Simonin (Paris: Gallimard, 1994) p. 1064, lines 855–860. See D. Ménager, *Ronsard. Le Roi, le Poète et les Hommes* (Geneva: Droz, 1979).
33. V. Hugo, *Les Châtiments*, in *Œuvres poétiques II*, ed. P. Albouy (Paris: Gallimard, 1967), p. 214.
34. A. d'Aubigné, *Les Tragiques*, in *Œuvres*, ed. H. Weber (Paris: Gallimard, 1969) p. 30, lines 386–390.
35. *Ibid.*, p. 31, lines 420–424.
36. J.-P. Sartre, "Orphée Noir," in Senghor, ed., *Anthologie de la nouvelle poésie nègre et malgache de langue française*, p. XLIV (my translation).
37. A. Breton, "Un grand poète noir" (préface de 1947), in A. Césaire, *Cahier d'un retour au pays natal* (Paris: Présence Africaine, 1983), p. 81 (my translation).
38. L. S. Senghor, *Chants d'ombre*, cited in Senghor (ed.), *Anthologie de la nouvelle poésie nègre et malgache de langue française*, p. 151.
39. A. Césaire, *Cahier d'un retour au pays natal*, pp. 46–47.
40. On these developments, see E. Anthony Hurley: *Through a Black Veil. Readings in French Caribbean Poetry* (Trenton, New Jersey: Africa World Press, 2000).
41. J. Mansour, *Rapaces* (Paris: Seghers, 1960), p. 17.
42. L. Labé, *Œuvres complètes*, ed. F. Rigolot (Paris: Garnier-Flammarion, 1986), p. 42.
43. *Ibid.*, p. 122, lines 1–4.
44. *Ibid.*, p. 131, lines 1–4.
45. This ambiguity is analyzed in F. Rigolot's "Préface," *ibid.*, pp. 22–23.
46. *Ibid.*, pp. 128–129, lines 1–2, 5–6, 9–14.

47. M. Desbordes-Valmore, *Œuvres poétiques I*, ed. M. Bertrand (Grenoble: Presses Universitaires de Grenoble, 1973) p. 178.

48. M. Riffaterre, *Semiotics of Poetry* (Bloomington: Indiana University Press, 1978), p. 1.

49. G. Miron, *L'Homme rapaillé* (Montréal: Presses de l'Université de Montréal, 1970), p. 48. I would like to thank Jean-Christian Pleau for focusing my attention on 'L'homme agonique' and on *L'homme rapaillé*'s double structure.

50. *Ibid.*, p. 61.

51. *Ibid.*, p. 108. I am grateful to Ève Therrien for her help with the translation of this quote.

52. J. Rabéarivelo, 'À Robert-Edward Hart,' in *Volumes* (Antananarivo: Imprimerie de l'Imérina, 1928), p. 24. I am indebted to Richard Serrano for bringing this poem to my attention, as well as for the translation and the point made here, which is developed in his upcoming book, *From Pillage to Posts: "Francophone" Writers at the Ends of French Empire*.

53. G. Miron, *L'Homme rapaillé*, p. 119 (my translation).

54. Christopher L. Miller develops this point in *Nationalists and Nomads. Essays on Francophone African Literature and Culture* (Chicago: The University of Chicago Press, 1998).

55. R. Char, *Œuvres complètes* (Paris: Gallimard, 1983), p. 173.

56. L. Aragon, *Le Musée Grévin* (Paris: Minuit, 1944), p. 29.

57. P. Éluard, *Œuvres complètes I*, ed. M. Dumas and L. Scheler (Paris: Gallimard, 1968), pp. 1105–1107, lines 1–8.

58. B. Péret, *Death to the Pigs and Other Writings*, trans. R. Stella (Lincoln and London: University of Nebraska Press, 1988), pp. 203–204.

59. *Ibid.*, p. 205.

60. *Ibid.*, pp. 205–206.

Chapter Five

1. R. Crisp, "Logos," in *Cambridge Encyclopedia of Philosophy*, ed. R. Audi (Cambridge: Cambridge University Press, 1995), pp. 448–449.

2. John 1:1, *The New Oxford Annotated Bible*, ed. B. Metzger and R. Murphy (New York: Oxford University Press, 1991), p. 125 NT.

3. V. Hugo, *Les Contemplations*, in *Œuvres poétiques II*, ed. P. Albouy (Paris: Gallimard, 1967), pp. 500 and 503.

4. Marguerite de Navarre, *Les Prisons*, ed. S. Glasson (Geneva: Droz, 1978), p. 179.

5. Marguerite de Navarre, Chanson 28, *Chansons spirituelles*, ed. G. Dottin (Geneva: Droz, 1971), p. 73, lines 1–2 and 6–11.

6. J. Du Bellay, Sonnet CXIII, *Œuvres poétiques I*, ed. H. Chamard (Paris: STFM, 1982), pp. 122–123.

7. Thomas M. Greene develops this point in *Poésie et magie* (Paris: Julliard, 1991), pp. 23–40.

8. F. de Saussure, *Cours de linguistique générale*, ed. T. de Mauro (Paris: Payot, 1972), p. 101.

9. P. J. Jouve, *Œuvres I*, ed. J. Starobinski (Paris: Mercure de France, 1987), pp. 696–697.

10. Plato, *The Republic*, ed. G. R. F. Ferrari, trans. T. Griffith (Cambridge: Cambridge University Press, 2000), p. 317.

11. A. de Vigny, *Poèmes antiques et modernes – Les Destinées*, ed. A. Jarry (Paris: Gallimard, 1973), p. 22, lines 102–106.

12. Both authors quoted in T. Todorov, *Théories du symbole* (Paris: Seuil, 1977), p. 235 (translation and emphasis mine).

13. See P. Lacoue-Labarthe and J.-L. Nancy, *L'Absolu littéraire: théorie de la littérature du romantisme allemand* (Paris: Seuil, 1978), and J. Rancière, *La Parole muette. Essai sur les contradictions de la littérature* (Paris: Hachette, 1998).

14. This distinction is developed in T. Todorov, *Théories du symbole*, pp. 235–260.

15. V. Hugo, *Les Contemplations*, in *Œuvres poétiques II*, p. 801, lines 12–20.

16. P. de Ronsard, *Les Hymnes, II*, in *Œuvres complètes II*, eds. J. Céard, D. Ménager, M. Simonin (Paris: Gallimard, 1994), p. 559, lines 9–16.

17. *Ibid.*, p. 561, lines 77–82.

18. J. Parmentier, *Œuvres poétiques*, ed. F. Ferrand (Geneva: Droz, 1971), p. 30.

19. C. Baudelaire, 'Richard Wagner et Tannhaüser à Paris,' *Œuvres complètes II*, ed. C. Pichois (Paris: Gallimard, 1976), p. 784.

20. Lines 8–11 rework, for example, a quotation from E. T. A. Hoffmann's *Kreisleriana*, which Baudelaire had also cited in a work of his own art criticism: the *Salon de 1846*. For a study of Baudelaire's general relationship to Hoffmann, see Rosemary Lloyd's *Baudelaire et Hoffmann: affinités et influences* (Cambridge: Cambridge University Press, 1979). For an overview and analysis of some of the sonnet's multiple connections with other nineteenth-century texts, see J. Culler, "Intertextuality and Interpretation: Baudelaire's 'Correspondances,'" in *Nineteenth-Century French Poetry: Introductions to Close Reading*, ed. C. Prendergast (Cambridge: Cambridge University Press, 1990), pp. 118–137. For a contemporary poetic response to the sonnet, see Jacqueline Risset's 'Promenade M' in *Petits éléments de physique amoureuse* (Paris: Gallimard, 1991).

21. Baudelaire, *Les Fleurs du mal*, in *Œuvres complètes I*, ed. C. Pichois (Paris: Gallimard, 1975), p. 11.

22. J. Culler notes the absence of any mention of God in "Intertextuality and Interpretation," p. 121.

23. *Ibid.*, p. 128.
24. P. de Man, *The Rhetoric of Romanticism* (New York: Columbia University Press, 1984), pp. 249–250.
25. A. Rimbaud, letter to Paul Demeny, *Œuvres complètes*, ed. A. Adam (Paris: Gallimard, 1972), p. 251.
26. S. Mallarmé, *Crise de vers*, in *Œuvres complètes*, ed. H. Mondor (Paris: Gallimard, 1945), p. 366.
27. Mallarmé, *Poésies*, in *Œuvres complètes I*, ed. B. Marchal (Paris: Gallimard, 1998), pp. 37–38.
28. *Ibid.*, p. 1189 (translation mine).
29. "Ptyx" may have been formed from the (feminine) Greek noun "ptux," meaning fold.
30. This last phrase is from M. Riffaterre, in *Semiotics of Poetry* (Bloomington: Indiana University Press, 1978), p. 18. Examples of the first two interpretations can be found respectively in B. Marchal's commentary on the poem in his edition, and in D. Grojnowski's and B. Sarrazin's implicit designation of the poem as a parody in *L'Esprit fumiste et les rires fin de siècle* (Paris: Corti, 1990), p. 63.
31. P. Valéry, *Variété*, in *Œuvres I*, ed. J. Hytier (Paris: Gallimard, 1957), pp. 1320, 1334, 1356.
32. Valéry cited in P. Brunel *et al.*, *Histoire de la littérature française* (Paris: Bordas, 1972), p. 437. See also *Variété*, in *Œuvres I*, p. 1274.
33. *Variété*, in *Œuvres I*, p. 1507.
34. *Ibid.*, p. 482.
35. *Tel quel*, *Œuvres II*, p. 478. Suzanne Nash analyses this "misappropriation" in "Other Voices: Intertextuality and the Art of Pure Poetry," in *Reading Paul Valéry*, eds. P. Gifford and B. Stimpson (Cambridge: Cambridge University Press, 1998), pp. 187–199.
36. *Charmes*, in *Œuvres I*, pp. 152–153, lines 1–8, 13–16, 25–32.
37. *Ibid.*, p. 151.
38. C. Pozzi, *Œuvre poétique*, ed. L. Joseph (Paris: La Différence, 1988), pp. 33–34, lines 1–5, 11–12, 16–25.
39. R. Desnos, *Corps et biens*, in *Domaine public* (Paris: Gallimard / Le point du jour, 1953), p. 95.
40. P. Éluard, *Œuvres complètes I*, ed. M. Dumas and L. Scheler (Paris: Gallimard, 1968), p. 232.
41. Hölderlin cited by M. Heidegger in "Hölderlin et l'essence de la poésie," in *Approche de Hölderlin*, trans. H. Corbin, M. Deguy and F. Fédier (Paris: Gallimard, 1973), p. 53. I quote Corbin's translation: it is this formulation that initially struck a chord.
42. Y. Bonnefoy, "L'Acte et le lieu de la poésie," in *Du mouvement et de l'immobilité de Douve* (Paris: Gallimard, 1970), p. 188. On Bonnefoy's theory of presence, see G. Gasarian, *Yves Bonnefoy, la poésie, la présence* (Seyssel: Champ Vallon, 1986).

43. "L'Acte et le lieu de la poésie," pp. 189 and 197.
44. *Ibid.*, p. 75, lines 1–6.
45. *Ibid.*, p. 79.
46. E. Guillevic, *Art poétique*, (Paris: Gallimard, 1989), pp. 122 and 153.
47. P. Jaccottet, *Poésie 1946–1967* (Paris: Gallimard, 1971) p. 56.
48. The poet and philosopher J.-C. Pinson has done this in *Habiter en poète* (Seyssel: Champ Vallon, 1995).
49. See J. Derrida, *Signéponge/Signsponge*, trans. R. Rand (New York: Columbia University Press, 1984).
50. F. Ponge cited by M. Collot in "D'un lyrisme objectif," in *Poétiques de l'objet*, ed. F. Rouget (Paris: Champion, 1999), pp. 452–453 (my translation).
51. F. Ponge, *Pièces*, in *Œuvres complètes I*, ed. B. Beugnot *et al.* (Paris: Gallimard, 1999), p. 793.
52. *Ibid.*, pp. 793–794.
53. M. Deguy, *La Poésie n'est pas seule. Court traité de poétique* (Paris: Seuil, 1987), pp. 95–152.
54. Deguy, *Gisants, Poèmes III 1980–1995* (Paris: Gallimard, 1999), pp. 235–237.
55. For a discussion of *Les Indes* and other transformations of the epic and the lyric, see J.-J. Thomas and S. Winspur, *Poeticized Language. The Foundations of Contemporary French Poetry* (University Park: Penn State University Press, 1999), pp. 239–264.
56. E. Glissant, 'Présentation,' in *Les Grands Chaos*, in *Poèmes complets* (Paris: Gallimard, 1994), p. 409.

Epilogue

1. Thibaut de Champagne, 'La Mort du rossignol,' in *Les Plus Beaux Manuscrits des poètes français* (Paris: Robert Laffont, 1991), p. 25, lines 1–7.
2. P. Valéry, *Œuvres I*, ed. J. Hytier (Paris: Gallimard, 1957), p. 1272 (translation mine).
3. See F. Mouret, "Art poétique et musication: de l'alternance des rimes," in *À haute voix*, ed. O. Rosenthal (Paris: Klincksieck, 1998), pp. 103–113.
4. E. Deschamps, *Œuvres complètes VII*, eds. A. Queux de Saint-Hilaire and G. Raynaud (Paris: Firmin-Didot, 1878–1903), pp. 269–271.
5. This point, along with much of the argument on Machaut and Chaucer that follows, draws on James I. Wimsatt's "Chaucer and Deschamps' 'Natural Music,'" in *The Union of Words and Music in Medieval Poetry*,

eds. R. A. Baltzer, T. Cable, and J. I. Wimsatt (Austin: The University of Texas Press, 1991), pp. 132–150.

6. *Ibid.*, p. 135.
7. *Ibid.*, pp. 138–139.
8. Guillaume de Machaut, *Le Livre du voir dit*, eds. P. Imbs and J. Cerquiglini-Toulet (Paris: Le Livre de Poche, 1999), p. 90, lines 697–702.
9. Wimsatt, "Chaucer and Deschamps," pp. 143–147.
10. J.-J. Rousseau, *Œuvres complètes V*, eds. B. Gagnebin and M. Raymond (Paris: Gallimard, 1995).
11. See Peter Collier's "Poetry and Cliché: Laforgue's 'L'Hiver qui vient,' " in *Nineteenth-Century French Poetry: Introductions to Close Reading*, ed. C. Prendergast (Cambridge: Cambridge University Press, 1990), pp. 199–224.
12. On the obscurity of Mallarmé's language, see M. Bowie, *Mallarmé and the Art of Being Difficult* (Cambridge: Cambridge University Press, 1978).
13. I develop this argument in *Performance in the Texts of Mallarmé: The Passage from Art to Ritual* (University Park: Penn State Press, 1993), and in "Apocalypse et modernisme," in *Le Livre total*, eds. A. Buisine and V. Kaufmann (*Revue des sciences humaines*, 1994–4), pp. 35–46.
14. See Mallarmé's preface to the *Cosmopolis* edition in *Œuvres complètes I*, ed. B. Marchal (Paris: Gallimard, 1998) pp. 391–392, and the definitive version of the poem, pp. 363–387.
15. J. Lemaire de Belges, *La Plainte du désiré*, ed. D. Yabsley (Paris: Droz, 1932), p. 71, lines 105–110.
16. F. Cornilliat develops this analysis in "Poésie et peinture, de Molinet à Lemaire," in *Poétiques de la Renaissance*, eds. P. Galand-Hallyn and F. Hallyn (Geneva: Droz, 2001), pp. 587–596.
17. Ronsard, *Œuvres complètes I*, ed. J. Céard, D. Ménager, and M. Simonin (Paris: Gallimard, 1993), pp. 152–156.
18. Du Bellay, *Œuvres poétiques II*, ed. H. Chamard (Paris: STFM, 1970), p. 68.
19. Roberto Campo relates this in *Ronsard's Contentious Sisters* (Chapel Hill: North Carolina Studies, 1998), pp. 244–246.
20. Campo quotes and discusses these remarks, *ibid.*, pp. 82–83.
21. Mallarmé, *Œuvres complètes I*, p. 1218.
22. Apollinaire, *Œuvres poétiques*, eds. M. Adéma and M. Décaudin (Paris: Gallimard, 1965), p. 213.
23. For a recent account of the interrelations of Prévert's poetics with his work in other art forms, see Michael Bishop's *Jacques Prévert: From Film and Theater to Poetry, Art and Song* (Amsterdam: Rodopi, 2002).
24. A. du Bouchet, *Dans la chaleur vacante* (Paris: Mercure de France, 1961).

25. See, for example, Claude Mouchard's analysis of Michaux' divergent use of space in verbal and visual art in "Michaux, métamorphoses d'espace," in *L'Art et l'hybride* (Saint-Denis: Presses Universitaires de Vincennes, 2001), pp. 83–102.

26. H. Michaux, *Œuvres complètes II*, eds. R. Bellour and Y. Tran (Paris: Gallimard, 2001), p. 263 (my translation).

27. *Œuvres complètes I*, eds. R. Bellour and Y. Tran (Paris: Gallimard, 1998), pp. 902–903. The caption is taken from a prose poem entitled 'La Lettre dit encore . . . ' in the collection *Épreuves, exorcismes* (*Ibid.*, p. 794).

Glossary

alexandrin (**alexandrine**): twelve-syllable verse; when regular, a line divided by a **caesura** into equal halves with fixed accents on syllables 6 and 12 and two other mobile accents.

alexandrin ternaire: a three-measure alexandrin with fixed accents on syllables 4, 8, and 12 (also called *trimètre romantique*).

allegory: a complex figurative representation, combining several **metaphors** and often employing personification; for German Romanticism, a conventional modality of representation (as opposed to **symbol**), in which the figurative sign conveys a concept as transparently as possible.

alliteration: the repetition of consonants, or of the first sound of several words in a sequence.

allusion: a literary or cultural reference to something outside the text.

anaphora: the repetition of a word or word-group at the beginning of a verbal sequence.

antithesis: a figure of contrast often framing an opposition within a parallel structure.

apocope: the dropping (or non-pronouncing) of a non-elided *e atone* at the end of a word.

apostrophe: a figure of address, often preceded by a declamatory "O."

archaism: an old-fashioned or obsolete word or word usage.

art poétique: a poem presenting the author's poetic theory.

assonance: the repetition of vowel-sounds; also line-terminal pairings of like vowels within tonic syllables containing different consonants (*nu/dur*).

autoreferentiality: a text's ability to focus our attention on its own formal existence.

ballade: medieval lyric form consisting of three **stanzas** and one closing half-stanza or *envoi*, each finishing on the same line or *refrain*; typically, three stanzas of eight **octosyllables** (patterned ababbcbc*) with a four-line *envoi* (bcbc*); or three stanzas of ten **decasyllables** (ababbccdcd*) with a five-line *envoi* (ccdcd*); the Romantic *ballade* is a much looser form often alluding to medieval themes or stories.

barbarisme: an incorrectly formed word.

blason: an epigram dedicated to the detailed description and praise of an object, such as a part of a woman's body. The *contre-blason* blames and mocks instead of praising.

caesura: see *césure*.

canso: the principal form of *Troubadour* poetry; a song exalting *fin'amor*, or courtly love.

canzoniere: originally Petrarch's collection of love poems celebrating Laura; subsequently applied to other collections modeled on Petrarch's.

catachresis: a **metaphor** or other **trope** whose figurative power has become "dead" due to lexical use by ordinary language (the "feet" of verse).

césure (caesura): the principal metrical (measure-separating) mark dividing the *alexandrin* and other long verses in two.

césure enjambante: a *césure* falling before a non-elided *e atone* (which is therefore counted with the following measure).

césure épique: a *césure* allowing a normally non-elided line-internal *e atone* to be "*apocopé*" (or dropped) just like the line-terminal one.

césure lyrique: a *césure* falling after a non-elided *e atone* (which is therefore counted with the previous measure).

chanson: lyric song form used by the *Trouvères* (after the *Troubadours'* "*canso*"); later any song form with variable number and patterns of rhymes.

chant royal: a late medieval form dedicated to a regal figure with five refrain-ending **stanzas** of eleven lines (patterned ababccddede*) and a five-line *envoi* (ddede*).

contre-rejet: the isolation, at the end of one line, of a short element that is syntactically bound to the next line.

coupe: the rhythmic mark dividing groups of syllables into measures; generally falls after an accented syllable.

coupe enjambante: a *coupe* falling before a non-elided *e atone* (which is therefore counted with the following measure).

coupe lyrique: a *coupe* falling after a non-elided *e atone* (which is therefore counted with the previous measure).

decasyllable: ten-syllable verse; when regular, divided by a **caesura** after the fourth syllable.

diérèse (diaeresis): the articulation in separate syllables of two contiguous vowel-sounds normally pronounced as one.

discours: a genre of political poetry developed by Ronsard (formally, a long poem composed of rhymed couplets of **alexandrines**).

dizain: a ten-line **stanza** or other unit of verse; in Scève, a fixed form (ababbccdcd).

ekphrasis: the figurative representation in literature of either real or imagined visual works of art.

elegy: in Antiquity, a plaintive poem often dealing with love, composed in a particular **meter**; from the Renaissance forward, a love poem of varying form with a mournful tone; in Romanticism, typically, a longish **heterometric** poem treating love nostalgically in a natural setting.

enjambement: the straddling of line-limits by syntax; one line runs into the next one without syntactical demarcation (the term often encompasses *rejet* and *contre-rejet*, but is sometimes reserved for the cases of straddling involving no particular emphasis).

enneasyllable: nine-syllable verse.

envoi: the closing of a *ballade* or *chant royal*, "sending" the poem to a prince or other addressee.

epic: a long, high-style poem narrating the heroic exploits of individuals or people.

épigramme **(epigram):** a short verse "inscription" that builds toward a crucial last line, or *pointe*.

épître **(epistle):** a fictitious or genuine letter in verse.

equivocation: the combination of two different meanings within one word.

euphemism: the understatement of something embarrassing or troubling.

fable: a tale containing a moral message, often employing allegories that personify plant and animals.

fin'amor **(courtly love):** medieval conception of love modeled on feudal service; the lover owes absolute fidelity and obedience to his Lady (who is often inaccessible or married to someone else).

haiku: a seventeen-syllable Japanese form in three lines (5+7+5), that normally evokes a clear image generating spiritual insight.

hemistich: a half-line of verse.

hendecasyllable: eleven-syllable verse.

heptasyllable: seven-syllable verse.

heterometric: a stanza or other unit containing lines of at least two different **meters.**

hexasyllable: six-syllable verse.

hiatus: contact between articulated vowels (as in the name *Pasiphaé* or the phrase *j'ai acheté*).

huitain: an eight-line unit of verse sometimes composed of two **quatrains**.

hymne: a genre celebrating cosmic forces or metaphysical concepts (formally, in Ronsard, a long poem composed of rhymed couplets of **alexandrines**).

hyperbole: the figure of exaggeration.

imparisyllable (*vers impair*): a line of verse composed of an odd number of syllables.

intertextuality: any mode by which one text refers to or engages itself with another.

inversion: an overturning of normal syntactical order (often to allow metrical regularity).

irony: figure consisting of saying one thing to imply the opposite.

isosyllabic: said of verse measured in terms of equal numbers of equal syllables, as opposed to "feet" containing variable numbers of syllables of different strength or duration.

laisse: an Old French epic stanza or varying length, built on **assonances**.

litote **(litotes):** understatement, saying less to imply more.

lyric poetry: the musical or musical-sounding expression of subjective emotions, experiences, and ideas.

metaphor: a **trope** substituting a figurative word (the **vehicle** or *comparant*) for a literal one (the **tenor** or *comparé*) on the basis of resemblance.

meter: regular rhythmic pattern in verse; by extension, the various types of verse, such as iambic pentameter, the **alexandrine**, etc.

metonymy: a **trope** substituting a figurative word for a literal one on the basis of contiguity (some connection or association exists between the two terms).

mimesis: the imitation, or representation, of reality in art.

mise en abîme: a mirroring effect stemming from some kind of formal self-reference.

neologism: a newly coined word.

octosyllable: eight-syllable verse.

ode: a lyric poem of varying form and genre, originally meant to be sung; a long poem publicly singing the praise of glorious feats, following a tripartite **stanzaic** structure; or a more loosely structured stanzaic poem, "singing" of personal emotions or down-to-earth pleasures.

onomatopoeia: the verbal imitation of natural sounds.

oxymoron: the joining of contradictory terms.

pentasyllable: five-syllable verse.

periphrasis: circuitously describes or alludes to an object rather than naming it.

pointe: a brilliant or witty conclusion; typically, of an **epigram**.

précieux: elitist, convoluted language, or the people using it.

prosimètre: a medieval narrative genre combining verse and prose.

prosody: the traits and rules of accent and rhythm in a given language; in a specialized sense, their application to poetry, for example, in constructing and using meters.

quatrain: four-line stanza.

quintil: five-line stanza.

referent: what a verbal or other sign refers to.

rejet: the isolation, at the beginning of one line, of a short element that is syntactically bound to the previous line.

rentrement: an abbreviated refrain including only the first part of the line.

rhyme (rime): the pairing of homophonous words in verse, generally at line-endings.

rime équivoque: a **rhyme** in which homophonous elements extend to entire words and beyond.

rime léonine: a very rich **rhyme** involving at least two syllables (*abolie/mélancolie*).

rime pauvre: a weak **rhyme** containing only one identical element – the tonic vowel (*bleu/feu*).

rime riche: a **rhyme** containing more than two elements in the tonic syllable (*pleine/haleine*).

rime suffisante: a **rhyme** containing two identical elements – the tonic vowel and a consonant (*rire/maudire*).

rimes croisées: a **rhyme** scheme alternating, or crossing, rhymes (abab).

rimes embrassées: a **rhyme** scheme embracing one pair within another (abba).

rimes plates: couplet **rhymes** (aabb).

rondeau: a medieval fixed form; twelve or thirteen lines built on two rhymes (a*b*ba aba*[b*] abbaa*); often the second line of the refrain is not repeated; later the refrain is reduced to a *rentrement*.

satire: a literary or other art work that mocks or attacks a person, group, event, social habit, political position or other aspect of reality (formally, often a long poem in rhymed couplets and familiar style).

sentiment de la nature: the projection of human feeling on a natural landscape.

signified: the meaning of a word or other sign.

signifier: the material (verbal or other) aspect of a sign.

simile (*comparaison*): a poetic comparison designating the similarity through an explicit term such as "like" or "as" (in French, "*comme*," "*pareil à*").

sizain: a six-line unit of verse.

sonnet: the dominant short form of Western poetry; fourteen lines of regular verse built on five (later seven) **rhymes**; generally divided into two *quatrains* (rhymed abba) and a *sizain* composed of two *tercets* (with various rhyme schemes: ccd eed, cdc ede, etc.).

stanza (*strophe*): a verse unit whose structure can be repeated, consisting of a set number of lines following a pattern of **meters** and **rhymes**; by extension, any isolated verse unit in a poem.

syllepsis: a figure whereby a part of speech performs two different functions simultaneously; for example, conveying at the same time a literal and figurative meaning.

symbol: something that represents something else, or the concretization of an abstract idea; in Saussure, a sign that retains some element of a natural link to its object; in Romanticism, a natural and motivated, sense-oriented type of sign (as opposed to **allegory**) that arrests our attention on its own modality even as it evokes something beyond itself.

syncope: the dropping (or non-pronoucing) of a non-elided *e atone* falling in the middle of a word.

synechdoche: a trope substituting a part for the whole or vice-versa.

synérèse **(synaeresis):** the articulation in one syllable of two contiguous vowel-sounds normally pronounced as two.

synesthesia: the exchange of different modes of sensorial experience.

tenor (*comparé*): the thing which is being compared in a **metaphor** or other comparison.

tercet: three-line stanza.

topos: an established or conventional subject matter, such as the beauty of a beloved woman or the return of spring.

trope: a figure that either changes or extends the literal meaning of a word to a figurative one.

vehicle (*comparant*): the thing to which the **tenor** (*comparé*) of a **metaphor** or other comparison is being compared.

vers composé: a line of verse divided by a **caesura**.

vers impair: see imparisyllable.

vers libres: lines of variable lengths and rhythms, which are neither systematically rhymed nor regularly accented.

vers mêlés: lines of variously mixed **meters** in regular verse (as opposed to *vers libres*).

***vers simple*:** a line of verse that is not divided by a **caesura**.

***verset*:** an intermediary line-structure between verse and prose.

***virelai*:** a medieval lyric form; often twenty-one lines of *quatrains* and *quintils* with refrains of varying lengths turning on the dominant rhymes of the first **stanza** (a*bba cdcd abbaa* cdcd abbaa*).

Bibliography

Allais, A., in D. Grojnowski and B. Sarrazin, eds., *L'Esprit fumiste et les rires fin de siècle*, p. 84.

Apollinaire, G., *Œuvres poétiques*, eds. M. Adéma and M. Décaudin (Paris: Gallimard, 1965).

Aragon, L., *Le Musée Grévin* (Paris: Minuit, 1944).

Aubigné, A. d', *Œuvres*, ed H. Weber (Paris: Gallimard, 1969).

Banville, T. de, *Petit traité de poésie française* (Paris: Fasquelle editeurs, 1935).

Baudelaire, C., *Œuvres complètes I, II*, ed. C. Pichois (Paris: Gallimard, 1975–1976).

Bellenger, Y., ed., *Le Sonnet à la Renaissance* (Paris: Aux Amateurs de Livres, 1988).

Benjamin, W., *Reflections*, ed. P. Demetz, trans. E. Jephcott (New York: Shocken Books, 1986).

Bishop, M., *Jacques Prévert: From Film and Theater to Poetry, Art, and Song* (Amsterdam: Rodopi, 2002).

Boileau, N., *Satires, epîtres, art poétique*, ed. J.-P. Collinet (Paris: Gallimard, 1985).

Bonnefoy, Y., *Du mouvement et de l'immobilité de Douve* (Paris: Gallimard, 1970).

Bowie, M., *Mallarmé and the Art of Being Difficult* (Cambridge: Cambridge University Press, 1978).

Breton, A., *Manifestoes of Surrealism*, trans. R. Seaver and H. R. Lane (Ann Arbor: The University of Michigan Press, 1969).

Breton, A., *Œuvres complètes I, II*, ed. M. Bonnet (Paris: Gallimard, 1988–1992).

Brunel, P., *et al.*, *Histoire de la littérature française* (Paris: Bordas, 1972).

Campo, R., *Ronsard's Contentious Sisters* (Chapel Hill: North Carolina Studies, 1998).

Cendrars, B., *Poésies complètes* (Paris: Denoël, 2001).

Césaire, A., *Cahier d'un retour au pays natal* (Paris: Présence Africaine, 1983).

Chanson de Roland (La), ed. G. Moignet (Paris: Bordas, 1989).

Char, R., *Œuvres complètes* (Paris: Gallimard, 1983).

Charles d'Orléans, *En la forêt de longue attente et autres poèmes*, ed. G. Gros (Paris: Gallimard, 2001).

Charles d'Orléans, *The French Chansons of Charles d'Orléans*, ed. S. Spense (New York and London: Garland Publishing, 1986).

Chénier, A., *Œuvres complètes II*, ed. G. Walter (Paris: Gallimard, 1966).

Chrétien de Troyes, *Œuvres complètes*, ed. D. Poirion *et al.* (Paris: Gallimard, 1994).

Christine de Pizan, *Œuvres poétiques I*, ed. M. Roy (Paris: Firmin Didot, 1886).

Claudel, P., *Cent phrases pour éventails* (Paris: Gallimard, 1942).

Claudel, P., *Cinq grandes odes* (Paris: Gallimard, 1975).

Collier, P., "Poetry and Cliché: Laforgue's 'L'Hiver qui vient,' " in C. Prendergast, ed., *Nineteenth-Century French Poetry: Introductions to Close Reading*, pp. 199–224.

Collot, M., "D'un lyrisme objectif," in *Poétiques de l'objet*, ed. F. Rouget and J. Stout (Paris: Champion, 1999), pp. 443–456.

Corneille, P., *Œuvres complètes III*, ed. G. Couton (Paris: Gallimard, 1987).

Cornilliat, F., "Poésie et peinture, de Molinet à Lemaire," in *Poétiques de la Renaissance*, eds. P. Galand-Hallyn and F. Hallyn (Geneva: Droz, 2001), pp. 587–596.

Cretin, G., *Œuvres poétiques*, ed. K. Chesney (Geneva: Slatkine, 1977).

Crisp, R., "Logos," in *Cambridge Encyclopedia of Philosophy*, ed. R. Audi (Cambridge: Cambridge University Press, 1995), pp. 448–449.

Culler, J., "Intertextuality and Interpretation: Baudelaire's 'Correspondances,' " in C. Prendergast, ed., *Nineteenth-Century French Poetry: Introductions to Close Reading*, pp. 118–137.

Damas, L.-G., in L. S. Senghor, ed., *Anthologie de la nouvelle poésie nègre et malgache de langue française*, pp. 5–25.

Defaux, G., "Rhétorique, silence et liberté dans l'œuvre de Marot," in *Bibliothèque d'Humanisme et Renaissance*, XLVI (Geneva: Droz, 1984), pp. 299–322.

Deguy, M., *Gisants, Poèmes III 1980–1995* (Paris: Gallimard, 1999).

Deguy, M., *La Poésie n'est pas seule. Court traité de poétique* (Paris: Seuil, 1987).

De Man, P., *The Rhetoric of Romanticism* (New York: Columbia University Press, 1984).

Derrida, J., *Signéponge / Signsponge*, trans. R. Rand (New York: Columbia University Press, 1984).

Desbordes-Valmore, M., *Œuvres poétiques I*, ed. M. Bertrand (Grenoble: Presses Universitaires de Grenoble, 1973).

Deschamps, E., *Œuvres complètes VII*, eds. A. Queux de Saint-Hilaire and G. Raynaud (Paris: Firmin-Didot, 1878–1903).

Desnos, R., *Domaine public* (Paris: Gallimard/Le Point du jour, 1953).

Du Bellay, J., *La Deffence et illustration de la langue françoyse*, ed. H. Chamard (Paris: STFM, 1970).

Du Bellay, J., *Œuvres poétiques I, II, V*, ed. H. Chamard (Paris: STFM, 1970–1983).

Du Bouchet, A., *Dans la chaleur vacante* (Paris: Mercure de France, 1961).

Éluard, P., *Œuvres complètes I*, ed. M. Dumas and L. Scheler (Paris: Gallimard, 1968).

Fontaine, M.-M., "Le Système des *Antiquités* de Du Bellay," in Y. Bellenger, ed., *Le Sonnet à la Renaissance*, pp. 67–81.

Fontanier, P., *Les Figures du discours* (Paris: Flammarion, 1977).

Fussell, P., *Poetic Meter and Poetic Form*, revised edition (New York: Random House, 1979).

Gasarian, G., *Yves Bonnefoy, la poésie, la présence* (Seyssel: Champ Vallon, 1986).

Gautier, T., *Émaux et camées*, ed. C. Gothot-Mersch (Paris: Gallimard, 1981).

Gendre, A., *Évolution du sonnet français* (Paris: Presses Universitaires de France, 1996).

Glissant, E., *Poèmes complets* (Paris: Gallimard, 1994).

Gordon, R. B., "The Lyric Persona: Nerval's *El Desdichado*," in C. Prendergast, ed., *Nineteenth-Century Poetry: Introductions to Close Reading*, pp. 86–102.

Goscinny, R. and A. Uderzo, *Astérix et Cléopâtre* (Paris: Dargaud, 1965).

Goudezki, J., in A. Velter, ed., *Les Poètes du Chat Noir* (Paris: Gallimard, 1996).

Gouvard, J.-M., *La Versification* (Paris: Presses Universitaires de France, 1999).

Goyet, F., "Le Sonnet français, vrai et faux héritier de la grande rhétorique," in Y. Bellenger, ed., *Le Sonnet à la Renaissance*, pp. 31–41.

Grangaud, M., *Poèmes fondus* (Paris: P.O.L., 1997).

Greene, T. M., *Poésie et magie* (Paris: Julliard, 1991).

Grojnowski, D. and B. Sarrazin, *L'Esprit fumiste et les rires fin de siècle* (Paris: Corti, 1990).

Guillevic, E., *Art poétique* (Paris: Gallimard, 1989).

Hegel, G. W. F., *The Philosophy of Fine Art*, IV, trans. F. P. B. Osmaton (New York: Hacker Art Books, 1975).

Heidegger, M., *Approche de Hölderlin*, trans. H. Corbin, M. Deguy, and F. Fédier (Paris: Gallimard, 1973).

Hugo, V., *Œuvres poétiques I, II*, ed. P. Albouy (Paris: Gallimard, 1964–1967).

Hugo, V., *Théâtre complet I*, ed. J.-J. Thierry and J. Mélèze (Paris: Gallimard, 1963).

Hurley, E. A., *Through a Black Veil. Readings in French Caribbean Poetry* (Trenton, New Jersey: Africa World Press, 2000).

Jabès, E., *Le Seuil le sable, Poésies complètes 1943–1988* (Paris: Gallimard, 1990).

Jaccottet, P., *Poésie 1946–1967* (Paris: Gallimard, 1971).

Jakobson, R. "Linguistics and Poetics," in *Style in Language*, ed. T. A. Sebeok (Cambridge, Mass.: MIT Press, 1960), pp. 350–377.

Jakobson, R. *Questions de poétique* (Paris: Seuil, 1973).

Jarrety, M., ed., *La Poésie française du Moyen Âge jusqu'à nos jours* (Paris: Presses Universitaires de France, 1997).

Jarry, A., *Tout Ubu* (Paris: Librairie Générale Française, 1962).

Johnson, B., *Défigurations du langage poétique* (Paris: Flammarion, 1979).

Jost, F., "Le Sonnet: sens d'une structure," in Y. Bellenger, ed., *Le Sonnet à la Renaissance*, pp. 57–65.

Jouve, P. J., *Œuvres I*, ed. J. Starobinski (Paris: Mercure de France, 1987).

Krysinska, M., in *Poèmes de femmes des origines à nos jours*, ed. R. Deforges (Paris: Le Cherche Midi, 1993), pp. 80–82.

Labé, L., *Œuvres complètes*, ed. F. Rigolot (Paris: Garnier-Flammarion, 1986).

Lacoue-Labarthe, P., and J.-L. Nancy, *L'Absolu littéraire: théorie de la littérature du romantisme allemand* (Paris: Seuil, 1978).

La Fontaine, J. de, *Œuvres complètes I*, ed. J.-P. Collinet (Paris: Gallimard, 1991).

Laforgue, J., *Œuvres complètes II*, eds. M. de Courten, J.-L. Debauve, P.-O. Walzer, and D. Arkell (Lausanne: L'Âge d'Homme, 1995).

Lamartine, A. de, *Œuvres poétiques complètes*, ed. M.-F. Guyard (Paris: Gallimard, 1963).

Lautréamont and G. Nouveau, *Œuvres complètes*, ed. P.-O. Walzer (Paris: Gallimard, 1970).

Lemaire de Belges, J., *La Plainte du désiré*, ed. D. Yabsley (Paris: Droz, 1932).

Lermina, J., and H. Levêque, *Dictionnaire thématique argot* (Paris: Bibliothèque Charcornac, 1897).

Lloyd, R., *Baudelaire et Hoffmann: affinités et influences* (Cambridge: Cambridge University Press, 1979).

Maber, R. G., *Malherbe, Théophile de Viau, and Saint-Amant: A Selection* (Durham: University of Durham, 1983).

Machaut, G. de, *Le Livre du voir dit*, eds. P. Imbs and J. Cerquiglini-Toulet (Paris: Le Livre de Poche, 1999).

Malherbe, F., *Commentaire sur Desportes*, ed. A. Sideleau (Montréal: Les Éditions Chantecler, 1950).

Malherbe, F., *Œuvres*, ed. A. Adam (Paris: Gallimard, 1971).

Mallarmé, S., *Œuvres complètes*, ed. H. Mondor (Paris: Gallimard, 1945).

Mallarmé, S., *Œuvres complètes I*, ed. B. Marchal (Paris: Gallimard, 1998).

Mansour, J., *Rapaces* (Paris: Seghers, 1960).

Marguerite de Navarre, *Chansons spirituelles*, ed. G. Dottin (Geneva: Droz, 1971).

Marguerite de Navarre, *Les Prisons*, ed. S. Glasson (Geneva: Droz, 1978).

Marot, C., *L'Adolescence clémentine*, ed. F. Lestringant (Paris: Gallimard, 1987).

Marot, C., *Œuvres poétiques II*, ed. G. Defaux (Paris: Bordas, 1993).

Marot, J., *Le Voyage de Gênes*, ed. G. Trisolini (Geneva: Droz, 1974).

Mazaleyrat, J., *Eléments de métrique française* (Paris: Armand Colin, 1974).

Ménager, D., *Ronsard. Le roi, le poète et les hommes* (Geneva: Droz, 1979).

Michaux, H., *Œuvres complètes I, II*, eds. R. Bellour and Y. Tran (Paris: Gallimard, 1998–2001).

Miller, C. L., *Nationalists and Nomads. Essays on Francophone African Literature and Culture* (Chicago: The University of Chicago Press, 1998).

Miron, G., *L'Homme rapaillé* (Montréal: Presses de l'Université de Montréal, 1970).

Molinet, J., *Faictz et Dictz*, ed. N. Dupire (Paris: SATF, 1936).

Morier, H., *Dictionnaire de poétique et de rhétorique* (Paris: Presses Universitaires de France, 1961).

Mouchard, C., "Michaux, métamorphoses d'espaces," in *L'Art et l'hybride* (Saint-Denis: Presses Universitaires de Vincennes, 2001), pp. 83–102.

Mouret, F., "Art poétique et musication: de l'alternance des rimes," in *À haute voix*, ed. O. Rosenthal (Paris: Klincksieck, 1998), pp. 103–113.

Mukherjee, M., "Symbolism and Orientalism in Rimbaud, Claudel, and Artaud" (New Brunswick, NJ: Rutgers University Ph.D., 2000).

Musset, A. de, *Contes d'Espagne et d'Italie*, ed. M. A. Rees (London: Athlone Press, 1973).

Nash, S., "Other Voices: Intertextuality and the Art of Pure Poetry," in *Reading Paul Valéry*, eds. P. Gifford and B. Stimpson (Cambridge: Cambridge University Press, 1998), pp. 187–199.

Nerval, G. de, *Œuvres complètes III*, eds. J. Guillaume and C. Pichois (Paris: Gallimard, 1993).

The New Oxford Annotated Bible, ed. B. Metzger and R. Murphy (New York: Oxford University Press, 1991).

Parmentier, J., *Œuvres poétiques*, ed. F. Ferrand (Geneva: Droz, 1971).

Péguy, C., *Œuvres poétiques complètes* (Paris: Gallimard, 1940).

Perec, G., *La Disparition* (Paris: Gallimard, 1989).

Péret, B., *Death to the Pigs and Other Writings*, trans. R. Stella (Lincoln and London: University of Nebraska Press, 1988).

Petrarca, F., *Canzoniere*, ed. G. Contini (Turin: Einaudi, 1982).

Pinson, J.-C., *Habiter en poète* (Seyssel: Champ Vallon, 1995).

Plantier, T., in *The Defiant Muse: French Feminist Poets from the Middle Ages to the Present*, pp. 180–183.

Plato, *The Republic*, ed. G. R. F. Ferrari, trans. T. Griffith (Cambridge: Cambridge University Press, 2000).

Ponge, F., *Œuvres complètes I*, ed. B. Beugnot *et al.* (Paris: Gallimard, 1999).

Pozzi, C., *Œuvre poétique*, ed. L. Joseph (Paris: La Différence, 1988).

Prendergast, C., ed., *Nineteenth-Century French Poetry: Introductions to Close Reading* (Cambridge: Cambridge University Press, 1990).

Queneau, R., *Bâtons, chiffres et lettres* (Paris: Gallimard, 1965).

Queneau, R., *Cent mille milliards de poèmes* (Paris: Gallimard, 1961).

Rabéarivelo, J.-J., *Volumes* (Antananarivo: Imprimerie de l'Imérina, 1928).

Racine, J., *Œuvres complètes I*, ed. G. Forestier (Paris: Gallimard, 1999).

Rancière, J., *La Parole muette. Essai sur les contradictions de la littérature* (Paris: Hachette, 1998).

Régnier, M., *Œuvres complètes*, ed. G. Raibaud (Paris: Nizet, 1982).

Richepin, J., *La Chanson des gueux* (Paris: Fasquelle, 1912).

Rifelj, C. de Dobay, *Word and Figure in Nineteenth-Century French Poetry* (Columbus: Ohio State University Press, 1987).

Riffaterre, M., *Semiotics of Poetry* (Bloomington: Indiana University Press, 1978).

Rimbaud, A., *Œuvres complètes*, ed. A. Adam (Paris: Gallimard, 1972).

Risset, J., *Petits éléments de physique amoureuse* (Paris: Gallimard, 1991).

Roche, D., *La Poésie est inadmissible* (Paris: Seuil, 1995).

Ronsard, P. de, *Œuvres complètes I, II*, eds. J. Céard, D. Ménager, and M. Simonin (Paris: Gallimard, 1993–1994).

Roubaud, J., *Poésie: (récit)* (Paris: Seuil, 2000).

Roubaud, J., *Quelque chose noir* (Paris: Gallimard, 1986).

Rousseau, J.-J., *Œuvres complètes V*, eds. B. Gagnebin and M. Raymond (Paris: Gallimard, 1995).

Rutebeuf, *Œuvres complètes I*, eds. E. Faral and J. Bastin (Paris: A. and J. Picard, 1959).

Said, E., *Orientalism* (New York: Vintage Books, 1979).

Saint-Amant, M.-A. de, *Œuvres complètes II*, ed. C. Livet (Paris: Jannet, 1855).

Saint-John Perse, *Œuvres complètes* (Paris: Gallimard, 1972).

Sartre, J.-P., "Orphée Noir," in L. S. Senghor, ed., *Anthologie de la nouvelle poésie nègre et malgache de langue française*, pp. ix–xliv.

Saussure, F. de, *Cours de linguistique générale*, ed. T. de Mauro (Paris: Payot, 1972).

Scève, M., *Œuvres complètes*, ed. P. Quignard (Paris: Mercure de France, 1974).

Scott, C., "Mallarmé's Mercurial E," in *Forum for Modern Language Studies*, 34 (1998), pp. 43–55.

Scott, C., *The Poetics of French Verse* (Oxford: Oxford University Press, 1998).

Scott, C., "The Mirage of Critical Distance: the Mallarmé of Yves Bonnefoy," in *Meetings with Mallarmé in Contemporary French Culture*, ed. M. Temple (Exeter: University of Exeter Press, 1998), pp. 199–226.

Sébillet, Th., *Art poétique françois*, in *Traités de poétique et de rhétorique de la Renaissance*, ed. F. Goyet (Paris: Le Livre de Poche, 1990).

Segalen, V., *Stèles* (Paris: Gallimard, 1973).

Senghor, L. S., ed., *Anthologie de la nouvelle poésie nègre et malgache de langue française* (Paris: Presses Universitaires de France, 1997); poems pp. 147–171.

Shaw, M. L., "Apocalypse et modernisme," in *Le Livre Total*, eds. A. Buisine and V. Kaufmann (*Revue des Sciences Humaines*, 1994), pp. 35–46.

Shaw, M. L., *Performance in the Texts of Mallarmé: The Passage from Art to Ritual* (University Park: Penn State University Press, 1993).

Stanton, D. C., ed., *The Defiant Muse: French Feminist Poets from the Middle Ages to the Present* (New York: The Feminist Press, 1986).

Thibaut de Champagne, in *Les Plus Beaux Manuscrits des poètes français* (Paris: Robert Laffont, 1991).

Thomas, J.-J, and S. Winspur, *Poeticized Language. The Foundations of Contemporary French Poetry* (University Park: Penn State University Press, 1999).

Todorov, T., *Théories du symbole* (Paris: Seuil, 1977).

Tzara, T., *Œuvres complètes I*, ed. H. Béhar (Paris: Flammarion, 1975).

Valéry, P., *Œuvres I, II*, ed. J. Hytier (Paris: Gallimard, 1957).

Verlaine, P., *Œuvres poétiques complètes*, eds. Y.-G. Le Dantec and J. Borel (Paris: Gallimard, 1962).

Viau, T. de, *Œuvres complètes III*, ed. G. Saba (Paris: Nizet/Rome: Edizioni dell'Ateneo and Bizzarri, 1979).

Vigny, A. de, *Poèmes antiques et modernes – Les Destinées*, ed. A. Jarry (Paris: Gallimard, 1973).

Villon, F., *Poésies complètes*, ed. C. Thiry (Paris: Le Livre de Poche, 1991).

Voiture, V., in *Anthologie de la poésie française du XVIIe siècle*, ed. J.-P. Chauvean (Paris: Gallimard, 1987).

Wimsatt, J. I., "Chaucer and Deschamps' 'Natural Music,' " in *The Union of Words and Music in Medieval Poetry*, eds. R. A. Baltzer, T. Cable, and J. I. Wimsatt (Austin: The University of Texas Press, 1991), pp. 132–150.

Winspur, S., *Saint-John Perse and the Imaginary Reader* (Geneva: Droz, 1988).

Index of notions

Index of names

Only names of primary authors and artists are indexed.